"For the millions of people whose lives are limited by social fears, this workbook by Antony and Swinson gives them the hope to control their future. The book is clear, practical, and easy to follow, and, above all, based on solid, scientific ground. The sections on troubleshooting are especially valuable to really help fine-tune the techniques. I would strongly recommend this book to anyone who is serious about overcoming their social fears."

—Ronald M. Rapee, Ph.D., Professor of Psychology, Macquarie University, Sydney, Australia, author of *Overcoming Shyness and Social Phobia: A Step-by-Step Guide*

"This volume, written by a team composed of a psychologist and a psychiatrist, provides an outstanding workbook for any individual suffering from social anxiety or shyness and wishing to undertake a structured self-help program to overcome it. The book can be used alone, or in conjunction with therapy. The authors are experts in the field and they offer strategies that are solidly grounded in the latest research literature. The workbook format provides readers with the exercises and worksheets they need to do the difficult work required to overcome their shyness and social anxiety."

—Jacqueline B. Persons, Ph.D., Director, San Francisco Bay Area Center for Cognitive Therapy and Associate Clinical Professor, Department of Psychiatry, University of California, San Francisco

# The Shyness & Social Anxiety Workbook

## PROVEN TECHNIQUES FOR OVERCOMING YOUR FEARS

MARTIN M. ANTONY, Ph.D.
RICHARD P. SWINSON, M.D.

New Harbinger Publications, Inc.

Distributed in Canada by Raincoast Books

Cover design by Blue Design
Edited by Kayla Sussell
Text design by Tracy Marie Powell-Carlson

Library of Congress Catalog Card Number: 00-134875

ISBN-10 1-57224-216-7
ISBN-13 978-1-57224-216-6

New Harbinger Publications' Web site address: www.newharbinger.com

09    08    07

20    19    18    17    16    15    14    13    12

*For our parents.*

—Martin M. Antony, Ph.D.

—Richard P. Swinson, M.D.

# Contents

# Acknowledgments

There are many people without whom this workbook would not have been possible. First, we wish to acknowledge those who were instrumental in developing and investigating the treatments described in this book. Dr. Aaron T. Beck pioneered many of the cognitive strategies that are used throughout the world to treat anxiety, depression, and many other conditions. We are also indebted to Drs. David Barlow, Isaac Marks, S. Rachman, Joseph Wolpe, and others who helped to develop and study the exposure-based strategies that are now commonplace for the treatment of anxiety. Finally, we thank Drs. Rick Heimberg, Sam Turner, Deborah Beidel, David M. Clark, and others, who adapted these cognitive and behavioral methods for the treatment of social anxiety.

We would like to thank our colleagues and students for their detailed comments on earlier drafts of chapters: Tim Ararat, Uppala Chandrasekera, Cynthia Crawford, Paul Harris, Michelle Jedrzkiewicz, Julian Lee, Andrea Liss, Randi McCabe, Karen Rowa, and Agnes Siwiak. We also extend a special thank-you to our clients and patients who made many helpful suggestions for improving parts of the book. Finally, we wish to express our gratitude to the staff at New Harbinger Publications (e.g., Matthew McKay, Amy Shoup, Kayla Sussell, Catharine Sutker) who worked closely with us through all the stages of developing, editing, and marketing this book.

Martin M. Antony, Ph.D.
Richard Swinson, M.D.
Toronto, Canada

# Introduction

Shyness and social anxiety are universal. From time to time, almost everyone has felt nervous speaking in front of a group or anxious when interacting with another person. We wonder if a presentation has gone well or whether we have made a good impression on a first date or a job interview. In fact, even some celebrities, who make their living in the public eye, have reported being excessively shy at times. A 1998 article on shyness in the *Toronto Star* reported that people such as Joan Rivers (comedienne), Richard Chamberlain (actor), James Cameron (director), Steffi Graf (tennis pro), and Eartha Kitt (entertainer) have all described themselves in interviews as being extremely shy and socially anxious. There have also been reports in the media about performers like Barbra Streisand, Carly Simon, and Donny Osmond suffering from performance anxiety. Even radio "shock jock" Howard Stern has described himself as being painfully shy when he is outside the safe confines of his on-the-air studio.

Shyness and social anxiety can range in intensity from being fairly mild to completely incapacitating. In extreme cases, social anxiety may prevent an individual from developing friendships, working, or even standing in a public place. Regardless of whether your fears are minor or completely overwhelming, the strategies described in this book will help you to deal more effectively with social anxiety.

We recommend that you read this workbook in the order in which the chapters appear. The initial chapters are designed to educate you about the nature of social anxiety and to teach you how to evaluate the main features of your own social anxiety. Then we discuss the costs and benefits of different treatment approaches and help you to select among available treatment options. Subsequent chapters provide detailed information about particular treatment strategies including medications, cognitive therapy for changing your anxious thoughts, using exposure to confront the situations you fear, and fine-tuning your communication and performance skills. The final chapter of the book discusses strategies for maintaining your improvements.

This book is different from other self-help books in a number of ways. Of the many books on social anxiety and shyness that you will find in your local bookstore, this is the first to be written in a workbook format. It is filled with exercises and practices designed to teach you basic strategies for overcoming shyness and social anxiety. We encourage you to fill in the blank worksheets and forms located throughout the text. In addition, we encourage you to make copies of the forms for your personal use, so you can continue to use them over the coming months.

This book also differs from many others because the strategies we recommend have all been investigated extensively in well-designed clinical studies. In addition to specializing in helping people deal more effectively with their anxiety, we also are actively involved in research on the nature and treatment of anxiety. It is a well-established fact that when the techniques described in this book are used in a therapeutic setting, people generally experience a significant decrease in their social and performance anxiety. Essentially, we have taken the strategies that have proven to be useful in therapy and adapted them to a self-help format. This workbook is designed so that it can be used alone, or along with regular visits to a professional therapist. In fact, one of our motives for writing this book was to have a good reference our own clients and patients can use as they progress through therapy.

The journey to overcoming your shyness and social anxiety may not be an easy one. Some aspects of your fear will be easier and quicker to overcome than others. Also, for every two or three steps forward, you may experience what feels like a step back. Nevertheless, the techniques described in this book have been shown to reduce social and performance fears in most people who use them consistently. With hard work and perseverance, these strategies will provide you with the opportunity to make big, positive changes in your life.

# Part I

# Understanding Your
# Social Anxiety

# Chapter 1

# Shyness and Social Anxiety

Rachel was a twenty-six-year-old woman who worked as an assistant manager of a small bookstore. She was referred to our Anxiety Treatment and Research Centre to obtain help for her intense anxiety about her upcoming wedding. Rachel wasn't afraid of being married (i.e., the commitment, living with her spouse, etc.); she was terrified of the wedding itself. The idea of being on display in front of such a large audience was almost unthinkable. In fact, she had postponed her wedding on two previous occasions because of her performance fears.

Rachel's anxiety encompassed more than just a fear of the wedding. She reported being shy from the time she was very young. When she was in high school, her anxiety around people had become increasingly intense and had affected her school life. She was convinced that her classmates would find her dull or boring or that they would notice her anxiety and assume that she was incompetent. Typically, she avoided doing oral reports at school and didn't take any classes where she felt her performance might be observed or judged by her classmates (e.g., gym). On a few occasions, she even went out of her way to obtain special permission to hand in a written essay instead of doing an oral report. Despite being an excellent student, she generally tended to be very quiet in class and rarely asked questions or participated in class discussions.

Throughout college, Rachel had difficulty making new friends. Although people liked her company and often invited her to parties and other social events, she rarely accepted. She had a long list of excuses to get out of socializing with other people. She was comfortable only with her family and several longtime friends, but aside from those, she tended to avoid significant contact with other people.

After college, she began working at a bookstore and over a short period of time was promoted to assistant manager. She was always comfortable dealing with the customers at her store and she gradually became more comfortable talking to her coworkers. However, she avoided eating lunch with the other staff members and never attended any social events such as the company's annual holiday party.

Rachel lived with her social anxiety for years, despite the ways in which it interfered with her functioning at school, work, and in her social life. It was not until the anxiety prevented her from having the kind of wedding she and her fiancé wanted that she decided to seek help.

Rachel's story is not that different from those of other people who experience intense feelings of shyness, social anxiety, and performance-related fears. The types of anxious beliefs and behaviors that she reported are similar to those that many socially anxious individuals describe. After her evaluation at our Centre, Rachel began a twelve-session course of cognitive behavior therapy (CBT) and gradually learned to cope with her anxiety more effectively. By the end of treatment, her avoidance of social situations had decreased significantly and she was much more comfortable in situations that previously made her very anxious.

Cognitive-behavior treatment involves (1) identifying the thought patterns and behaviors that contribute to a person's negative feelings such as anxiety, and (2) teaching that person new ways of thinking and behaving to better manage the anxiety. The strategies commonly used in CBT for social anxiety are described throughout this book. Before exploring those strategies, however, we will begin this chapter in the same way we usually begin treatment with the individuals we see in our program, i.e., with an overview of the nature of fear and anxiety in general, and of social anxiety in particular.

## Anxiety, Worry, Fear, and Panic

Everyone knows what it feels like to be afraid. Fear is a basic human emotion. In humans, fear seems to be controlled, in part, by an area of the brain called the limbic system. The limbic system includes some of the deepest, most primitive structures of the brain—structures shared by many less "evolved" animals. In fact, there is reason to believe that the emotion of fear is present across most, if not all, animal species. Most organisms display specific patterns of behavior when confronted with danger and often these "fearful" behaviors include forms of aggression or escape. Therefore, the intense feelings we experience when we are exposed to an immediate danger often are called the "fight or flight" response.

Although most people use the terms "anxiety" and "fear" interchangeably, behavioral scientists who study emotions tend to assign somewhat different meanings to these and other related terms (Antony and Barlow 1996). *Anxiety* is a future-oriented feeling of dread or apprehension associated with the sense that events are both uncontrollable and unpredictable. In other words, anxiety is a nagging feeling that occurs when a person believes a negative event may occur in the future and that nothing can be done to prevent it.

People who feel anxious tend to dwell upon and ruminate about the possibility of danger. This tendency to dwell on future negative events is called *worry*. Anxiety is also associated with uncomfortable physical feelings such as arousal (e.g., sweatiness, increased pulse), tension (e.g., tight muscles), and pain (e.g., headaches).

There is no question that when anxiety is too intense it can interfere with performance; however, mild to moderate amounts of anxiety are actually helpful. If you never became even slightly anxious under any circumstances, you probably wouldn't bother doing the things that must be done. Why would you bother preparing an assignment on time, dressing nicely for a date, or eating healthy food if you weren't concerned about the consequences of not doing these things? In part, it is anxiety that motivates us to work hard, prepare for challenges, and protect ourselves from possible threats.

In contrast to anxiety, fear is a basic emotion that occurs when an individual is confronted with an immediate, real or imagined danger. Fear leads to a sudden, intense physiological alarm reaction that essentially has one purpose: to get the person away from the danger as quickly as possible. When someone feels fearful, his or her body goes into overdrive to ensure that escape is fast and successful. Heart rate and blood pressure increase to transfer blood to the large muscles. Breathing quickens to improve the flow of oxygen throughout the body. The individual sweats to cool off the body and perform more efficiently. In fact, all of these symptoms of arousal and fear are designed to make escape easier, allowing for survival in the face of danger.

*Panic attack* is the clinical term used to describe the experience of intense fear that takes place when no realistic danger is actually present. Panic attacks can be triggered by specific situations that people fear (e.g., giving an oral presentation, being in a high place, seeing a snake) or they sometimes occur "out of the blue," without any obvious trigger. Panic attacks are discussed in more detail later in this chapter.

To summarize, fear is an emotional reaction to an immediate danger, whereas anxiety is a state of apprehension about some future threat. For example, worrying about giving a presentation that is a week away is anxiety, whereas experiencing an adrenaline rush while in the midst of giving a presentation is usually an example of fear.

Here are a few points to remember:

1. Anxiety and fear are normal emotions everyone experiences from time to time;

2. Anxiety and fear are time-limited, in that even though they may feel as though they may continue forever, they always decrease over time; and

3. Anxiety and fear are designed to perform a helpful function in that they prepare you for future threats and protect you from danger. So, your goal should not be to rid yourself of all fear and anxiety. Rather, your goal should be to reduce your anxiety to a level that no longer interferes significantly with your life.

# What Is a Social Situation?

Any situation in which you and other people are present is a social situation. Social situations can include times during which you are interacting with others (e.g., parties, conversations), situations in which you are the focus of attention (e.g., giving a presentation, playing the piano at a family gathering), or situations in which people may notice you (e.g., sitting on a bus or subway, walking through a busy mall). Table 1-1 lists additional examples of social situations.

## Table 1-1: Examples of Social Situations

**Interpersonal Situations (i.e., interacting with others)**

Asking someone out on a date

Initiating or maintaining a conversation

Going to a party

Having friends over for dinner

Meeting new people

Talking on the telephone

Expressing a personal opinion

Having a job interview

Being assertive (e.g., asking someone else to change their behavior)

Returning an item to a store

Sending back food in a restaurant

Making eye contact

**Performance Situations (i.e., being observed by others)**

Public speaking

Speaking in meetings

Playing sports or participating in aerobics

Getting married

Performing music or acting on a stage

Eating or drinking in front of others

Using public bathrooms with others in the room

Writing with others watching (e.g., filling out a form)

Making a mistake in public (e.g., falling down, dropping your keys, etc.)

Walking or jogging in a public place (e.g., on a busy street)

Introducing yourself (e.g., saying your name) in front of a group

Shopping in a busy store

# What Is Social Anxiety?

Social anxiety refers to the tendency to be nervous or uncomfortable in social situations, usually because of fear about doing something embarrassing or foolish, making a bad impression, or being judged negatively by others. For many people, social anxiety is limited to certain types of social situations. For example, some people are very uncomfortable in formal work-related situations (e.g., presentations, meetings) but are quite comfortable in more casual situations (e.g., parties, socializing with friends). Others may show the exact opposite pattern, with formal work situations being easier than unstructured social gatherings. In fact, it is not unusual to hear of a celebrity who is quite comfortable performing in front of large audiences but who has described him or herself as shy and nervous when interacting with people one-on-one or in small groups.

The intensity of social anxiety and the range of feared social situations varies from person to person. For example, some people experience fear that is fairly manageable, whereas others are completely overwhelmed by the intensity of their fear. For some people, the fear is limited to a single social situation (e.g., using public rest rooms, public speaking), whereas for others, the social anxiety occurs in almost all social situations.

The experience of social anxiety is related to a number of common personality styles and traits including shyness, introversion, and perfectionism. People who are shy often feel uncomfortable in certain social situations, particularly when they involve interacting with others or meeting new people. People who are introverted tend to be quieter and more withdrawn in social situations and may prefer being alone, compared to people who are extroverted or outgoing. However, introverted people are not necessarily anxious or fearful when socializing. Finally, the trait of perfectionism is associated with a tendency to hold overly high standards for oneself that are difficult or impossible to meet. Perfectionism can lead people to feel anxious in public for fear that other people will notice their "flaws" and judge them negatively. Perfectionism is discussed again later in this chapter.

## *How Common Is Social Anxiety?*

It is difficult to obtain accurate estimates of the prevalence of social anxiety because different studies have tended to define social anxiety differently and used different questions when interviewing people about their anxiety. Nevertheless, researchers have consistently found that shyness and social anxiety are common among men and women of all ages. A 1982 survey of almost 400 fifth-graders found that 36 percent labeled themselves as shy, 59 percent reported that they would rather be less shy, 46 percent reported that being shy was a personal problem, and 47 percent reported being interested in joining a counseling group to overcome their shyness (Lazarus 1982).

Surveys of adults have confirmed that shyness is a common trait. For example, in a surveys of more than 1,000 people from across the United States and elsewhere, psychologist Phillip Zimbardo and his colleagues (Carducci and Zimbardo 1995; Henderson and Zimbardo 1999; Zimbardo, Pilkonis, and Norwood 1975) found that 40 percent of those who were asked currently considered themselves to be chronically shy, to the point of it being a problem. Another 40 percent reported that they had previously considered themselves to be shy. Fifteen percent more considered themselves to be shy in some situations and only 5 percent reported that they were never shy. More recent surveys suggest that the prevalence of shyness may be even higher (for a review of studies on the prevalence of shyness, see Henderson and Zimbardo 1999).

Researchers have also begun to study the prevalence of social phobia (a condition associated with extreme social anxiety that will be described later in this chapter). In a recently published survey of more than 8,000 Americans (Kessler, McGonagle, Zhao, Nelson et al. 1994), more than 13 percent of people reported having the necessary symptoms to receive a diagnosis of social phobia. In fact, social phobia was the third most prevalent psychological problem. Other studies suggest that this may be an overestimate, with the true prevalence of social phobia being closer to 7 percent (Stein, Walker, and Forde 1994). Either way, it is clear that social phobia is a common problem and the trait of shyness affects almost everyone at one time or another.

## Effects of Gender on Shyness and Social Anxiety

Shyness and social anxiety are common across both genders, although there is some evidence that they are more common in females than in males (see Beidel and Turner 1998 for a review). In samples of school children, 70 percent of those with a diagnosis of social phobia are female. In adult community samples, the ratio of men to women with social phobia is about the same as in children, although some studies have tended to find smaller prevalence differences between genders. Interestingly, among those who actually seek treatment for their social anxiety, the ratio of males to females is about equal (both for adults and children).

There are a number of plausible explanations why women are more likely than men to report fearing social situations. (Incidentally, even greater sex differences have been found for a broad range of phobias, including fears of animals, driving, enclosed places, etc.). First, there is evidence that men underreport their fears, compared to women (Antony and Barlow 1997). It is possible that men are actually more anxious in social situations than they are willing to admit. Also, in Western societies, women are often expected to be more socially active than men. Therefore, men may be able to avoid certain types of social situations more easily than women, without being harassed about their absence and without experiencing as much social pressure from others in their day-to-day lives.

## *Effects of Culture on Shyness and Social Anxiety*

It is challenging to measure social anxiety across cultures because signs of social anxiety in one culture may have a very different meaning in another culture. For example, whereas some cultures may view poor eye contact as a sign of shyness or social anxiety, other cultures often avert their eyes from contact with another as an appropriate sign of respect (Antony and Barlow 1997; Beidel and Turner 1998). Cultures also differ with respect to their use of pauses and silence during conversation, the preferred physical distance from others, and the appropriate tone of voice.

Despite the difficulties in measuring social anxiety across cultures, studies generally suggest that social anxiety and shyness are common across different ethnic groups. However, it should be noted that in the United States and Canada, the majority of people who seek treatment for social phobia tend to be white and have a European background. Although people from nonwhite, non-European backgrounds are just as likely to experience problems with social anxiety, they are less likely to seek treatment.

# How Does Social Anxiety Affect People's Lives?

In this section, we will discuss how a person's social anxiety can affect relationships, work and school, and other day-to-day activities. After reading each section, take a few moments to consider how your social anxiety affects each of these life domains and then describe this in the space provided.

## *Relationships*

Social anxiety can make it difficult for people to establish and maintain healthy relationships. It can affect all levels of relationships, from those with strangers and casual acquaintances to those with family and significant others. For many individuals, even the most basic forms of social interaction (e.g., making small talk, asking other people for directions, saying hello to a neighbor) are very difficult. For such a person, dating may be completely out of the question. Social anxiety may be more manageable around more familiar people, such as close friends and family—but not always. For some people, anxiety may actually increase as a relationship becomes more intimate. Also, social anxiety can interfere with existing relationships, particularly if a socially anxious person's partner wants to socialize with others on a more regular basis. The following case examples illustrate how social anxiety can have a negative impact on a person's relationships.

- William has never been in a romantic relationship. Although others have expressed interest in dating him, he always makes excuses not to go out and usually doesn't return their phone messages. William wants desperately to be in a relationship, but he just can't find the courage to take the initial steps.

- Cindy is generally comfortable with her male colleagues at work and she has several male friends with whom she socializes occasionally. However, as her relationships with men become closer, she is increasingly fearful that the other person will discover the "real" Cindy and reject her. She has ended several relationships with men just as they were becoming close.

- Jerry frequently argues with his girlfriend about his unwillingness to spend time with her friends. Although he was quite shy and anxious when they first started dating, recently his social anxiety has put more of a strain on their relationship. Because of his anxiety, they have been spending a lot of time alone while she has been wanting to socialize as a couple with other people.

- Norm has gradually lost many of his friends over the years. For a while after finishing high school, he kept in touch with his closest friends. However, because of his anxiety, he often dreaded returning their calls and almost never accepted their invitations to get together. Eventually, his friends stopped calling him.

- Alison's roommate consistently plays loud music after midnight making it impossible for her to sleep. Despite feeling very frustrated and angry, Alison avoids asking her roommate to turn down her music for fear that her words won't come out right or that her roommate will disapprove of her.

- When talking to people whom she doesn't know well, Julia tends to speak very quietly, keep her distance, and avoid eye contact. As a result, people at work have learned to leave her alone and rarely invite her to lunch anymore.

In the space below, record the ways in which social anxiety has affected your friendships and relationships.

*Shelly wants to socialize more*

## Education and Career

Significant social anxiety usually has an impact on a person's education and career. It can affect the types of courses taken in school and the types of jobs a person seeks. It can also affect a person's job performance as well as his or her enjoyment of school or work. Consider the following case examples:

- Naveen turned down a promotion at work that involved significant supervisory responsibilities including chairing a weekly staff meeting and training groups of staff. Although the job would have provided him with a significant increase in salary, Naveen was terrified of speaking in front of groups and he couldn't even imagine being able to lead the weekly meetings.

- Ruth dropped out of college partway through her third year. As a freshman and sophomore, Ruth had been able to be anonymous in her large classes. However, when her classes became smaller in her junior year, she felt increased pressure to participate in class and began avoiding her lectures, and eventually left school.

- Len dreads going into work each day. He is terrified to speak to his coworkers and avoids speaking to his boss at all costs. Although he never misses work, Len keeps the time he must talk to others at a minimum. He rarely takes a break for fear that others will ask him to have lunch or to spend their breaks with him.

- Cheryl has been out of work for two years. Although she often hears of jobs that might be interesting, the thought of having to go through a formal interview is completely overwhelming. On several occasions she has arranged for job interviews and then failed to show up because of her social anxiety.

- People at work think that Jason is a snob. He tends to be very serious and speaks very little to others. Even when someone asks him a question, he tends to answer with only one or two words. In reality, he is not a snob; he is just very shy and anxious around people at work.

In the space below, record the ways in which social anxiety has affected your work or education:

Seen as conceited in his.

## *Other Day-to-Day Activities*

Just about any activity that involves contact with other people can be affected by social anxiety. The following examples illustrate the range of situations and activities that are often difficult for people who are socially anxious.

- Sita avoids going shopping on Saturdays because the stores are so crowded and she is fearful of having other people watch her. In fact, just walking down a busy street is sometimes difficult.

- Michael screens all of his phone calls. He is very anxious when speaking to people on the phone because it is more difficult to know how they are reacting to what he says, as compared to speaking in person.

- Kalinda has stopped going to the gym. She was finding that exercising in front of other people was causing her too much anxiety. Instead she exercises at home, where no one can see her.

- Reid noticed a small hole in a sweater that he had just purchased. Although he had not worn the sweater and it still had all the original tags, he was unable to return the sweater for fear of looking foolish in front of the salesperson.

In the space below, record the ways in which social anxiety has affected your day-to-day functioning:

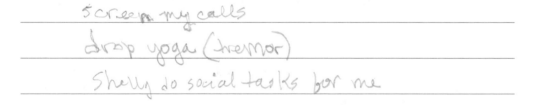

Screen my calls

drop yoga (tremor)

Shelly do social tasks for me

# Social Phobia (Social Anxiety Disorder)

When social anxiety becomes particularly severe, it may develop into a condition known as social phobia. Social phobia (also called social anxiety disorder) is one of several anxiety disorders listed in the Diagnostic and Statistical Manual of Mental Disorders, Fourth Edition (American Psychiatric Association 1994). The DSM-IV is the guide used by mental health practitioners (primarily in North America) to identify and diagnose various types of psychological problems. The DSM-IV diagnoses do not tell us much about the causes of the disorder. Instead, the disorders listed in the DSM-IV are simply descriptions of specific behavior clusters that cause impairment or distress in a person's life. In short, they are a way of classifying certain types of problem behaviors.

Although there is strong evidence that some of the DSM-IV disorders (e.g., schizophrenia, Alzheimer's disease) are associated with a biological dysfunction, the evidence is much less clear for other disorders (e.g., phobias of snakes or spiders). The problems listed in the DSM-IV range from severe mental illnesses to disorders that most people consider to be "bad habits." In fact, the DSM-IV even includes such problems as impaired sleep due to jet lag or shift work and nicotine dependence.

If your anxiety symptoms meet the diagnostic criteria for social phobia, that does not mean that you are sick, have a disease, or are mentally ill. What it does mean is that you are experiencing social anxiety at a level that distresses you or interferes with aspects of your functioning. Remember that almost everyone experiences social anxiety, shyness, or performance anxiety in one situation or another. The social anxiety experienced by people with social phobia is associated with the same types of anxious thoughts and behaviors that most people experience. The difference is that people with social phobia experience social anxiety at a more intense level, in a wider range of situations, and more frequently than people without social phobia. Fortunately, social phobia responds extremely well to the types of treatment discussed throughout this book.

## Diagnostic Criteria for Social Phobia

To meet the DSM-IV criteria for social phobia, a person must have an intense and persistent fear of one or more social or performance situations. Typically, the fear is related to anxiety over being scrutinized by others, or doing something embarrassing or humiliating. In addition, the fear must distress the individual or cause significant interference in his or her life. In other words, a person who has a strong fear of public speaking but doesn't need to speak in front of groups and doesn't care about the fact that he or she has the fear would not receive a diagnosis of social phobia. On the other hand, a person who is terrified of public speaking and needs to speak in front of groups (e.g., a school teacher) might receive a social phobia diagnosis as long as all of the other criteria are met.

In addition, it is important to note that if the social anxiety is related exclusively to a fear of having people observe the symptoms of another problem, it is not social phobia. Social anxiety is often an aspect of other problems. For example, people with eating disorders may be nervous about having other people notice their unusual eating habits. People who wash their hands excessively due to obsessive compulsive disorder (OCD) may avoid people either for fear of being contaminated by others or for fear of having other people notice their OCD symptoms (e.g., frequent washing, red hands from washing, etc.). People with panic disorder (a problem associated with unexpected panic attacks that occur out of the blue) may be concerned about other people noticing their panic symptoms. In these examples, the social anxiety is seen as part of the eating disorder, OCD, or panic disorder, respectively. For social phobia to be diagnosed as a separate problem, there must also be extreme social anxiety that is separate and unrelated to the other problem. For example, the individual might have a general fear of looking stupid, appearing boring to others, or making mistakes in front of other people—over and above the anxiety about having others observe his or her panic attacks, compulsive washing, or unusual eating habits.

Diagnosing social phobia is a complicated task. The information outlined in this section gives you an idea of how mental health professionals distinguish different types of problems from social phobia. However, this overview will probably not be enough for the purpose of self-diagnosis. If you want to be sure about whether your symptoms meet the diagnostic criteria for social phobia, we recommend that you see a psychiatrist or psychologist who has experience and expertise in the assessment of anxiety disorders.

Unfortunately, even professionals sometimes have difficulty agreeing about whether the diagnostic criteria for a particular disorder are met. For many people, the criteria outlined in the DSM-IV don't fit as neatly as we might like, which makes diagnosis especially challenging. Fortunately, the exact diagnosis isn't always necessary for selecting an effective treatment. The strategies described in this book will be useful for overcoming shyness and performance anxiety regardless of whether the full criteria for social phobia are met.

One final note about the diagnosis of social phobia: If all of the criteria for social phobia are met and the person is fearful of almost all social situations, the person is said to have *generalized social phobia*. Professionals sometimes use the term *discrete social phobia* to describe social anxiety that is limited to a single situation such as public speaking.

## Avoidant Personality Disorder

The DSM-IV includes another disorder that is very similar to social phobia. *Avoidant Personality Disorder* (APD) is a condition in which a person feels socially inhibited, inferior, personally unappealing, inadequate, and extremely sensitive to criticism from others. People with APD tend to avoid activities that involve contact with other people for fear of criticism, disapproval, or rejection. In fact, they are often preoccupied with the possibility of being criticized or rejected in social situations. They may also avoid getting involved with other people (including intimate relationships) or taking social risks, unless certain of being liked.

If you compare the criteria for social phobia and avoidant personality disorder, you will find that the two problems share many features. In fact, most experts agree that they are probably not even different conditions. If anything, avoidant personality disorder is just a more intense form of social phobia. For a review of research on the relationship between social phobia and avoidant personality disorder, see Antony and Barlow (1997) or Widiger (1992).

# Three Components of Social Anxiety

In an effort to define shyness, Cheek and Watson (1989) surveyed 180 shy individuals about the types of experiences that are associated with shyness and social anxiety. Eighty-four percent of the participants' responses to the survey fell into one of three categories: the physical aspects of social anxiety (e.g., uncomfortable feelings and sensations), the cognitive aspects of social anxiety (e.g., anxious thoughts, expectations, predictions), and the behavioral aspects of social anxiety (e.g., avoidance of social situations).

Cognitive-behavioral treatments for overcoming social anxiety encourage people to think of their social anxiety in terms of these three components. In other words, when people are feeling anxious, they are encouraged to pay attention to the things that they feel, think, and do. One of the first steps in overcoming problems with social anxiety is to break the anxiety down into its parts. Viewing your social anxiety in terms of these smaller components will help to make the problem seem less overwhelming, will help you to understand the variables that contribute to your anxiety, and will provide a context in which to use the specific strategies outlined in this book.

---

# Table 1-2: Physical Feelings Associated with Social Anxiety

Racing or pounding heart

Breathlessness or feelings of being smothered

Dizziness or lightheadedness

Difficulty swallowing, choking feelings, or a "lump" in the throat

Quivering or shakiness (e.g., in the hands, knees, lips, or whole body)

Blushing

Nausea, diarrhea, or "butterflies" in the stomach

Excessive sweating

Trembling or quavering voice

Tearfulness, crying

Nervous laughter, smiling

Poor concentration (e.g., forgetting what you are trying to say)

Blurred vision

Numbness and tingling sensations

Feelings of unreality or being detached

Tightness or weakness in the muscles (e.g., wobbly legs, sore neck)

Chest pain or tightness in chest muscles

Dry mouth

Hot flushes or chills

## Physical Feelings and Social Anxiety

Table 1-2 includes a list of physical feelings that are typically associated with anxiety and fear in social situations. Although these feelings include a broad range of arousal symptoms, people who are socially anxious are often especially fearful of symptoms that may be noticeable to other people. These include symptoms such as shaky hands, sweating, blushing, and a trembling voice.

People who are socially anxious differ from one another with respect to the ways in which they experience these feelings when they are anxious. Some people report many different physical symptoms. Others report only a few of these feelings. In fact, some people are not aware of any physical sensations when they are anxious.

There is also evidence that people are often not able to accurately report the intensity of these sensations. People who are socially anxious often report that their physical symptoms are very intense, particularly those symptoms that might be visible to other people. This is, however, often not the case. For the majority of people who are socially anxious, their symptoms are much less noticeable than they think. For example, a recent study by Mulkens, de Jong, Dobbelaar, and Bögels (1999) found that when socially anxious individuals are exposed to a stressful social situation, they are more likely than nonanxious individuals to report a belief that they are blushing. However, in reality, the study also found that there were no differences between socially anxious and nonanxious people with respect to the actual intensity of blushing.

Although in most cases, people's anxiety symptoms are less noticeable than they think, there is no question that a small number of individuals have a tendency to blush, shake, or sweat that is clearly excessive and may actually be quite noticeable to other people. In other words, some people blush easily and others don't. Some people have shakier hands than others and some people perspire more than others. However, not everyone who blushes, sweats, and shakes excessively also experiences intense fear when around other people. In fact, many people are not terribly concerned about experiencing these symptoms in front of other people.

In other words, it is not the fact that you experience these symptoms that is the problem. Rather, *it is your beliefs about the meaning and possible consequences of these symptoms that contributes to your social anxiety.* If you didn't care whether other people noticed your physical anxiety symptoms you would probably be much less anxious in social and performance situations. Furthermore, you would probably experience fewer of these uncomfortable symptoms.

Not surprisingly, the physical sensations that you experience when you are anxious or fearful are similar to those that you experience during any intense emotion, including excitement and anger. The differences between fear, excitement, and anger are not so much in the way they feel physically, but rather in the types of thoughts and behaviors associated with each of these emotions. It is to these aspects of social anxiety that we now turn our attention.

## Social Anxiety and Thinking

Strictly speaking, people don't react emotionally to the situations and events in their lives. Rather, they react emotionally to their *beliefs* and *interpretations* regarding these events and situations. In other words, given an identical situation, several people might have completely different emotional responses, depending on their beliefs about the situation.

Consider the following example. Imagine that you have interviewed for a job and are waiting to hear about the outcome of the interview. You were told that you would hear within a week. Two weeks have passed and you still have not heard from anyone about whether you landed the position. How would you feel? What emotions would you be experiencing? The examples below illustrate how particular interpretations regarding this specific situation might lead to very different emotional responses.

| Your Interpretation | Your Emotion |
| --- | --- |
| The interviewer didn't like me. I will never find a good job. | Sad |
| I am being treated unfairly. I was promised a call within a week and I am entitled to the courtesy of a phone call, regardless of the outcome. | Angry |
| Maybe this is a bad sign. If they wanted me, they would have called me by now. | Anxious |
| Maybe I gave the interviewer the wrong phone number. | Anxious |
| I suppose it is a good sign that I haven't been called yet. At least I am still in the running for the position. | Optimistic |
| I suppose that the decision is taking longer than the interviewer expected. He will probably call next week. | Neutral |
| Maybe the interviewer is very busy. I will call him to follow up and we'll take things from there. | Neutral |

Often our beliefs are accurate; however, sometimes our beliefs are exaggerated or incorrect. For example, some people who are socially anxious are quick to assume that another person doesn't like them just because he or she seems uninterested during a conversation. In reality, there are many reasons why a person might look uninterested when talking to you. Some of these include the following:

- The other person is not interested in the topic of the conversation, but still likes you as an individual.

- The other person is hungry.

- The other person is in a hurry (e.g., he or she is late for an appointment).

- The other person is tired.

- The other person is feeling sick or unwell.

- The other person is shy or socially anxious.

- The other person is thinking about something stressful that happened earlier in the day.

- The other person is worrying about something that is coming up.

- The other person is someone who generally doesn't enjoy conversations.

## Table 1-3: Examples of Anxious Beliefs about Social Situations and Relationships

- It is important that everybody like me
- If my boss doesn't like me, I will be fired
- If I give a presentation, I will make a fool of myself
- If I make a mistake, people will become angry with me
- People are untrustworthy and nasty
- People should always be interested in what I say
- People should not look at me the wrong way
- If I am not liked by a particular person, I am unlikable
- If someone rejects me, I deserve it
- It is awful to blush, shake, or sweat in front of others
- People can tell when I am anxious
- People find me unattractive
- If I speak to my boss, I will look incompetent
- I should be able to hide my anxiety symptoms
- If my hands shake at work, it will be a disaster
- Anxiety is a sign of weakness
- I should not appear anxious
- If I am too anxious, I will not be able to speak

Adapted from M. M. Antony and R. P. Swinson. 2000. *Phobic Disorders and Panic in Adults: A Guide to Assessment and Treatment.* Washington, DC: American Psychological Association. Used with permission.

- The other person is someone who always looks somewhat uninterested, even when he or she is having a good time.

- You are incorrectly assuming that the other person is uninterested even though he or she is showing all the usual signs of interest.

If you are anxious in certain social situations, the chances are good that you are either interpreting the situation as threatening in some way or are predicting that something negative is likely to occur. The more often that you experience social or performance anxiety, the more often you probably engage in anxious patterns of thought. Common beliefs held by people who are socially anxious are listed in Table 1-3. A more detailed discussion of the role of thoughts in social anxiety is provided in chapter 6.

## Social Anxiety and Behavior  "Safety behaviors"

The most common behavioral responses to feeling anxious or frightened are to avoid the anxiety-provoking situation or to engage in other behaviors to reduce the anxiety as quickly as possible. The reason that you engage in these anxious behaviors is because they are very effective at reducing your discomfort—in the short term. However, in the long term, these behaviors have the effect of maintaining your fear and anxiety in social situations because they prevent you from learning that your anxious predictions are unlikely to come true. Examples of anxious behaviors are provided in Table 1-4.

## Interactions Among the Three Components

The cycle of fear and anxiety can begin with any of the three components discussed in the previous sections. For example, you may be talking to a colleague at work when you notice yourself perspiring slightly (physical component). That may lead to anxious thoughts about whether your colleague is noticing your sweaty brow and wondering if there is something wrong with you (cognitive component). As your anxiety increases, the intensity of your physical sensations increases and you continue to think anxious thoughts. Eventually, you may make an excuse to leave the situation (behavioral component).

Alternatively, the cycle may begin with the cognitive component. For example, before giving a presentation, you may tell yourself that you are going to lose your train of thought and that others will notice how uncomfortable you are. You imagine that the others will interpret your discomfort as a sign of weakness (cognitive component). As you continue to dwell on these anxious thoughts, you notice your face beginning to feel flushed and your heart rate increasing (physical component). Finally, you make a decision to read your presentation word for word to be sure that your anxiety doesn't cause you to lose your place during the presentation (behavioral component).

Finally, the cycle may start with the behavioral component, namely avoidance. By putting off getting together with friends for a long time (behavioral

# Table 1-4: Examples of Anxious Behaviors

| Anxious Behavior | Examples |
| --- | --- |
| Refusing to Enter the Situation | Turning down an invitation to a party |
| | Making an excuse not to have dinner with a friend |
| | Never answering questions in class /groups |
| Escaping from the Situation | Always arriving late for meetings and leaving early to avoid making "small talk" |
| | Offering to help with the dishes at a party to avoid talking to the guests |
| | Making an excuse to get off the telephone with a friend or coworker |
| Subtle Avoidance Behaviors | Distracting yourself from your anxious thoughts |
| | Keeping the room dark during your presentations to keep the audience focused on the slides rather than on you |
| | Filling out a check before arriving at a store to avoid writing in front of others |
| | Avoiding eye contact and speaking very softly when conversing with others |
| Overprotective Behaviors | Wearing makeup and a turtleneck sweater to hide your blushing |
| | Always attending the holiday office party with a close friend, spouse, or other safe person even though your coworkers tend to attend alone |
| | Always arriving early for meetings to ensure that it will not be necessary to enter the room after everyone else is already seated |
| Drug or Alcohol Use | Having a couple of glasses of wine before meeting another person for a date |

component), you are more likely to experience anxious thoughts (cognitive component) about what might happen when you see them, as well as uncomfortable physical feelings when you are actually in the situation (physical component).

Although avoiding anxiety-provoking situations can be comforting in the short term, it also can have the effect of making the situation even more uncomfortable when you finally confront it. The longer you put off an unpleasant task, the harder it is to start the task when you finally decide to do it. For example, a lot of people find that the hardest day to drag themselves into work is Monday. We are even less motivated to return to work or school after a long vacation. The reason is simple. Avoidance makes it more difficult to do things.

### Exercise

Over the next week or so, use the following form to record your anxiety in terms of the three components of fear. Try to complete the form each time you encounter a feared social situation (if possible, at least three times in the next week). In the first column, record the situation (e.g., time and place). In the second column, record the intensity of your fear using a scale from 0 (no fear) to 100 (maximum fear). In the third column, record the physical sensations that you experienced in the situation. In the fourth column, record any anxious thoughts or predictions that you are aware of regarding the situation. Finally, in the fifth column, record any avoidance behaviors or any other anxious behaviors used to reduce your anxiety. In addition to the blank form, a sample completed form is included.

# Other Problems and Features Associated with Social Anxiety

Social anxiety is often associated with a number of additional problems. These may include panic attacks in social situations, excessively high standards and perfectionism, depressed mood, a negative body image, substance abuse, and difficulty trusting others. Each of these associated difficulties is discussed below.

## *Panic Attacks*

If you experience intense social anxiety, the chances are good that you have had panic attacks in social and performance situations. As discussed at the beginning of this chapter, a panic attack is a rush of fear that occurs in the absence of any realistic danger. According to the definition of a panic attack, the fear must peak within ten minutes, although it usually peaks immediately or within a few seconds. Also, to meet the full criteria for a panic attack, there must be at least four symptoms from a list of thirteen, including racing heart, chest discomfort, dizziness, breathlessness, shaking, stomach discomfort, sweating, choking feelings, hot flashes or chills, feelings of unreality or detachment, numbness or tingling, and fears of dying, going crazy, or losing control.

# Three Components of Social Anxiety Monitoring Form

| Place/Situation, Date/Time | Fear (0–100) | Sensations | Anxious Thoughts | Anxious Behaviors |
|---|---|---|---|---|
| | | | | |
| | | | | |
| | | | | |

Adapted from M. M. Antony and R. P. Swinson. 2000. *Phobic Disorders and Panic in Adults: A Guide to Assessment and Treatment.* Washington, DC: American Psychological Association. Used with permission.

# Three Components of Social Anxiety Monitoring Form (Sample)

| Place/Situation, Date/Time | Fear (0–100) | Sensations | Anxious Thoughts | Anxious Behaviors |
|---|---|---|---|---|
| March 3 At a party | 55 | Blushing, Started sweating | I will have nothing to say People will think I'm strange People will notice that I'm anxious People will think I'm stupid | Kept to myself and didn't talk to anyone Made an excuse to leave early |
| March 7 Talking to my boss | 90 | Heart pounding Blushing Sweating | My boss will think I'm incompetent My anxiety will show | Avoided eye contact Apologized excessively |
| March 9 Spoke in class | 70 | Heart pounding Sweating | I sound stupid People will laugh at me | Spoke very quietly Said no more than I felt I had to |

Adapted from M. M. Antony, and R. P. Swinson. 2000. Phobic Disorders and Panic in Adults: A Guide to Assessment and Treatment. Washington, DC: American Psychological Association. Used with permission.

For those who suffer from social anxiety, panic attacks tend to be triggered by exposure to feared social situations or sometimes even to just thinking about being in a feared situation. In addition, people who are socially anxious are often fearful of experiencing panic attacks and related symptoms. Because panic attack symptoms are often incorrectly viewed as a sign that one is about to lose control, it is no wonder that people who are socially anxious would want to avoid having panic attacks in front of others. Even though people who experience panic attacks often are afraid of losing control, going crazy, fainting, having a heart attack, or experiencing some other physical or social catastrophe, such consequences are extremely unlikely. In other words, panic attacks are very uncomfortable, but are not dangerous. In fact, the symptoms often are not even noticeable to other people.

## Perfectionism

Research from our Centre and elsewhere (Antony, Purdon, Huta, and Swinson 1998; Antony and Swinson 1998) has consistently found that social anxiety is associated with elevated levels of perfectionism. Perfectionism may be defined as the tendency to hold standards that are unrealistically high and overly rigid. Perfectionists tend to have exaggerated concerns about making mistakes and often go out of their way to ensure that mistakes are avoided.

In social anxiety, people tend to place too much importance on making a perfect impression on others. If they are not assured of being liked or approved of by others, people who are socially anxious tend to avoid socializing. Or, if they don't avoid socializing, they tend to experience high levels of discomfort when exposed to feared social situations. Perfectionism is different from simply having high standards. High standards are often useful because they motivate us to work hard and succeed. In the case of perfectionism, however, the standards are so high and so inflexible that they actually interfere with performance by causing a person to overprepare for tasks (e.g., spending many hours rehearsing a presentation), procrastinate (e.g., putting off preparing for a presentation), or be overly critical of his or her own performance.

## Depression

Given the impact of social anxiety on a person's functioning, it is no wonder that a substantial number of people with social phobia also experience depression. Severe social anxiety can lead to isolation, loneliness, and deep sadness. Social phobia can prevent a person from living up to his or her potential, which, in turn, can lead to feelings of hopelessness and depression. Depression can also increase the severity of social anxiety.

People who are depressed are often embarrassed about feeling down, may assume that others don't want to be around them, and may avoid being around other people. Social anxiety and depression are associated with similar thought patterns as well—specifically, negative thoughts about oneself and about one's relationships. Finally, there is reason to think that social phobia and depression may be related to similar biological processes in the brain. Consistent with this observation that social anxiety and depression are related, the treatments discussed in this book (including both psychological treatments and medications) have been shown to be useful for both anxiety and depression.

### Body Image Problems

People who are unhappy with their physical appearance may feel anxious when socializing or being watched by others. For example, people with eating disorders such as anorexia nervosa and bulimia nervosa may avoid activities that involve eating in front of others or showing their bodies (e.g., wearing shorts, swimming, exercising in public). People who are overweight may also be concerned about having their physical appearance judged negatively by others. In fact, dissatisfaction with any aspect of one's physical appearance (e.g., losing your hair, not liking your nose, etc.) can lead some people to experience social anxiety.

### Substance Abuse Problems

Some people who experience excessive levels of social anxiety use alcohol or other drugs to help cope with social situations. In most cases, this may involve only having an extra glass of wine at a party or having a beer when eating out with friends. However, for some people, using alcohol or drugs to manage anxiety can become a problem if the drug or alcohol use becomes excessive. If you frequently use excessive amounts of alcohol or drugs to feel more comfortable in social situations, it may be important to address this issue at the same time that you are working on your social anxiety.

### Anger and Mistrust of Others

In addition to fearing negative judgment from others, some people with social phobia may also be mistrustful of others. They may avoid confiding in other people, not only for fear of being judged, but also for fear that the other person will not be able to keep a secret. Social phobia is also sometimes associated with elevated levels of anger and irritability. For example, some people with social phobia may become very angry or hostile when they are being looked at by others. They may also become angry at perceived rejections by other people.

## Overcoming Social Anxiety

Two main types of strategies have been shown to be useful for overcoming social anxiety. They include psychological strategies and certain medications, each of which is discussed briefly below.

## Psychological Strategies

Although there are many different types of psychotherapy practiced by mental health professionals, there are only a small number of strategies that have been shown to be effective for reducing social anxiety in a relatively brief amount of time. The chapters in this book discuss three general approaches that repeatedly have been shown to be effective for treating social phobia.

1.  Exposure-based strategies will teach you to approach feared situations gradually, over and over again, until they no longer provoke fear.

2.  Cognitive strategies will be used to help you to identify your anxious thoughts and to replace them with more realistic ways of thinking.

3.  Instruction in basic communication skills will teach you to communicate more assertively, meet people more easily, give effective presentations, and use nonverbal communication appropriately.

## Medication

There are a number of medications that have been shown to be effective in decreasing the symptoms of social phobia. These include a range of antidepressants as well as certain tranquilizers. As long as the person continues to take the medication, these treatments are about as effective as some of the psychological strategies discussed earlier. For some people the combination of medication and psychological treatment is the most effective combination. (See chapter 5 for a discussion of the benefits and costs of using particular medications for treating your social anxiety.)

# Chapter 2

# Why Do You Have
# These Fears?

## Biological Factors

As with any emotion or personality trait, our biology affects how we feel and behave. In cases of extreme social anxiety, biological processes that have been proposed as contributing factors include natural selection or evolution, genetics, and alterations in the levels of certain neurotransmitters in the brain. Each of these is discussed below.

### Natural Selection: The Evolutionary
### Function of Social Anxiety

In 1994, Drs. Randolph Nesse and George Williams published a book called *Why We Get Sick: The New Science of Darwinian Medicine*. The essential argument made in the book is that many of the illnesses from which humans suffer developed according to the same laws of natural selection that are thought to have guided the more "positive" aspects of human evolution. Natural selection is the process by which members of a species who are best able to adapt to the environment are the most likely to reproduce successfully, thereby causing the species to evolve gradually and to survive over a long period of time.

The book discusses how a number of uncomfortable conditions such as sneezing from allergies, suffering from colds or fevers, and experiencing pain from injuries all serve to protect us from potential dangers. For example, the same processes that lead to allergies, colds, and fever also help the body to rid itself of potentially dangerous toxins and parasitic viruses. Pain following an injury is a warning sign that prevents us from moving our bodies in ways that could worsen the injury.

Nesse and Williams also discuss the role that evolution and natural selection may play in predisposing people to develop problems with anxiety. As mentioned in chapter 1, the "fight or flight" response associated with fear and panic protects us from potential danger. When we are afraid, our bodies quickly become mobilized either to meet the danger head on or to escape from the danger as quickly as possible. All of the sensations that we experience when we are frightened (e.g., increased pulse, faster breathing, sweating, hyperventilation, etc.) are designed to help us meet the physical demands of fighting the threat or escaping to safety.

It makes sense that humans would develop a propensity for experiencing social anxiety. We are social beings, and as such, we are very much dependent on those around us. None of us could survive without the help of others. As infants and children, we are completely dependent on our parents for food, shelter, comfort, and education. As we grow up, we continue to depend on other people. We depend on our employers to provide us with money for food and shelter. We depend on other people to build our homes, grow our food, heal our injuries, entertain us, and to help us meet most of our day-to-day needs. Because of our dependence on other people, we learn at a very young age that it is important to get along well with people. Essentially, we want other people to like us. Consistently making a bad impression on other people can lead to isolation, unemployment, and many other negative consequences.

Feeling anxious in social situations serves to remind each of us to pay attention to the effects our behavior have on those around us. If we didn't think about the effects of our behavior on others, we would probably get into trouble more often than not. We wouldn't bother dressing nicely or being polite. We might always say exactly what's on our mind, without considering whether it might be hurtful. Feeling anxious in social situations protects us from offending other people and from having other people judge us in negative ways. In fact, many of us find the qualities associated with mild shyness (e.g., modesty, a lack of pushiness) to be attractive. It is normal and often helpful to feel shy or socially anxious from time to time.

Of course, social anxiety and shyness are not always helpful. Extreme social anxiety may lead to impaired concentration, which, in turn, can cause a person to make more errors at work or school. In addition, socially anxious people often avoid taking social risks and may therefore find it difficult to make friends or to find work. Whereas mild to moderate levels of social anxiety are completely normal and often even helpful, extreme social anxiety can interfere with a person's functioning.

So, from an evolutionary perspective, people with social phobia do not have an illness per se. Rather, they have *too much of a good thing*. Social anxiety is helpful in small doses, but when it is too intense, it can make life more difficult.

## Genetics and Social Anxiety

Social phobia appears to run in families. For example, a recent study by Stein, Chartier, Hazen, Kozak, et al. (1998), found that having a first-degree relative (e.g., a parent, sibling, or child) with *generalized* social phobia (i.e., extreme anxiety in most social situations) made an individual ten times as likely to have social phobia. In contrast, *specific* social fears (e.g., discrete fears of public speaking) were less likely to run in families.

Of course, the existence of social phobia in multiple family members does not necessarily mean that the social anxiety is transmitted by genes. As we will discuss shortly, there is evidence that social anxiety also can be transmitted through learning. In other words, just being around others who are shy can teach a child to be more socially anxious.

To tease out genetic influences from the effects of environment, typically research involving twin studies, adoption studies, genetic linkage studies, and gene association studies is used. Of these, only twin studies have been conducted for people suffering from social phobia. Essentially, twin studies involve examining the *concordance rate* for social phobia in pairs of identical twins (i.e., those twins who share 100 percent of the same genetic makeup) and fraternal twins (twins who on average share only 50 percent of the same genetic makeup). (The term "concordance rate" refers to the probability of one person having a particular problem if his or her twin also has the problem.) Because twin pairs tend to be raised in similar environments regardless of whether they are identical twins or fraternal twins, a higher concordance rate in identical twins than in fraternal twins is thought to be evidence that genetics may have played a larger role in the development of that particular problem.

In the case of social phobia, twin studies have been inconsistent, with some showing a greater influence of genetics and others showing a greater influence of environmental influences. Interestingly, however, two personality traits closely related to social anxiety appear to be highly heritable, with heritability estimates (the extent to which the transmission of a trait across generations is due to genetics) being close to 50 percent across a wide range of studies (Plomin 1989). One of these traits, called *neuroticism,* is a general tendency to feel distressed, anxious, nervous, and worried. The other trait, called *introversion,* is a tendency to be inwardly focused and socially withdrawn. Not surprisingly, shyness and social anxiety tend to be associated with both of these personality styles (Briggs 1988). For further discussion of the role of genetics in social anxiety, see Antony and Swinson (2000).

If genetics does in fact play a role in causing social anxiety, does that mean that social anxiety cannot be changed? Not at all. Out genetic makeup affects just about every aspect of who we are, including physical fitness, academic ability, depression, weight, personality, and even our interests and hobbies. Yet we all know that our behavior and experiences still play an important role in determining our performance in these various areas.

For example, regardless of whether an individual is genetically predisposed to be athletic, training hard will improve his or her performance as a long-distance runner. Furthermore, the environment (e.g., the exercise habits that he or she learns while growing up) may have a profound effect on whether he or she exercises regularly as an adult. Still, there are differences between people with respect to how hard they must train to become physically fit. For some people it comes easier than for others—in part, because of their genetic makeup.

The same reasoning holds true for social anxiety. A genetic predisposition to have high levels of social anxiety and shyness simply means that you may have to work harder at overcoming the problem than someone who doesn't have such a predisposition.

### Effects of the Brain and Neurotransmitters

Compared to other psychological problems, including other anxiety disorders, studies examining the biological factors underlying social anxiety often have failed to obtain significant findings. Research examining hormonal factors, sleep patterns, and heart functioning has consistently failed to find differences between people with social phobia and people without significant social anxiety. However, in contrast to the negative results obtained in most biological research on social anxiety, a recent study by Schmidt (1999) found unique patterns of brain electrical activity associated with the personality traits of shyness and sociability. Specifically, shyness and sociability were both associated with specific patterns of electrical activity in the front areas of the brain. The implications of this finding are unclear, and these results remain to be replicated by other researchers.

Studies examining the role of neurotransmitters (the chemicals responsible for transmitting information throughout the brain) in social anxiety have yielded mixed results. Some studies suggest that the neurotransmitter dopamine may be involved (King, Mefford, and Wang 1986; Lewis, Gariepy, and Devaud 1989), whereas other studies have failed to replicate these findings (Tancer 1993; Tancer, Mailman, Stein, Mason, et al. 1994/95).

Studies regarding the role of serotonin (another neurotransmitter) also have yielded mixed findings. Interestingly, medications that work on the serotonin system are helpful for decreasing the symptoms of social phobia. Books by Antony and Swinson (2000) and Schmidt and Schulkin (1999) provide a more detailed review of the role of biology in social anxiety and shyness.

## Psychological Factors

In addition to biological factors, a person's learning experiences and beliefs also contribute to whether he or she will develop difficulties with social anxiety and shyness. The ways in which learning and beliefs contribute to social anxiety are discussed below.

## How Learning Contributes to Social Anxiety

A large number of studies suggest that learning plays an important role in the development of fear. We learn to fear objects and situations through three main routes. First, directly experiencing a trauma or some negative consequence in a particular situation can lead to fear. For example, being bitten by a dog can teach a person to be afraid of dogs. Second, observing other people who are afraid of a situation can teach a person to be nervous. For example, people are more likely to be nervous behind the wheel if they grew up with a parent who was an anxious driver. Finally, hearing or reading about the dangers of a particular situation can help to cause or maintain a person's fearfulness. For example, reading about airline crashes can help to strengthen a person's fear of flying.

### Learning by Direct Experience

A history of negative experiences in social situations can increase a person's shyness and social anxiety. Examples of social traumas include such events as the following:

- Being severely teased

- Being bullied by other children while growing up

- Having parents, friends, teachers, or employers who are overly critical

- Doing something embarrassing in a social situation (e.g., making an obvious mistake, vomiting, having a panic attack, etc.)

In the space below, list examples of negative consequences that you have experienced in social situations that may have contributed to, or helped to maintain, your social anxiety.

*Examples of Negative or "Traumatic" Experiences That May Have Contributed to My Social Anxiety*

_____

_____

_____

_____

### Learning by Observing Others

Observation is a powerful way of learning to fear specific objects and situations. This form of learning (also called *vicarious* learning) includes developing a fear by observing role models who themselves are anxious in social situations. Another form of observational learning involves witnessing another person experience a trauma in a social situation. Examples of observational learning experiences that could lead to the development of social anxiety include the following:

- Growing up with family members who are very shy and who rarely socialize

- Watching a classmate be severely criticized by a teacher following a presentation

- Seeing coworkers become very anxious while giving presentations

- Witnessing a friend being teased by other students at school

In the space below, list examples of observational learning experiences that may have contributed to, or helped to maintain, your social anxiety.

*Examples of Observational Learning Experiences That May Have Contributed to My Social Anxiety*

_____

_____

_____

_____

### Learning Through Information and Indirect Means

People can learn to fear social situations by reading about or being warned about the dangers of making a bad impression on others. Examples of situations that could lead to developing social anxiety through the transmission of information include the following:

- Being repeatedly told by one's family that it is very important to always make a good impression

- Being exposed to messages in magazines and on television that your image is the most important aspect of your being, and that you are only as attractive as other people think you are

In the space below, list examples of informational learning experiences that may have contributed to, or helped to maintain, your social anxiety.

*Examples of Indirect or Informational Learning Experiences That May Have Contributed to My Social Anxiety*

---

---

---

---

## Why Only Some People Develop Extreme Social Anxiety

Although negative experiences, observational learning, and informational learning are common routes by which people develop fears, they are not enough to explain why some people develop social anxiety and others do not. Almost everyone is exposed to negative experiences in social situations. At one time or another most of us are teased. We are all exposed to anxiety-provoking messages at home as well as through the media. And yet, not everyone develops a problem with social anxiety. Why is this so?

Most likely, there are other factors that influence whether a particular person develops problems with social anxiety following one or more negative social experiences. These can include biological factors, such as a person's genetic makeup. Previous learning experiences and the ways in which someone deals with his or her negative social experiences may also influence the development of fearfulness. For example, a person who is ridiculed the first time he or she gives a presentation may be more likely to develop a fear of public speaking than someone who is ridiculed on a single occasion after having given many successful presentations previously.

Similarly, someone who is severely teased at school may be "protected" from developing problems with social anxiety if he or she receives support from close friends after the episode. Finally, avoiding a social situation following a traumatic experience may increase the chances of developing social anxiety. You have probably heard that the best thing to do after falling off a horse is to get back on as soon as possible to avoid developing a fear of horses. The same is true of social anxiety. If you avoid a social situation following a traumatic experience, you may be increasing your chances of developing a fear of that situation.

# How Beliefs Contribute to Social Anxiety

As discussed in chapters 1 and 6, people with elevated social anxiety tend to think about social situations in a more negative way than do those people who are less anxious. Anxious thoughts, interpretations, and predictions can lead someone to feel fear and anxiety in social situations.

There are numerous studies investigating the role of thinking in social anxiety. There is also evidence that helping people to change their anxious beliefs is an effective way of decreasing their social anxiety. We have reviewed the research on thinking and social anxiety elsewhere (Antony and Swinson 2000). Some of the highlights of this research include the following findings:

- People with social phobia tend to pay more attention to information that represents social threat than to nonthreatening information, compared to people who are less anxious. For example, when asked to look at lists of words, people who are socially anxious spend more time looking at words that are related to social anxiety (e.g., "blush," "party") than do those who are less anxious.

- Social anxiety is associated with a tendency to have a better memory and recognition for other people's faces, particularly if the expression on the face appears to be negative or critical.

- Social anxiety is associated with a tendency to rate ambiguous or neutral faces as having a more negative expression.

- People with social anxiety are more likely than less anxious people to assume that others will interpret their physical symptoms (e.g., shaking, sweating, etc.) as a sign of a serious problem with anxiety or some mental illness. In contrast, people who are not socially anxious are less concerned about others noticing their physical arousal symptoms. Instead, people without significant social anxiety assume that others will interpret their physical symptoms as normal (e.g., perhaps a sign of feeling hot, being hungry, etc.).

- Social anxiety is associated with a tendency to rate your own performance more critically, when compared to how other observers rate your performance.

- People with social phobia are more likely than nonanxious people to think that social events are more likely to take place and more likely to have severe negative consequences.

- When asked to imagine a social interaction, people with social phobia are more likely than nonanxious individuals to take an observer's perspective (i.e., to visualize the interaction as if it is being watched by a third person). In other words, when imagining a conversation with a colleague, a person with social phobia observes him or herself in addition to the person he or she is talking to. Nonanxious people are more likely just to visualize the person to whom they are speaking. This finding is consistent with the idea that people with social phobia are overly concerned with how they come across to others, and that they tend to see themselves from other people's perspectives.

Taken together, these studies suggest that social anxiety and social phobia are associated with thinking styles that may actually make the problem worse. Chapter 6 discusses ways to change your anxious thoughts and replace them with less anxious and more realistic ways of thinking.

## How Behaviors Contribute to Social Anxiety

As discussed in chapter 1, avoidance of social situations can have the effect of increasing social anxiety over the long term. In other words, the main strategy that people who are socially anxious use to cope with their fear may actually make the problem worse.

Some behaviors that people use to "protect" themselves in social situations can actually lead to the very outcome that people with social phobia fear most—a negative reaction from others. For example, if when talking to other people at a party, you speak very quietly, avoid eye contact, and avoid expressing your views and opinions, people may choose to talk to someone else. They may interpret your behavior as a sign that you are not interested in talking or that you are a difficult person to get to know. See chapters 7 through 9 for a discussion of strategies for stopping avoidance behavior and for approaching feared situations in a safe and controlled way. Chapter 10 discusses strategies for improving communication and social skills.

# Chapter 3

# Getting to Know Your Social Anxiety

## Why Conduct a Self-Assessment?

Before any psychologist, psychiatrist, or other mental health professional begins to help an individual with a particular problem, there is an initial period of evaluation and assessment. This evaluation process involves collecting information needed to better understand the nature and extent of the problem so that the best possible treatment plan can be formulated. This initial assessment almost always involves an interview and may also include various questionnaires and standard tests. Sometimes, the therapist may ask the person to start keeping a diary to monitor specific thoughts or behaviors.

In the case of social anxiety, a clinician might spend the first session (or even the first few sessions) asking questions about the client's social anxiety, about other difficulties he or she might be experiencing, and about the person's general background. The individual also may be asked to answer a series of questionnaires that measure social anxiety and related problems. In addition, diaries are often completed between sessions to measure the person's anxiety in social situations, his or her feelings of depression, and any other aspects of the problem.

The assessment process helps the clinician get to know the client and is essential for identifying and understanding that person's problems. The findings from the assessment are essential for choosing and implementing a course of treatment.

In the same way, a detailed self-assessment will help you to understand and address your difficulties with social anxiety. We strongly recommend that before you begin working on changing your own social anxiety, you engage in a careful self-assessment. This assessment process will have the following four main benefits. It will:

1. Allow you to measure the severity of your social anxiety.

2. Help you to identify key problem areas.

3. Make it easier to choose the most appropriate treatment strategies.

4. Provide you with an opportunity to measure your improvement as you use the strategies described in this book.

Now we will discuss each of these issues in greater detail.

## Measuring the Severity of Your Social Anxiety

The term "severity" takes into account such variables as (1) the intensity of your fear in social and performance situations, (2) the range of different situations that precipitate your social anxiety, (3) the frequency with which you experience intense social anxiety, (4) the effect of your social anxiety on your day-to-day life, career, and relationships, and (5) the extent to which being socially anxious bothers you. Generally, as the severity of social anxiety increases, typically, so does the intensity of the fear, the number of situations that are affected, the frequency with which anxiety is experienced, the level of interference with day-to-day functioning, and the extent to which a person is bothered by having the fear.

## Identifying Which Problems to Work On

If you are like many people, you probably experience anxiety in a number of different social situations. A comprehensive self-assessment will help you to decide which fears to work on first. First, it will be important to identify which situations you fear and avoid. Next, you will need to identify your priorities, that is, which aspects of the problem you want to begin to address first. When choosing your priorities, here are some suggestions to keep in mind.

- Begin working on problems for which you are likely to see quick changes. Early improvements will help to motivate you to work on more difficult situations.

- Try to work on fears that interfere the most with your day-to-day life. Being able to confront the most disabling fears will have a much bigger impact on your life than working on fears that are less important to you.

- If one of your treatment aims is very important to you but is just too overwhelming to deal with, divide that goal into smaller, more manageable objectives. For example, if you are afraid of dating, you could work on your fear by breaking the situation down into steps (e.g., saying hello to an attractive classmate, sitting beside the classmate for several weeks in a row, speaking with the classmate after class, offering to study with the classmate, asking the classmate to have dinner with you after class).

## Choosing the Best Strategies for Change

A self-assessment also can help you to decide which treatment strategies to use. In many cases, the specific treatment approaches you select will be directly related to factors you identify in your self-assessment. Consider the following examples of how an assessment can help you to select the best approaches for treatment.

- Identifying which situations you fear and avoid will help to choose which situations to select for exposure practices (as described in chapters 7 and 8).

- Identifying the extent to which you are fearful of the physical feelings that you experience when you are anxious will help determine whether you should practice exposure to uncomfortable physical sensations (as described in chapter 9).

- Assessing honestly those areas in which your social skills can be improved will help you to decide whether to spend time working on the skills involved in assertiveness, public speaking, dating, or general communication. (See chapter 10 for strategies for improving various types of social and communication skills.)

- If you decide to take medications for your social anxiety, the choice of which medication to try will depend on your previous response to medications, possible interactions with other medications you are taking, medical conditions you may have, side effects that you are willing to tolerate, as well as a number of other factors. If you are considering using medications, thinking about these issues should be part of your self-assessment (see chapter 5).

## Measuring Your Improvement

Assessment is not only for the initial phase of your treatment. Rather, the process of assessment should continue throughout treatment and even after treatment has ended. Continuing the assessment process throughout treatment will provide you with a way of measuring how much your social anxiety has improved as a result of using the strategies described in this book. Also, conducting occasional self-assessments after treatment has ended will provide you with evidence as to the extent to which you have maintained your improvements.

# Step-by-Step Guide for Conducting a Self-Assessment

Therapists and clinicians who treat social anxiety use a number of tools to assess clients and patients. The most common of these include the following:

**Clinical Interviews:** Interviews involve asking a person specific questions about his or her background, anxiety symptoms, and related problems. It is an easy way of getting to know someone and learning about his or her difficulties simply by talking.

**Questionnaires:** Questionnaires include paper-and-pencil tests that a person completes before beginning treatment, and perhaps again during treatment and after treatment ends. They are used to provide additional information not covered in the interview, as well as to confirm and expand upon the information provided in the interview.

**Diaries:** Diaries are completed on a day-to-day basis, between therapy sessions. They are useful because they provide the individual with an opportunity to record his or her thoughts and feelings as they occur, rather than having to remember all of the details of a complex event later.

**Behavioral Assessment:** Behavioral assessment involves directly observing a person's behavior or asking the person to perform a specific behavior, and then measuring the thoughts and feelings that arise in that situation. The most common types of behavioral assessment for social anxiety are the *behavioral approach test* and *behavioral role-play*. These involve having a person enter a feared social situation (behavioral approach test) or act out a feared situation in a role-play (behavioral role-play) and having the person report his or her fear level, anxious thoughts, and other experiences.

Although these assessments are usually conducted by a psychologist, psychiatrist, or other professional, each can be adapted as part of your self-assessment. We recommend that your assessment include all of the following three steps:

- *Conduct a Self-Interview* (i.e., answering important questions about your anxiety and related problems).

- *Complete Anxiety Diaries* (to start, we recommend that you complete the Three Components of Social Anxiety Monitoring Form, which was included in chapter 1. We recommend that you fill this out several times per week for at least two weeks).

- *Complete a Behavioral Approach Test or Role-Play.*

## Conducting a Self-Interview

Any professional contact with a psychologist, psychiatrist, or other mental health professional typically begins with a clinical interview, during which the clinician asks the client or patient a list of questions about his or her problems. Clinical interviews tend to differ in a number of ways, including the following:

- **Duration:** The interview portion of the assessment usually consists of one or two sessions, each lasting an hour. However, sometimes the interview is very brief (as short as fifteen minutes) and other times it can be quite lengthy (several hours), depending on the level of detail required by the clinician.

- **Degree of structure:** Typically, the interview is at least somewhat structured, in that the clinician has a pretty good idea of what types of questions he or she will ask. In some settings, the interview will be completely structured, with the clinician actually reading questions from a manual, in a predetermined order. Other times, the interview may be quite unstructured, going in whatever direction the client wishes to take.

- **Types of questions asked:** The types of questions asked may depend on such factors as the *therapy orientation* of the clinician (in other words, the specific topics discussed will depend on the clinician's beliefs regarding the underlying causes and best treatments for the problem); the therapist's level of experience with assessing and treating social anxiety and related problems; and the professional background of the clinician (e.g., physician, psychologist, social worker, etc.).

The purpose of the clinical interview is to identify the problems that the individual is experiencing, to discover the factors that may be causing or contributing to the problem, and to identify the variables important for choosing appropriate treatment strategies. Some of the topics typically covered during a clinical interview for someone suffering from social anxiety include the following:

- What is the major problem? Is the person suffering from social phobia, or is the social anxiety related to some other problem?

- Are there associated problems, such as depression, alcohol or drug abuse, marital difficulties, elevated job stress, or medical conditions?

- How and when did the problem develop?

- What has the course of the problem been over the years? For example, has it ever gone away for a period of time?

- How intense is the fear in social situations? Does the person experience panic attacks (see chapter 1 for a definition of panic attacks)?

- How does the social anxiety affect day-to-day functioning at work or school, at home, and in relationships?

- Which variables (e.g., the size of a group, etc.) affect the individual's fear in particular situations?

- What are the specific thoughts, beliefs, and predictions that contribute to the person's social anxiety?

- What social situations does the individual avoid?

- Are there subtle ways (e.g., distraction) in which the person avoids feeling anxious in social situations? Does he or she engage in overprotective behaviors (e.g., having a couple of glasses of wine to cope with anxiety at parties)?

- Has the person had treatment in the past, and if so, what type of treatment? Was the treatment effective?

- Do other members of the person's family have the same problem? If so, what types of treatment have they found helpful?

- Might the person's family members be able to help with the process of overcoming the social anxiety? Conversely, are there ways in which family members might interfere with treatment?

- Are there basic social skills (e.g., assertiveness, effective communication) that the person needs to improve?

For your self-interview, we recommend that you ask yourself similar questions and try to provide answers. To help you with this, we have identified ten basic questions you should try to answer at the start of your self-assessment. The answers to these questions will help you to do the following: decide whether social anxiety is in fact a problem for you; identify the factors that contribute to your social anxiety; and choose the specific situations that you need to work on most. At the beginning of chapter 4, we will suggest additional questions that will help you to develop a treatment plan.

## 1. Which Social Situations Do You Fear and Avoid?

For each of the following situations (divided into interpersonal situations and performance situations, as defined in chapter 1), record a number ranging from 0 to 100 to rate (1) the extent to which you fear the situation during a typical or average exposure and (2) the extent to which you typically avoid the situation. For example, if you have an intense fear of making presentations, but you avoid the situation only about half the time, your fear rating might be an "80" and your avoidance rating might be a "50." If the situation is one that you never encounter, base your ratings on how fearful you imagine you would be in the situation and how much you would avoid the situation if it was one that came up from time to time. Use the following scales to rate your fear and avoidance levels.

**Fear**

| 0 | 10 | 20 | 30 | 40 | 50 | 60 | 70 | 80 | 90 | 100 |
|---|----|----|----|----|----|----|----|----|----|-----|

| *No Fear* | | *Mild Fear* | | | *Moderate Fear* | | *Extreme Fear* | | *Very Extreme Fear* | |

**Avoidance**

| 0 | 10 | 20 | 30 | 40 | 50 | 60 | 70 | 80 | 90 | 100 |
|---|----|----|----|----|----|----|----|----|----|-----|

| *Never Avoid* | | *Rarely Avoid* | | | *Sometimes Avoid* | | *Often Avoid* | | | *Always Avoid* |

**Interpersonal Situations (i.e., interacting with others)**

| Fear | Avoidance | Item |
|------|-----------|------|
| _____ | _____ | Asking someone out on a date |
| _____ | _____ | Starting a conversation with a classmate or coworker |
| _____ | _____ | Going to a party |
| _____ | _____ | Having friends over for dinner |
| _____ | _____ | Being introduced to new people |
| _____ | _____ | Talking on the telephone with a friend |
| _____ | _____ | Talking on the telephone with a stranger |
| _____ | _____ | Expressing a personal opinion (e.g., expressing your views about a movie you saw recently or a book that you read) |
| _____ | _____ | Being interviewed for a job |
| _____ | _____ | Being assertive (e.g., refusing an unreasonable request) |
| _____ | _____ | Returning an item to a store |
| _____ | _____ | Sending back food in a restaurant |
| _____ | _____ | Making eye contact |
| _____ | _____ | Other (specify) _____ |
| _____ | _____ | Other (specify) _____ |
| _____ | _____ | Other (specify) _____ |

**Performance Situations (i.e., being observed by others)**

| Fear | Avoidance | Item |
|------|-----------|------|
| _____ | _____ | Making a toast at a party or family gathering |
| _____ | _____ | Speaking in meetings at work or school |
| _____ | _____ | Playing sports or participating in aerobics in front of others |
| _____ | _____ | Standing in a wedding party at someone else's wedding |
| _____ | _____ | Singing or performing music in front of others |
| _____ | _____ | Eating or drinking in front of others |
| _____ | _____ | Using public bathrooms with others in the room |
| _____ | _____ | Writing with others watching (e.g., signing a check) |
| _____ | _____ | Making a mistake in public (e.g., mispronouncing a word) |
| _____ | _____ | Walking or jogging in a busy public place |
| _____ | _____ | Introducing yourself (e.g., saying your name) in front of a group |
| _____ | _____ | Shopping in a busy store |
| _____ | _____ | Other (specify) _____ |
| _____ | _____ | Other (specify) _____ |
| _____ | _____ | Other (specify) _____ |

## 2. Which Variables Make Your Anxiety Better or Worse?

An important step in your self-assessment is to become aware of the variables that make your fear better or worse in a given situation. For example, if you are fearful of eating with other people, there are many factors that may influence your fear in this situation, including the type of person with whom you are eating, the location of the meal, and the types of food being eaten (e.g., messy "finger" foods are worse for some people). Identifying the variables that affect your level of fear in a particular situation will help you to set up appropriate practices when you begin to use the exposure-based techniques discussed later in this book.

Below is a list of variables that sometimes affect a person's fear and anxiety in social situations. For each item, record a number ranging from 0 to 100 to rate the extent to which the variable listed affects your level of fear or discomfort in the types of social situations that you fear. For example, if you are much more anxious when talking to a woman than when talking to a man, you might rate the effect of the other person's gender on your anxiety at about a 75 or 80. Use the following scale to obtain your rating.

**Effect on Your Discomfort**

| 0 | 10 | 20 | 30 | 40 | 50 | 60 | 70 | 80 | 90 | 100 |
|---|----|----|----|----|----|----|----|----|----|-----|
| *No Effect* | | *Mild Effect* | | | *Moderate Effect* | | | *Large Effect* | | *Very Large Effect* |

**Aspects of the Other Person and Their Effect on Your Discomfort**

| Effect on Your Discomfort | Item |
|---|---|
| _____ | Age (e.g., whether the other person is older, younger, or the same age as you) |
| _____ | Gender of the other person (e.g., same sex, opposite sex) |
| _____ | Relationship status of the other person (e.g., married, single) |
| _____ | Physical attractiveness of the other person |
| _____ | Nationality or ethnic background of the other person |
| _____ | How confident the other person seems |
| _____ | How aggressive or pushy the other person seems |
| _____ | How intelligent or educated the other person appears to be |
| _____ | How rich or "upper class" the other person seems to be |
| _____ | Other (specify) _____ |
| _____ | Other (specify) _____ |

**Your Relationship with the Other Person and Its Effect on Your Discomfort**

| Effect on Your Discomfort | Item |
|---|---|
| _____ | How well you know the other person (e.g., family member, close friend, acquaintance, stranger, etc.) |
| _____ | How intimate and close you are to the other person |
| _____ | Whether there is a history of hostility and conflict between yourself and the other person |
| _____ | The type of relationship between you and the other person (e.g., supervisor, coworker, employee) |

| | Other (specify) _____ |
|---|---|
| _____ | |
| _____ | Other (specify) _____ |

## Aspects of How You Feel and Their Effect on Your Discomfort

| Effect on Your Discomfort | Item |
|---|---|
| _____ | How tired you are overall |
| _____ | General level of stress in your life at the time |
| _____ | How familiar you are with the topic being discussed |
| _____ | How prepared you are before entering the situation (e.g., Have you had a chance to rehearse your presentation?) |
| _____ | Other (specify) _____ |
| _____ | Other (specify) _____ |

## Aspects of the Situation and Their Effect on Your Discomfort

| Effect on Your Discomfort | Item |
|---|---|
| _____ | Lighting |
| _____ | How formal the situation is (e.g., eating at a wedding reception vs. a casual dinner with friends) |
| _____ | Number of people involved (e.g., presenting to a few coworkers vs. presenting to an auditorium full of people) |
| _____ | Activity involved (e.g., eating, speaking, writing, etc.) |
| _____ | Your physical position (e.g., seated, standing, etc.) |
| _____ | Whether you can use alcohol or drugs to feel more comfortable |
| _____ | How long you are stuck in the situation |
| _____ | Other (specify) _____ |
| _____ | Other (specify) _____ |

## 3. What Physical Feelings Do You Experience When You Are in a Feared Social Situation and How Frightened Are You of Experiencing These Feelings in Front of Others?

Below is a list of physical feelings that people sometimes experience when they are feeling anxious, worried, or frightened. For each item, you should first record a number (from 0 to 100) that reflects the intensity of the feeling during a typical exposure to an anxiety-provoking social situation. A rating of 0 means that typically you do not experience the sensation at all, and a rating of 100 means that the sensation typically is extremely intense when you encounter social situations that are a problem for you.

Next, using a scale from 0 to 100, rate the extent to which you are fearful of experiencing the sensation in front of other people. A rating of 0 means that you are not at all concerned about experiencing the sensation in front of others and a rating of 100 means that you are extremely fearful of experiencing the sensation in front of others.

**Intensity of the Physical Sensations**

| 0 | 10 | 20 | 30 | 40 | 50 | 60 | 70 | 80 | 90 | 100 |
|---|----|----|----|----|----|----|----|----|----|-----|

*Not at all*        *Mild*            *Moderate*            *Extreme*            *Very Extreme*

**Fear of Having the Physical Sensations in Front of Others**

| 0 | 10 | 20 | 30 | 40 | 50 | 60 | 70 | 80 | 90 | 100 |
|---|----|----|----|----|----|----|----|----|----|-----|

*No Fear*        *Mild Fear*            *Moderate Fear*        *Extreme Fear*        *Very Extreme Fear*

| Intensity of Sensation | Your Fear of Sensation | Sensation |
|---|---|---|
| _____ | _____ | Racing or pounding heart |
| _____ | _____ | Breathlessness or smothering feelings |
| _____ | _____ | Dizziness or lightheadedness |
| _____ | _____ | Difficulty swallowing, choking feelings, or a "lump" in the throat |
| _____ | _____ | Quivering or shakiness (e.g., in the hands, knees, lips, or whole body) |
| _____ | _____ | Blushing |
| _____ | _____ | Nausea, diarrhea, or "butterflies" in the stomach |
| _____ | _____ | Excessive sweating |
| _____ | _____ | Shaky voice |
| _____ | _____ | Tearfulness, crying |
| _____ | _____ | Poor concentration (e.g., forgetting what you are trying to say) |
| _____ | _____ | Blurred vision |
| _____ | _____ | Numbness and tingling sensations |

| | | |
|---|---|---|
| _____ | _____ | Feelings of unreality or being detached from your body or from things around you |
| _____ | _____ | Tightness, soreness, or weakness in the muscles |
| _____ | _____ | Chest pain or tightness in chest muscles |
| _____ | _____ | Dry mouth |
| _____ | _____ | Hot flushes or chills |
| _____ | _____ | Other (specify) _____ |
| _____ | _____ | Other (specify) _____ |
| _____ | _____ | Other (specify) _____ |

## 4. What Are Your Anxious Beliefs, Predictions, and Expectations?

As discussed in chapter 1, your beliefs have an enormous impact on how you feel in social situations. For example, if you expect that others will think you are stupid, weak, or unattractive, you are bound to feel anxious around other people. On the other hand, if you are not especially concerned about what others think about you in a particular situation, you are much more likely to feel comfortable. Often, our beliefs and predictions are not based on reality. For people who experience elevated anxiety in social and performance situations, beliefs and expectations regarding these situations are often negative. These thoughts tend to exaggerate the likelihood of danger and lead the person to expect the worst, even when there is no reason to do so.

Cognitive therapy involves teaching people to identify and change their anxious beliefs, predictions, and expectations by considering more realistic alternative beliefs. Before you can change your thoughts, however, you need to be able to observe them and to decide whether they are unrealistic and perhaps making your anxiety worse.

Chapter 1 lists examples of thoughts and expectations that contribute to social anxiety. Some of these include basic assumptions such as "It is important that everyone like me" and "Nobody will ever think I am interesting." Other anxious thoughts may be more focused on a particular situation, such as "If I arrive at class early, I won't be able to think of anything to say" and "People will think I am weird if they notice my hands shaking."

To identify your own anxious thoughts, we recommend the following steps. First, review some of the examples of anxious thoughts listed in chapter 1. These will give you an idea of the types of thoughts that are often associated with social anxiety. Next, think of social situations that you find particularly difficult (e.g., talking to strangers, eating with other people, speaking at meetings) and try to answer the questions below. Your answers to these questions will give you an idea of the types of thoughts, predictions, and expectations that help to maintain your anxiety.

What are you afraid will happen in the situation?

_____

_____

_____

What might people think about you in the situation?

_____

_____

_____

Is it almost always important that you make a good impression? Why?

_____

_____

_____

How will you react in the situation (what symptoms will you exhibit)?

_____

_____

_____

What if your expectations come true? What might that lead to?

_____

_____

_____

Are you aware of any other beliefs or predictions that contribute to your anxiety?

_____

_____

_____

### 5. What Are Your Anxious Behaviors?

**Avoidance of Social Situations.** Are there situations that you refuse to enter? For example, do you avoid going to parties, particularly when you don't know people? When the telephone rings, do you avoid answering it? Do you turn down opportunities to do presentations even when they are important? Avoidance is one of the most common behaviors that help to maintain your fear and anxiety. Earlier in this chapter you rated the extent to which you fear and avoid various social situations. As part of this review of your anxious behaviors, look over that list again and note which situations you tend to avoid at least some of the time. If there are any other situations that come to mind, list them below.

_____

_____

_____

_____

**Subtle Avoidance and Overprotective Behaviors.** Are there subtle ways in which you avoid situations or protect yourself from feeling anxious in social situations? These would be small things that you do in the situation either to manage your anxiety or to manage other people's impressions of you.

For example, if you have to give a presentation, do you stand in a particular place? Do you wear certain clothes to hide "defects" that you perceive in your appearance? Do you purposely end the presentation late so that there is no time for questions? Do you use videos or slides during the presentation so that the focus won't be on you? Do you avoid making eye contact with the audience?

If you are attending a party, do you purposely stay close to your spouse so that you won't have to talk to other people? Do you have a drink or two as soon as you get to the party so that your anxiety stays in check? Do you offer to help serve food or clean dishes so you won't have to talk to the other guests? Do you take frequent bathroom breaks to avoid being with everyone else? When you are talking to other guests at the party, do you ask the other person lots of questions to keep the focus of the conversation away from you?

All of these are examples of subtle avoidance strategies that people sometimes use in social situations. As discussed in chapter 1, these behaviors may decrease your anxiety in the short term by helping you to feel safer. However, in the long term, they typically have the effect of preventing your anxiety from decreasing naturally over time because they prevent you from learning that the situation can be safe and manageable even without relying on subtle avoidance strategies. In the spaces below, list examples of subtle avoidance behaviors that you use to manage your anxiety in social situations. Because these behaviors may differ from situation to situation, there is space to record these behaviors for each of a number of different social situations.

| Specify Social Situation | Subtle Avoidance and Overprotective Behaviors |
| --- | --- |
| _____ | _____ |
| | _____ |
| | _____ |
| _____ | _____ |
| | _____ |
| | _____ |
| _____ | _____ |
| | _____ |

**Comparing Yourself to the "Wrong" People.** One of the ways in which we evaluate ourselves is to make comparisons with other people. In school, we ask our classmates how they did on their exams to get an idea of how our own work compares to that of others. We are curious about our coworkers' salaries, in part, because having that information is a way of knowing whether we are being paid fairly.

Research (Suls and Wills 1991) has consistently found that most people compare themselves to others whom they perceive to be either similar to themselves or slightly better on a particular dimension.

For example, an average student is likely to compare his or her grades to those of other average students or to slightly better-than-average students. Similarly, a top athlete tends to compare his or her performance to other top athletes in order to judge the quality of his or her own performance. This pattern of social comparison makes sense because it is most likely to provide information you can use to gauge your own performance. Comparing yourself to someone whom you perceive to be much better or much worse than you on a particular dimension will provide information that isn't especially relevant to you. For example, if you are a musician who plays mostly in local clubs, it doesn't make sense to compare your success to that of the most popular and successful musicians in the world. Making such comparisons is likely to cause you to feel inadequate, because you will perceive that you can't possibly compete with the best.

Preliminary research from our center suggests that people who are particularly socially anxious make different types of social comparisons than do those who are less anxious. Specifically, social anxiety is associated with a tendency to make more frequent "upward" comparisons. In other words, people who are socially anxious are more likely to compare themselves to people they perceive as better than they are. (Similarly, a comparison to someone who is perceived to be worse off on a particular dimension is called a "downward" comparison.) The tendency to make upward comparisons increases the likelihood that an individual will feel worse after making the comparison.

Can you think of recent examples when you have compared yourself to someone whom you perceived to be more attractive, more competent, less anxious, stronger, or smarter than you are? Or, did you make an "upward" comparison on some other dimension? How did you feel afterward? Do you often tend to compare yourself to people whom you perceive to be ideal or perfect on a certain dimension, rather than people whom you perceive to be typical or average? In the space below, describe an example of a time when you compared yourself to someone who was much "better" than you in some way.

---

---

---

**Overcompensating for Perceived Deficits.** Are there ways in which you try extra hard in social situations to compensate for flaws or faults that you perceive yourself to have? For example, do you overprepare for presentations by putting together too much material, memorizing the presentation, or reading the presentation word for word from your notes? Do you rehearse everything that you are going to say before meeting a friend for dinner, just in case you become overly anxious and lose your train of thought? Do you go out of your way to talk a lot to appear outgoing, just so people won't notice that you're anxious? Each of these is an example of how people sometimes overcompensate to cover up what they perceive to be flaws. If you can think of examples of times when you have overcompensated in social situations for what you thought were flaws or faults, list them below.

---

---

---

**Excessive Checking and Reassurance Seeking.** Social anxiety, shyness, and performance anxiety sometimes can lead people to engage in frequent checking and reassurance seeking behaviors. Examples include frequently looking in the mirror to make sure that your hair is perfect, and continually asking your friends to reassure you that you are interesting or smart.

Although it is helpful to seek reassurance from time to time, constant reassurance seeking can have a negative impact by helping to maintain your fear. By asking for reassurance over and over again, you may strengthen the belief that there is something wrong with you (why else would you need to check so often?).

Also, you run the risk of never learning to provide yourself with the reassurance that you may need. Finally, constantly asking others for reassurance may cause some of your greatest fears to come true by negatively affecting how others view you. Other people may get tired of always having to provide you with reassurance. Also, if you constantly ask others to make judgments about you (e.g., to tell you how smart, attractive, or interesting you are), you may actually be training them to be more observant and scrutinizing of you than they might otherwise be.

In the space below, list some examples of times when you have engaged in excessive checking or reassurance seeking.

---

---

---

## 6. Could You Benefit from Improving Your "People Skills"?

Everyone has times during which they give off the wrong impression simply because they did not know how to communicate a particular message to another person or group. Generally, this is not a big problem unless it happens frequently or in situations where there is a lot at stake.

In most cases, people who are socially anxious have quite adequate social skills. But they tend to assume that their social skills are much worse than they actually are. Furthermore, as their anxiety decreases and they obtain more practice interacting with others in the situations that they fear, their skills tend to improve over time.

Below are some examples of areas where you may want to consider working on improving your skills. This may prove to be particularly helpful for situations that you have tended to avoid over the years and therefore may not have had the opportunity to learn some of the subtleties of navigating your way through the situation. For example, if you have never dated, you may need some practice before knowing how to ask someone out on a date to maximize your chances of a positive response. As you read through the examples, try to identify "people skills" that you may want to work on. There is space at the end of this section to record your responses.

**Assertiveness.** Do you have difficulty being assertive? In other words, is it hard for you to say "no" if someone asks you to do something that you don't want to do? Is it difficult to ask someone to change their behavior if he or she is treating you unfairly or is not doing their share of the work? Most people have some difficulty at times dealing directly and assertively with situations like these. However, the more difficulty that you have in situations that call for assertive communication, the more you have to gain from learning assertiveness skills.

**Body language, tone of voice, and eye contact.** Do you have difficulty making eye contact with other people? Does your tone of voice or body language send the message that you are not open to interacting with others? Behaviors that convey such messages may include speaking very quietly or letting your voice drop off at the end of your sentences, standing far away from other people when you are talking with them, answering questions with very short responses, and displaying a "closed" body posture (e.g., crossing your arms and legs). Although you may use these behaviors to "protect" yourself in social situations, they may actually have the opposite effect by turning others away. If you send the message to others that you are unavailable, they will be more likely to leave you alone.

**Conversation skills.** Do you have difficulty knowing what to say when talking to people at work or school? Is it hard to know how or when to end conversations? Do you find it difficult to know where the fine line is between appropriate self-disclosure and talking too much about yourself? Do you often offend other people with comments that you make? If you have difficulty making small talk or engaging in casual conversations, you may benefit by working on improving these skills.

**Meeting new people.** Do you have difficulty knowing what to say when you want to initiate contact with new people? Do you have difficulty asking someone out on a date? Are you at a loss for knowing how and where to meet new people? There are lots of different places to meet new people and lots of tricks to making meeting new people easier. The first step is identifying whether this is an area that you would like to work on.

**Presentation skills.** Speaking effectively in public involves a number of complex skills and behaviors. It is not enough to be calm and confident. An effective speaker also knows how to maintain the audience's interest by using humor and effective audio-visual aids and handouts, stimulating audience participation, and conveying his or her own interest in the topic. If you fear making presentations, part of overcoming your fear of public speaking may include learning how to improve your speaking skills.

In the space below, list any social or communication skills that you might like to work on.

## Social Skills That You Would Like to Develop or Improve

_____

_____

_____

_____

### 7. How Much Does Your Social Anxiety Bother You or Interfere with Your Life?

Everyone has situations or objects that they fear. In most cases, people live with the fear and it doesn't really have a major impact on how they live their lives. For example, for most people who are fearful of public speaking, the opportunity to give presentations rarely comes up and it is very easy to avoid the situation without any significant cost. Similarly, most people who are uncomfortable speaking to their supervisors are just as happy to stay that way either because the situation rarely arises or because the discomfort and hard work that would be needed to overcome the fear wouldn't be worth the relatively small impact that the change would likely have on the person's life.

As we discussed in chapter 1, social anxiety, shyness, and performance-related fears are only a problem if they interfere with aspects of your functioning or if having the fear is troublesome for you. For example, someone who is terrified of giving presentations and who has to give presentations on a regular basis clearly has a problem.

So, as part of your self-assessment, it is important for you to determine which aspects of your fear trouble you and which don't. Are there particular situations for which you are most interested in overcoming your fear? For example, it may be important for you to overcome your fear of socializing with friends, but relatively less important for you to overcome your fear of speaking in front of large groups if that situation never arises.

In the space below, record (1) the ways in which your social anxiety interferes with your functioning (including work or school, social life, relationships, hobbies and leisure activities, home and family life), (2) the specific aspects of your social anxiety that you most want to change, and (3) any aspects of your social anxiety that you are not interested in working on.

### Ways in Which Social Anxiety Interferes with Your Life

_____

_____

_____

### Aspects of Your Social Anxiety That You Want to Change

_____

_____

_____

**Aspects of Your Social Anxiety That You Don't Want to Change**

_____

_____

_____

## 8. How and When Did Your Social Anxiety Begin?

How old were you when you recall having significant anxiety first in social situations? What was going on at that time in your life?

_____

_____

_____

How old were you when you first recall that your social anxiety began to interfere with aspects of your life? What was going on at the time?

_____

_____

_____

What has the course of your social anxiety been over the years? Has it improved, stayed the same, or worsened? Are you aware of factors that may have caused it to change over the years (e.g., getting married, moving to a new neighborhood, etc.)?

_____

_____

_____

Are there specific events that initially caused you to become more nervous in social situations or made your social anxiety worsen? Examples may include experiences such as presentations that didn't go well, being teased while growing up, or doing something embarrassing or humiliating in public.

_____

_____

_____

### 9. Does Anyone Else in Your Family Have This Problem?

Are you aware of anyone else in your family having problems with shyness, social anxiety, or performance-related fears? If so, do you think that this had an influence on how you feel in these situations? If yes, how?

---

### 10. Are There Any Physical Conditions That Contribute to Your Social Anxiety?

For some individuals, certain physical or medical conditions may influence their tendency to experience social anxiety. For example, people who stutter may be more nervous when talking to others compared to people who don't stutter. Often, their fear is exclusively related to a concern that they will stutter and that others will notice. Similarly, people suffering from other medical conditions (e.g., shaking due to Parkinson's disease, having to move about in a wheelchair, not being able to write neatly due to severe arthritis) may be self-conscious about having others observe their symptoms.

Other people, although they may not be suffering from a medical condition, may still have a greater tendency than others to have shaky hands, blush easily, or sweat excessively, independent of their fears. For these individuals, these reactions tend to be very intense and may often occur even outside of social situations, and when they are not particularly anxious. Although many people who experience these symptoms at such an extreme level are not concerned about others noticing, for some, having these extreme symptoms contributes to their social anxiety.

Do you suffer from any physical conditions or medical illnesses that add to your anxiety around other people? If so, record the details below.

---

## Diaries

The diaries used to assess social anxiety usually are just forms on which an individual records his or anxiety-related symptoms, including frequency of exposure to feared situations, anxiety levels (using a numeric scale such as 0–100), uncomfortable physical sensations such as blushing or shaking, anxious thoughts and predictions (e.g., "I will make a fool of myself during this presentation"), and anxious behaviors such as avoidance and distraction. An example of such a diary is the Three Components of Social Anxiety Monitoring Form, which is reproduced in chapter 1. As discussed earlier, we suggest that you complete this form several times per week for at least two weeks before starting your treatment. Numerous other forms and diaries are included throughout this book as well. They are designed to be used while trying the specific treatment techniques described in later chapters.

## Behavioral Assessments

The most commonly used type of behavioral assessment for social anxiety is the Behavioral Approach Test (BAT). This assessment method involves physically entering a feared situation and measuring your anxiety and associated symptoms. For example, if you are afraid of public speaking, you might force yourself to speak at a staff meeting. After the meeting, you can record the particulars of the situation (who else was there, how long you spoke for, etc.), your fear level (e.g., 80 out of 100), your anxious thoughts (e.g., my words will come out all jumbled), and whether you engaged in any avoidance behaviors (e.g., avoiding eye contact).

If it is too frightening to try this in a real-life situation, or if it is impossible to do so for another reason, the assessment can be completed in the form of a role-play. In a role-play, the person acts out the feared situation with the therapist or another individual present, instead of being in the real situation. For example, if you are afraid of job interviews, you might try to practice a job interview with another person (friend, family member, or therapist) taking the role of the interviewer. Following the practice, you would again record the particulars of the situation, your fear level, your anxious thoughts, and your avoidance behaviors.

Therapists use behavioral assessments because they have several advantages over traditional forms of assessment such as interviews and questionnaires. First, they are less likely to be influenced by people's difficulties in remembering the details of their fears. For example, some people may overestimate or underestimate their fear levels if they are asked to describe their fear during past exposures to feared situations. Their memories may be influenced by a particularly negative experience in a feared situation and, as a result, they may report that their fear is actually higher than it typically is. Also, people's memories regarding their reactions in the situations they fear may be poor simply because they typically avoid the fearful situation, making it difficult to know for sure how they feel when they are exposed to the situation.

Another advantage of the behavioral approach test is that it allows the therapist and the individual to directly observe the anxious thoughts and behaviors that might otherwise go unnoticed. It also allows the therapist to independently assess the extent to which the client's shaking, blushing, or sweating is actually noticeable to others.

Can you think of a behavioral approach test or role-play that you can set up for yourself? For example, if you are fearful of speaking up in a meeting, try doing it anyway. Immediately after the meeting, record your physical symptoms, anxious thoughts, and the avoidance behaviors that took place while you were conducting the practice. Did it go better than you expected it to go? Was it worse? Was it about what you expected?

# Trouble Shooting

You may find that your self-assessment does not go as smoothly as you might like. Here are some common problems that may arise during your self-assessment as well as some solutions, suggestions, and words of reassurance.

*Problem:*     I didn't know the answer to all the questions.

*Solution:*    That's to be expected. As you progress with the treatment, you will have an opportunity to become better acquainted with your social anxiety. Self-assessment is an ongoing process and it's not necessary to have all the answers before you start to work on changing your social anxiety. In fact, there may be some questions that you will never know the answers to and that is okay. The purpose of this chapter is just to help you better understand the areas that are causing you the most difficulty.

*Problem:*     Answering these questions increased my anxiety.

*Solution:*    This is quite common. Conducting a self-assessment forces you to pay attention to the thoughts that contribute to your anxiety. This effect of increased anxiety tends to be temporary. As you progress through the treatment procedures discussed throughout this book, it is likely you will find that focusing on the thoughts and feelings associated with your social anxiety will become less anxiety-provoking over time.

*Problem:*     My answers to these questions depend on many different variables, so I find it difficult to come up with a response to certain questions.

*Solution:*    This concern is often raised by people who are undergoing an assessment. Frequently questions are difficult to answer because they depend on so many different factors. For example, the question, "How fearful are you of public speaking?" may depend on such things as the topic of the presentation, the number of people in the audience, the lighting in the room, the length of the presentation, how prepared you are, and many other factors. We suggest that you handle difficult questions by estimating your response based on a typical or average situation. So, if your fear of public speaking ranges from 30 to 70, depending on the situation, you could put down "50." If you prefer, you could just record the range "30 to 70," which would be more precise.

After reading this chapter, you should have a better understanding of the nature of your social anxiety. You should be more aware of the types of social situations that you fear and avoid, the variables that affect your discomfort level, the physical sensations that you experience when you are anxious, the thoughts and behaviors that contribute to your fear, and the ways in which social anxiety interferes with your life. Understanding these aspects of your social anxiety will help you to choose the best strategies for overcoming your fear as you work your way through the rest of this book.

# Part II

# How to Overcome Social Anxiety and Enjoy Your Life

# Chapter 4

# Making a Plan for Change

This chapter will help you to consider the range of factors that are important for developing a treatment plan. These factors include deciding whether this is the best time for you to work on your social anxiety, selecting treatment goals, trying to understand why treatment may or may not have worked in the past, and understanding your current options for treatment.

## Is Now the Best Time to Start This Program?

In some ways, it may seem as if there is never a good time to begin a new project. Almost always there are competing demands that make it difficult to find free time or extra energy to start something new. Work may be unusually busy; you may be getting over a cold; or your children may be a handful right now. Although the time may not be perfect, you will need to decide whether it is even a possibility for you to start this program given your current life circumstances. Your chances of getting the most out of this book will depend on your answering "yes" to the following questions:

- Are you motivated to become less shy or to decrease your social anxiety? Is this something you really care about?

- Are you willing to feel even more anxious in the shortterm, in order to feel more comfortable in social and performance situations in the future?

- Are you able to put aside, at least to some extent, other major problems and stresses in your life (e.g., family problems, work stresses), so that you can focus on learning to manage your social and performance anxiety?

- Are you able to set aside several blocks of time several days per week to practice the techniques described in this book?

Hopefully, after carefully considering these questions, you will make a commitment to work on overcoming your social anxiety. However, you may also decide that this is not the best time for you to work on the problem and that you would rather wait until your life situation changes. If that is the case, you may still find reading this book helpful because it contains strategies that can be used from time to time, as you need them. However, making big changes will require using the techniques described in this book frequently and consistently.

## Benefits and Costs of Overcoming Your Anxiety

For the majority of people, the benefits of using the strategies described in this book outweigh the costs. Examples of possible benefits include the following:

- Learning to feel more comfortable in feared social and performance situations

- Meeting new friends

- Improving the quality of your relationships

- Learning to network more comfortably in situations related to your job or career

- Expanding the possible options for what you can do in your leisure time

- Improving your job prospects (e.g., realizing new opportunities to get a promotion or to seek a higher paying position)

- Opening up opportunities for self-improvement by furthering your education

- Learning to increase your enjoyment of life

- Feeling more confident

- Increasing your ability to express yourself

- Learning strategies that you may be able to apply to other problems, such as anger, depression, or a troubled relationship

Can you think of other benefits that would result from overcoming your social anxiety? If so, record them in the space below.

_____

_____

_____

In addition to these benefits, however, there are also possible costs to the treatment, especially early in the process. For example, if you choose to use medications, you will have to remember to take them regularly and you may experience side effects. Depending on the medication, side effects may include fatigue, headaches, changes in weight and appetite, and changes in sexual functioning. Also, newer medications may be expensive, particularly if they are not covered by your health plan. (See chapter 5 for a more detailed discussion of medications and their side effects.)

Psychological treatments, such as confronting the situations that you fear, are also associated with costs. First, they are time-consuming. To get the most out of exposure-based treatments, for example, you will need to practice for an hour or more, three to five days per week. In addition, conducting exposure practices is almost guaranteed to make you feel anxious and uncomfortable, particularly at the start. Although the exercises are designed so that the discomfort is usually manageable, at times your fear will probably be quite intense.

In addition to feeling uncomfortable, you may feel more tired, especially on days when you practice confronting situations that make you uncomfortable. You also may feel irritable and perhaps even have anxiety-provoking dreams. Finally, your improvement may not follow a smooth course. It is likely the changes will take time and you may have periods (e.g., days, weeks, or even months) during which you feel as though you are slipping backwards. For many people this is a normal part of the process of overcoming social anxiety. By continuing to use the strategies described in this book, however, your anxiety should continue to improve over time.

Overcoming your anxiety may also have an impact on other areas of your life. In most cases, the impact will be positive, but there may be some costs associated with these changes as well. For example, if you are in a long-term relationship, you may find that your partner will need time to adjust to the changes you are making. For example, as you become more comfortable socializing, you may be out more often with friends or coworkers. If your partner is accustomed to having you around most of the time, this may require some new adjustments. We recommend that you discuss the changes that you are making openly with your partner, friends, and family members, if appropriate. This will demonstrate to them that you are sensitive to how the improvements in your social anxiety may affect them.

Can you think of other possible costs of overcoming your social anxiety, shyness, or performance-related fears? If so, record them in the following space.

_____

_____

_____

Now that you have had a chance to consider the costs and benefits of working on your social anxiety, you are in a better position to make a commitment to working on overcoming your fears. Assuming that you have decided to go ahead as planned, the remainder of this chapter will help you consider the strategies best suited to your individual needs.

# Setting Goals for Change

Without setting specific goals or objectives, it will be impossible for you to evaluate whether you are making the changes that you hope to make. Goals can be described in a number of different ways. First, goals can reflect either short-term or long-term changes that you would like to accomplish. For example, if you have a fear of public speaking, a reasonable one-week goal might be to ask a single question at a meeting at work, regardless of how anxious you feel. A six-month goal might be to give a thirty-minute presentation without feeling significant anxiety. As you go through the process of overcoming your social anxiety, it is important to identify short-term goals (e.g., What do you want to accomplish this week?), medium-range goals (e.g., What do you want to accomplish over the next few months?), and long-range goals (e.g., What do you want to accomplish over the next year or two?).

Goals also can be described either as *specific* or *general*. A specific goal is more detailed than a general one. Therefore, specific goals are often better suited for selecting appropriate treatment strategies, compared to general goals. Also, with more specific goals, it is easier to measure whether your objectives are being met. Although it is okay to have a few general goals, you also should try to generate as many specific goals as possible. Examples of general and specific goals are listed below.

| General Goal | Specific Goal |
|---|---|
| To be more comfortable during presentations at my weekly sales meetings | To have my fear level during presentations decrease from a level of 100 out of 100 to a level of 40 out of 100 |
| To ask someone out on a date sometime | To ask John (or Jane) to have dinner with me by the end of this month |

| | |
|---|---|
| To have more friends | To meet at least three new friends by the end of this year, with whom I can see movies or watch sports |
| To be comfortable in crowds | To be able to walk through a crowded mall or on a crowded street with my fear below a 30 or 40 out of 100 |
| To cope better with criticism | To be able to tolerate negative feedback on my annual performance review at work without becoming very upset and while still paying attention to all my positive achievements over the year |
| To ask questions in class | To ask at least one question during each class over the rest of this semester |
| To deal better with groups | To be able to make small talk at a party while maintaining eye contact and making sure that I speak loudly enough for others to hear |

Now, think about what types of changes *you* would like to make. Specifically, think about aspects of your social anxiety (e.g., anxious beliefs, situations that you avoid, etc.) that you would like to change. Try to be realistic. Also, recognize that your goals may change. For example, right now you may not need to make presentations in your daily life. However, if you take a job that involves public speaking, your goals may have to be revised to reflect this change.

We have included space for you to record your goals for the next month as well as your goals for one year from now. Of course, if you prefer, you may choose other time periods. The main point to remember is that you may have different short-term and long-term goals. Although some goals may be realistic targets for a year or two from now, they may not be realistic goals for one week or one month from now.

**One-Month Goals**

1. _____

2. _____

3. _____

4. _____

5. _____

6. _____

7. _____

8. _____

9. _____

10. _____

**One-Year Goals**

1. _____

2. _____

3. _____

4. _____

5. _____

6. _____

7. _____

8. _____

9. _____

10. _____

# Reviewing Previous Attempts to Treat Your Social Anxiety

This section has two purposes. First, if you have tried to overcome your social anxiety in the past, it will help you review the treatments that worked for you and those that were not especially helpful. Second, this section will help you to identify possible reasons why certain previous attempts to overcome your social anxiety were not useful, if this was your experience. By identifying the reasons for previously successful and not-so-successful treatment attempts, you will be able to make more educated decisions about what types of strategies to try now. If a treatment has worked well in the past, you may want to try it again. If you did not benefit from a particular treatment previously, you may want to try something new. However, you should still consider giving a particular treatment another try if you didn't give it a fair chance the first time.

In the spaces below, check off any treatments that you have tried in the past. Also, describe the treatment and record whether the outcome was helpful.

### Record of Previous Treatments

| Yes | No | Treatment |
|-----|-----|-----------|
| _____ | _____ | **Medications**<br>If yes, list drug names, duration of treatment, and maximum dosage for each drug. Also, describe any side effects that you experienced and the outcome of the treatment. In other words, did it help? |

_____

_____

_____

| _____ | _____ | **Exposure to Feared Situations**<br>If yes, describe the treatment (e.g., frequency of exposures, duration of treatment, types of situations practiced in, outcome). |

_____

_____

_____

| _____ | _____ | **Cognitive Therapy** (see definition later in this chapter).<br>If yes, describe the treatment (e.g., duration of treatment, outcome). |

_____

_____

_____

| _____ | _____ | **Skills Training** (e.g., assertiveness training, public speaking or communications course). If yes, describe the treatment (e.g., duration of treatment, outcome). |

_____

_____

_____

_____    _____    **Insight Oriented Therapy** (i.e., therapy that is focused on early childhood experiences, and on helping you to understand the deep causes underlying a particular problem). If yes, describe the treatment (e.g., duration of treatment, outcome).

_____

_____

_____

_____    _____    **Supportive Therapy** (i.e., therapy that is usually fairly unstructured, in which the client describes his or her experiences over the past week and the therapist offers support and perhaps suggestions for solving problems that arise from week to week). If yes, describe the treatment (e.g., duration of treatment, outcome).

_____

_____

_____

_____    _____    **Self-Help Books.** If yes, describe the treatment (e.g., What book did you read? What approach did the book take? Did it help?)

_____

_____

_____

Now that you have identified specific treatments you have tried in the past, the next step is to understand why a treatment was ineffective or only partially effective, if that was your experience. Listed below are some of the reasons why psychological treatments and medications are occasionally not helpful.

## Why Psychological Treatments Sometimes Don't Help

- It is an ineffective therapy for the specific problem. Some psychological treatments (particularly cognitive-behavior therapy) have been shown to be more effective than others for treating social anxiety.

- The therapist is inexperienced either with the type of therapy being offered or the type of problem being treated.

- The frequency and intensity of practices is too low. For example, if an individual practices exposure to social situations too infrequently, he or she is less likely to see results.

- The treatment does not last long enough (e.g., the person drops out of treatment or the treatment ends before positive results can be seen).

- An individual expects the treatment to be ineffective. There is evidence that a person's expectations can affect the outcome of psychotherapy (Safren, Heimberg, and Juster 1997).

- The person does not comply with the treatment (e.g., missing sessions, not completing homework).

- There are other problems or stresses in the person's life that interfere with treatment (e.g., severe depression, alcohol abuse, stressful job).

## Why Medications Sometimes Don't Help

- It is the wrong medication for the problem. Some medications have been shown to be more effective than others for treating social anxiety (see chapter 5). Furthermore, a medication that works for one person may not be the best choice for someone else.

- The medication dosage is not high enough.

- The treatment does not last long enough. Some medications can take up to six weeks to have an effect. Also, stopping certain medications too soon can increase the chances of the anxiety coming back.

- An individual expects the treatment to be ineffective. As with psychotherapy, there is evidence that a person's response to medication is affected by his or her expectations.

- The side effects are unmanageable.

- The person is using drugs, drinking alcohol, or taking other medications that interact with the effects of the medication for social anxiety.

- The person does not comply with the treatment (e.g., misses pills, etc.).

If you have tried to overcome your social anxiety in the past, but found treatment to be ineffective or only partially effective, do you have any guesses about why it may not have worked as well as you had hoped it would?

1. _____

2. _____

3. _____

Based on your previous experiences with therapy or medication, are there strategies that you want to try again?

1. _____

2. _____

3. _____

Are there strategies that you definitely don't want to try again?

1. _____

2. _____

3. _____

# Proven Strategies for Overcoming Social Anxiety

There are hundreds of different approaches that people have used to overcome emotional difficulties, behavior problems, and bad habits. Some of these approaches include psychotherapy, medications, prayer, relaxation training, yoga, hypnosis, distraction, drinking alcohol or using drugs, exercise, changing diet, reward and punishment, herbal remedies, education and reading about the problem, past-life regression, and so forth. Furthermore, each of these methods can be subdivided into even more categories. For example, there are many different types of psychotherapy and medications, some of which are more useful than others for a particular problem. Given all of the different available options, it can be very difficult for a consumer to select the best approach for overcoming a particular problem.

For most of the methods listed above, there is almost no controlled research examining their use in treating anxiety in general, and social anxiety in particular. The term "controlled" is used to describe studies in which the investigators have examined the effects of a particular treatment while taking steps to ensure that any improvements that occur are, in fact, due to the treatment, rather than to other factors. Note that a lack of controlled research does *not* mean that a particular treatment is ineffective. It simply means we just don't know whether the treatment works or how well it works.

Even if someone seems to improve after using one of the methods named above, it is difficult to know whether it was the treatment that had a beneficial effect, or whether other factors contributed to the change. For example, as mentioned earlier, someone's expectations of improving during treatment can affect his or her improvement. Other reasons why people might improve with a particular treatment may include the passage of time. For some types of problems (e.g., depression), the symptoms may improve naturally over time, regardless of whether the sufferer receives any specific treatments.

Changes in a person's normal routines (e.g., a reduction of stress at work) also can contribute to improvements over and above any treatment effects.

Properly controlled research can help to determine whether the effects of a treatment are indeed due to the treatment rather than to other factors. One strategy used by researchers is the inclusion of a control group. For example, research studies that examine the effects of a medication on a particular problem usually give a percentage of the individuals in the study a *placebo*, which is, essentially, a pill that contains no real medication. This group is called the *placebo control group*. Typically, neither the doctor nor the patient knows whether the person is taking a placebo or the real medication until after the study ends.

The test of whether a medication is helpful depends on how well people taking the medication respond, compared to those who are taking placebo. Including a placebo control group allows the researcher to directly measure the effects of the medication over and above the effects of the individual's expectations regarding the treatment. Properly conducted studies examining the effects of psychological treatments also include appropriate control groups to aid in understanding why a particular treatment may appear to work.

In this book, we have chosen to focus on techniques that have been shown in controlled research to be effective for helping people to overcome problems with social anxiety, shyness, and performance-related fears. In other words, these techniques have been shown to be effective compared to no treatment, placebo treatments, other forms of psychotherapy, or other appropriate control groups. The techniques we will focus on include two main groups of strategies: cognitive-behavior therapy and medications.

## Cognitive-Behavior Therapy

Cognitive-behavior therapy, or CBT, includes a group of techniques that are usually used together as a package. Numerous studies have shown that CBT is an effective way of overcoming social anxiety (for a review, see Antony and Swinson 2000). Cognitive-behavior therapy differs from other more traditional forms of therapy in the following ways:

- CBT is directive. In other words, the therapist is actively involved in the therapy and makes very specific suggestions.

- CBT's focus is on changing a particular problem. Some other forms of therapy focus on helping the individual develop insight (i.e., understanding) into the deep-rooted causes of a problem, but do not offer specific strategies for overcoming the problem.

- CBT has a relatively brief duration. The typical course of CBT for social anxiety is ten to twenty sessions.

- CBT focuses on current beliefs and behaviors, which are thought to be responsible for maintaining the problem. Some traditional therapies tend to focus more on early childhood experiences.

- In CBT, the therapist and client are "partners" and work together during treatment.

- In CBT, the client chooses the goals for therapy, with input from the therapist.

- CBT usually includes strategies for measuring progress so that treatment techniques can be altered for maximum effectiveness.

- CBT involves changing beliefs and behaviors so that the client is able to better manage anxiety and to navigate anxiety-provoking situations.

Cognitive-behavior therapy for social anxiety includes three main types of strategies. Treatment almost always includes cognitive therapy and exposure to feared situations. In addition, social skills training is sometimes included.

### Cognitive Therapy

The word "cognition" means "thought." The term "cognitive" refers to anything having to do with assumptions, beliefs, predictions, interpretations, visual imagery, memory, and other mental processes related to thinking. Cognitive therapy is a way of helping people replace their negative and unrealistic thoughts with a more realistic way of thinking.

The basic underlying assumption of cognitive therapy is that negative emotions occur because people interpret situations in a negative or threatening way. For example, people who are convinced that others will judge them in a negative way or who are overly concerned about the opinions of others are bound to feel anxious or uncomfortable in certain social situations. Cognitive therapy teaches individuals to be more aware of their negative thoughts and to replace them with less negative thoughts. People are taught to treat their beliefs as guesses about the way things may be, rather than as facts . They are taught to examine the evidence supporting their anxious beliefs and to consider the possibility that an alternative belief is true.

For example, if Henry is very hurt and angry because a friend didn't return his call, these negative feelings might stem from Henry's belief that the friend doesn't care about him. In cognitive therapy, Henry would be taught to consider alternative explanations for the friend's behavior, including the possibility that the friend never received the message, forgot to return the call, or is out of town. After all, there are many possible reasons why a caring friend might not have returned Henry's call quickly.

At the beginning of treatment, diaries are used to record anxious thoughts and to counter them with more realistic predictions and interpretations. As people become more comfortable with the methods of challenging their unrealistic negative beliefs, their new ways of thinking become more automatic and the diaries are no longer needed. People learn to manage their anxious thoughts before they get out of control. Cognitive therapy techniques are described in detail in chapter 6.

### Exposure

Exposure involves gradually but repeatedly confronting feared situations, until they no longer trigger fear. In most cases, exposure is viewed as a necessary component of CBT. In fact, exposure may be even more powerful than cognitive therapy as a way of changing anxious negative thinking. By exposing yourself to situations you fear, you will learn that the risk in these situations is minimal. Through direct experience, many of your anxious predictions and beliefs will be proven incorrect. You will also learn to better tolerate situations in which some of your beliefs actually may be true (e.g., when another person actually does judge you negatively). Finally, exposure will provide you with an opportunity to practice your cognitive therapy skills and to improve upon any social or communication skills that may be rusty from having avoided social situations for so long. See chapters 7 through 9 for detailed instructions for designing and implementing exposure exercises.

### Improving Social Skills

Social skills training refers to the process of learning to improve the quality of your communication as well as other social behaviors, so there will be an increased likelihood of obtaining a positive response from others. Note that most people who are socially anxious have better social skills than they think they do. In fact, formal social skills training is often not included in CBT programs, and people undergoing the treatment still respond quite well. Still, there is evidence that some people can benefit from learning a few new techniques to become more assertive, make small talk more effectively, improve their eye contact, and learn basic skills for dating or meeting new people. Chapter 10 describes strategies for improving social and communication skills.

### Medications

Numerous medications have been shown to be effective for treating social phobia (Antony and Swinson 2000). These include certain antidepressants (e.g., Paxil, Nardil) that also target anxiety, and certain anti-anxiety drugs (e.g., Klonapin). Typically, medications are taken on a daily basis. To varying degrees, all medications are associated with certain side effects. However, for most people, these side effects are quite manageable and most tend to decrease over time.

## Choosing Among Treatment Options

If you decide to try medications, you will need to get a prescription from a physician—usually your family doctor or a psychiatrist. A visit to your family doctor is a good place to start. He or she can make a referral to a psychiatrist if needed. If you are interested in trying a psychological treatment, such as CBT, you have the option of trying to overcome the problem on your own or of seeking professional help.

## Self-Help or Professional Help?

For mild social anxiety, a self-help approach such as that described in this book may be sufficient. However, many people find that the added structure and support provided by a therapist is helpful. If you decide to seek professional help, this book can still help to reinforce what you learn in therapy. An important part of CBT involves educating the client (often using self-help readings) and encouraging the client to practice the various CBT techniques between sessions. In other words, even CBT conducted with a therapist often includes a self-help component, especially compared to other forms of professional therapy. For more information on finding a therapist, see the section on seeking professional help that appears later in this chapter.

## Cognitive-Behavior Therapy or Other Psychotherapy?

In almost all cases, we recommend cognitive therapy and exposure as the psychological treatment of choice for social phobia. Adding social skills training to the program may be useful for some individuals as well. As for other psychological therapies, although they certainly have a place for treating certain types of problems, they are not proven when it comes to treating social phobia and other anxiety-related conditions.

Some people with whom we have worked have reported benefits from combining CBT with another form of psychotherapy. In these cases, typically they have seen one therapist for CBT and another for dealing with other issues (e.g., marital problems, coping with childhood abuse). Although this approach sometimes works well, we recommend that your two therapists stay in close contact with each other so that they can ensure they are not giving you contradictory messages during therapy.

## Medication or CBT?

Relatively few studies have compared medications to CBT for social phobia, and the few studies that have been published have examined only a small number of medications (Antony and Swinson 2000). The most common finding is that medications and CBT work about equally well, while the person is involved in the treatment. There is also reason to believe that medications may work more quickly than CBT for some people with social phobia. However, after treatment has ended, the advantages of CBT over medication become more apparent. After ending CBT, people usually maintain their improvements over time. In contrast, people are more likely to have their anxiety return after stopping medication. In other words, for treating social phobia in the long-term, there may be an advantage of CBT over medication.

Another option is to combine medication and CBT. Currently, there are no published studies on the effectiveness of combining CBT and medication for social phobia, compared to using either alone. However, several studies are underway and we should soon know more about the advantages of combined treatment. Based on our clinical experience, some people seem to respond best to the combination of these two approaches. The approach we usually recommend is to start with either CBT or medication (usually CBT), and then introduce the other treatment after several months, if needed.

## Group or Individual Therapy?

Cognitive-behavior therapy can be delivered either individually or in groups. Both approaches work well, although each has advantages over the other. Group treatment gives people an opportunity to meet other people with the same problem. This can offer you the opportunity to learn from the mistakes and successes of others while reminding you that you are not the only one suffering from this problem. Group treatment also provides clients with opportunities to interact with other individuals who can participate in exposure exercises and role-play practices. For example, group members can be an audience to practice giving presentations to.

The cost is another advantage of group therapy. Because you are sharing the therapist's time with other people, the cost per session often is lower than for individual therapy. If you decide to enter group treatment for social anxiety, we recommend that you try to find a group that focuses exclusively on social anxiety (rather than one that includes people who suffer from different problems). You are most likely to find a specialized social anxiety group at an anxiety disorders specialty clinic.

Now that we have sold you on the advantages of group therapy, we must remind you that individual therapy also has advantages. First, it can be less scary than group therapy, particularly at the beginning. As you can imagine, people with social phobia are often quite terrified of starting group treatment, although anxiety about speaking in front of the group usually diminishes after the first few weeks. Furthermore, with individual therapy, you don't have to share your time with other group members. And, because there is more time to focus on you, the program can be individually tailored to suit your personal needs. Individual therapy also has advantages from a scheduling perspective. If you miss a session due to illness or vacation, usually you can just reschedule an individual appointment. In contrast, if you miss a group session, catching up on the material that you missed may be more complicated.

Whether you decide to seek group or individual treatment should depend on a careful weighing of all of these factors. Keep in mind, however, that you may not have a choice. Although the availability of CBT is increasing, this form of therapy is still hard to find in some places, either in a group or individual format. We would like to emphasize that, when choosing a therapy, the most important factor is finding a therapist who has experience in providing CBT for social anxiety. Whether you choose group or individual therapy should be a secondary issue, since both seem to work well.

# The Importance of Regular Practice or "Homework"

Although simply reading about how to overcome social phobia may be helpful, to make big changes in your social anxiety, it will be necessary for you to actually practice the techniques described throughout this book. For example, you will get more out of the cognitive strategies described in chapter 6 if you complete the monitoring forms and diaries and frequently take advantage of opportunities to challenge your anxious beliefs.

To get the most out of exposure practices, it will be important to enter feared situations as frequently as possible and to stay in the feared situations until your fear has decreased. Many of your exposure practices can be conducted during the course of your everyday life (e.g., having lunch with coworkers instead of eating alone), but other practices may require you to set aside time just for the exposure exercises.

## *Including a Helper or Cotherapist*

It may be helpful to involve a helper or "cotherapist" in your treatment, for example, a friend, coworker, or family member. Your helper can provide you with opportunities to practice role-play exposures, such as presentations, simulated job interviews, making small talk, or asking another person out on a date. In addition, he or she can provide you with honest feedback about your performance and offer suggestions for improvement.

When choosing other people to help you out, we suggest that you select people whom you trust. The other person should be someone who is supportive and unlikely to become frustrated or angry if things move slowly or if you are finding a particular situation difficult or anxiety-provoking. If possible, your helper should read relevant sections of this book so that he or she has a better understanding of the treatment and how it works. If this is not practical, an alternative option would be to have you describe to your helper what his or her role will be during the practices.

# Seeking Professional Help

If you are interested in seeking professional help for your social anxiety, here are some additional suggestions to keep in mind.

## *How to Find a Therapist or Doctor*

One of the most difficult aspects of finding a therapist or doctor is knowing where to look. A good place to begin is with your family doctor, who will likely be aware of psychiatrists, psychologists, and anxiety specialty clinics in your area. You may also want to call nearby hospitals and clinics to see if they have programs that offer either CBT or medication for social anxiety. Check with your insurance company or managed care health organization about the rules regarding coverage for treatment of psychological conditions. Your plan may have restrictions with respect to whom you can see and the number of sessions that are covered.

Another way to find help is to contact a national organization that focuses either on anxiety-related problems or CBT. For example, the Anxiety Disorders Association of America offers information about treatment options and self-help groups across the USA and Canada. The Association for Advancement of Behavior Therapy is an international organization that also has information on social anxiety and options for treatment. Information on how to contact these and other organizations is provided in the Resources section at the back of this book. You may also contact your state psychological or psychiatric associations to get information about psychologists or psychiatrists in your area.

When choosing a professional, don't be afraid to ask questions. Before making a commitment, here are some issues that you should clarify:

- The type of treatment being offered. For example, if you are interested in a psychological treatment, you should ask whether the person is experienced in providing CBT for social and performance anxiety.

- The typical number of sessions recommended for treating this problem, recognizing that it is often difficult to know this before conducting a thorough assessment.

- The length of each session.

- The frequency of sessions.

- The cost per session and preferred method of payment. Are the fees flexible?

- The location and setting. For example, is the treatment conducted in a private office? A hospital? A university clinic? A community clinic? A research center?

- The availability of group versus individual treatments for social anxiety.

- Who provides the treatment? A psychologist? Psychiatrist? Psychology student or psychiatric resident? How experienced is the person? Where was he or she trained? If it is a student therapist, how closely is he or she supervised? How experienced is the supervisor? Can you meet with the supervisor if you wish?

## Types of Professionals

If you are interested in trying medication, most likely you will need to see a psychiatrist or family doctor. Although psychologists in the United States have actively lobbied to obtain limited prescription privileges, currently, medications are almost always prescribed by a physician.

If you are interested in receiving a nonpharmacological-based therapy, your options are much wider. Your therapist can be a psychologist, physician, nurse, social worker, or professional from any number of other backgrounds. However, keep in mind that most practicing clinicians, regardless of their background, do not have extensive experience in providing CBT for anxiety-related problems. It is much more important that you find someone who is familiar with treating social anxiety using cognitive and exposure-based strategies and treatments than what degree the person has. Currently, psychologists are often the most likely to have this background, but other disciplines are increasingly being trained in providing cognitive and behavioral treatments.

Understanding the differences between the different types of therapists often can be confusing. A brief description of some of the main professionals who sometimes provide CBT and related treatments is provided below:

**Psychologist.** In most places, psychologists who specialize in treating psychological disorders usually have a doctoral degree in clinical or counseling psychology. Often, this degree is a Ph.D. (which includes significant training in providing clinical care and research), although it may also be a Psy.D. (indicating a primary training focus on providing clinical services, and relatively less emphasis on research), or an Ed.D. (indicating training that stems from an educational psychology perspective). Typically, training of a psychologist includes an undergraduate bachelor's degree (four years) followed by an additional five to eight years of graduate training.

In most places, people with a master's degree (usually an MA or MS) in clinical or counseling psychology also can offer clinical services. A master's degree typically involves two years of graduate training. Rules vary across American states and Canadian provinces with respect to what individuals with a master's in psychology can call themselves. In some places, they are called psychologists. In other areas, they are called psychological associates. Some states and provinces may not have a formal designation for people with master's level training. In such cases, master's level clinicians often call themselves psychotherapists or psychometrists, neither of which are protected terms (in other words, anyone can refer to themselves using these labels).

**Psychiatrist.** A psychiatrist is a physician who has specialized in treating mental health problems after completing four years of medical school. Typically, this specialty training includes a five-year residency and also may include additional fellowship training. Psychiatrists are more likely than other types of clinicians to understand and treat anxiety from a biological perspective, although increasingly, psychiatric training programs are including training in CBT. Advantages of being treated by a psychiatrist over other types of professionals include the opportunity to obtain medications in addition to other forms of therapy, as well as the opportunity to be assessed by a physician who is uniquely qualified to recognize medical conditions that may be contributing to the problem.

**Social worker.** Social workers are trained to do many different things including helping people to deal better with their relationships, solve their personal and family problems, and learn to cope better with day-to-day stresses. They may help people to deal with the stresses of inadequate housing, unemployment, lack of job skills, financial distress, serious illness or disability, substance abuse, unwanted pregnancy, and other hardships. Most social workers specialize, and some end up providing psychotherapy either in a private practice or a hospital or agency setting. Although CBT is seldom a formal part of social work training programs, some social workers obtain specialized training in CBT following their formal schooling.

**Occupational therapist.** Occupational therapists help individuals to achieve independence in all aspects of their lives by teaching them specific skills to deal more effectively with their home and work environments. They often work in medical settings (e.g., helping people who have recently suffered a stroke to compensate for their deficits) as well as settings specializing in mental health services. As with social workers, occupational therapists rarely receive training in CBT as part of their formal education, although they may obtain experience with CBT after completing their degree in occupational therapy.

**Other professions.** Professionals from a variety of other groups may be trained to provide CBT or other forms of psychotherapy. These include some family physicians, nurses, clergy or other religious leaders, and even psychotherapists without any formal degree in a mental health–related field.

As mentioned earlier, it is more important to know whether the person you are seeing has the experience and expertise in treating social anxiety using strategies that have proved useful than whether the person is a nurse, family doctor, psychologist, psychiatrist, or a student in one of these fields.

## Final Questions Regarding Treatment of Social Anxiety

**How long does treatment take?** As mentioned earlier, cognitive-behavioral treatment for social and performance anxiety typically takes between ten and twenty sessions. Sometimes, a person may make significant gains after just three or four sessions, particularly if the fear is very mild. Other times, treatment may last many months or even years. If you are being treated with medication (particularly antidepressants), it is usually recommended that you stay on the medication for six months to a year or more, before slowly decreasing the dosage and eventually discontinuing the medication. If the symptoms return, it may be necessary to resume taking the medication or to try a different form of treatment.

**Are the effects of treatment long-lasting?** As discussed earlier, the effects of CBT tend to be relatively long-lasting, although you may experience some bad days occasionally. In contrast, stopping medication treatment suddenly is more likely to lead to a return of the anxiety. You can protect against this to some degree by staying on the medication for a longer period (perhaps at a reduced "maintenance" dosage) and by stopping the medication very gradually. Also, stopping certain types of medications is more likely to lead to a return of symptoms than stopping other medications, as reviewed in chapter 5.

**Will you be completely "cured"?** A small percentage of people who have significant social anxiety are able to reach a point at which they rarely experience any social anxiety at all. Similarly, a small percentage of people do not obtain any benefit from either CBT or medications. For most people, however, the result of treatment is somewhere in between these two extremes. It is realistic to expect that proper treatment is likely to lead to a significant decrease in your social anxiety, avoidance behaviors, and impairment of day-to-day life. However, it is also likely that there will remain some situations that will still be anxiety-provoking, at least to some extent. This outcome may not seem too bad if you remember that most people experience social and performance anxiety from time to time.

**What if you don't like your therapist or doctor?** Although it is unrealistic to expect to be feeling better after only a few weeks, you should know after one or two meetings whether you are comfortable working with your therapist or doctor. If you are not pleased with how things are going, consider trying someone else. Within six to eight weeks after beginning either CBT or medication, you should begin to see changes. If changes have not occurred after two months, you should talk to your doctor or therapist about the possible reasons for the lack of improvement and consider other treatment options.

# Measuring Change During Treatment

Chapter 3 emphasized the importance of monitoring your progress throughout your treatment program. We recommend that periodically (i.e., every few weeks) you reflect on your progress by considering what types of changes you have made and what changes remain to be accomplished. You may decide to revise your treatment plan, depending on your progress. You may also decide to update your treatment goals. We recommend that you occasionally complete some of the forms in chapter 3 as a way of assessing whether your social anxiety is improving.

# Developing a Comprehensive Treatment Plan

In chapters 1 and 2, you learned about the nature and causes of social anxiety. In chapter 3, you completed a thorough assessment of your own anxiety symptoms. The self-assessment process was continued throughout this chapter, as you reviewed your previous attempts at treatment and developed your treatment goals. You are now ready to develop a treatment plan. By now, you should have a good idea of what you need to work on and whether you will try to overcome your social anxiety on your own, or with the help of a professional therapist or physician.

If you are considering trying medication, we recommend that you read chapter 5 next. Chapter 5 reviews the various medications that have been shown to be useful for treating social and performance anxiety. If you are interested in trying the cognitive-behavioral techniques, we suggest that you develop a treatment schedule for the next few months. The following list is one example of such a schedule:

- In the next week, read chapter 6 and begin to work on changing your negative thinking patterns. Chapter 6 includes a number of effective cognitive strategies as well as diaries that you should complete several times per week.

- Continue to practice the cognitive strategies for two to three weeks before moving on to the exposure-based techniques (chapters 7 through 9).

- When you are ready to begin exposure practices, begin reading chapters 7 and 8. As you read these chapters, you will have the opportunity to plan exposures designed specifically for your own pattern of fear and avoidance. We recommend that you practice the situational exposure strategies for five or six weeks before moving on to chapter 9.

- At the same time that you are practicing exposures, you should continue to practice using the cognitive strategies that you will learn in chapter 6. By using the cognitive strategies and practicing exposures to feared situations, you should notice your fear beginning to decrease.

- After five or six weeks of practicing exposure to feared situations, read chapter 9 to learn more about how to expose yourself to feared physical sensations. If you are frightened of feeling certain sensations when you are anxious, we recommend that you spend two to three weeks practicing the strategies described in chapter 9. At the same time, continue to practice the cognitive and exposure techniques from the earlier chapters.

- If there are social skills that you would like to improve, this will be the time to use the exercises described in chapter 10. Again, we recommend that you do not stop using the skills that you learned earlier, particularly the cognitive and exposure-based strategies.

At this point, several months will have passed and your anxiety will be likely to have improved significantly. We recommend that you now read chapter 11, which discusses ways of maintaining the gains you have made so far.

If you are curious and you want to read later sections in the book now, that's fine. However, it is important that you go back and practice the strategies in each chapter before moving on to the next set of techniques. These strategies are the building blocks that eventually will lead to an improvement in your social anxiety. After completing this chapter a number of issues should be clearer to you. First, you should have a better idea of whether this is the best time for you to work on overcoming your social anxiety. Second, you should have formulated a number of treatment goals, both for the short term and the long term. Finally, it is likely that you will have considered the various treatment options and identified your own treatment preferences. The remaining chapters in this workbook provide more detailed instructions in how to take advantage of particular strategies for managing social anxiety.

# Chapter 5

# Medications for Social Anxiety and Social Phobia

## Deciding to Take Medication

As discussed in earlier chapters, two approaches have been shown to be useful for overcoming social anxiety: medications and cognitive-behavioral therapy (CBT). Chapter 4 reviewed the key points to keep in mind when deciding whether to use drug treatments to overcome your symptoms of social anxiety. Medications and CBT (see chapters 6 through 10) have been shown to be about equally effective in the short term for treating social anxiety. Still, each approach has advantages and disadvantages.

### Advantages of Medications Compared to CBT

- Medications are often easier to obtain. Any physician (e.g., family doctor or psychiatrist) can prescribe medications. In contrast, professionals who have specialized training in providing CBT are often more difficult to find.

- Drug treatments are easy to use and do not take up much time. You just need to remember to take the pill. In contrast, CBT requires a lot of hard work and is typically time-consuming.

- Medications may work more quickly than CBT. Depending on the type of drug, behavioral changes are often observed in as little as an hour (for treatment with anti-anxiety medications) and as much as four to six weeks (for treatment with antidepressant medications). Typically, CBT takes weeks to months before significant changes take place.

- Medications may be less expensive in the short term. Visits to the doctor can be infrequent once a stable dosage is reached. At that point, the only cost is the medication itself. In contrast, CBT usually requires more frequent visits to the therapist throughout the treatment and therefore can be costly, especially if you have no health insurance.

## Disadvantages of Medications Compared to CBT

- Anxiety is more likely to return after stopping medication than after stopping CBT. In other words, the effects of CBT appear to be longer lasting.

- Medication may be more expensive than CBT over the long term. Because medication is typically used for a longer period (sometimes years), the costs are likely to add up to more than the cost of CBT, which generally lasts only several months.

- Many people experience side effects when taking medications. Although these are often manageable and improve after the first few weeks, some people experience more severe side effects, making treatment with medication unpleasant or impossible. The only significant side effect of CBT is an increase in anxiety during exposure to feared situations.

- Medications for social anxiety may interact with alcohol or with other medications. They may also cause problems in people who have certain medical illnesses. CBT does not interact in the same ways with alcohol, medications, or medical illnesses.

- Some medications are difficult for people to stop taking because they may cause intense (although temporary) withdrawal symptoms during discontinuation. This is particularly a problem with certain anti-anxiety medications. Medications with the potential for dependence should be discontinued slowly. In contrast, physical dependence and withdrawal problems are not associated with CBT.

- Some medications (e.g., monoamine oxidase inhibitors) require a restricted diet. CBT does not require any food restrictions.

- Most medications must be used cautiously during pregnancy or if you are breast-feeding a baby. CBT can be used safely in either of these situations.

## Summary

In deciding whether to try medications, you should consult with your doctor. Keep in mind, however, that your doctor's advice regarding this issue is likely to be influenced by his or her own expertise and preferences. In reality, it is very difficult to predict who is most likely to respond to CBT versus medication, or a combination of the two approaches. Although medication is an appropriate option for severe, impairing social anxiety, CBT is also an effective treatment. In fact, we generally recommend that people try CBT initially, if it is available, because the benefits tend to be longer lasting than those of medication.

# Choosing Among Medications

If you decide to try medications, there are three general classes of drugs effective for social anxiety: antidepressant medications, anti-anxiety medications and, to a lesser extent, beta-adrenergic blockers (beta-blockers). Each of these approaches will be discussed later in this chapter.

When selecting among these medications, you and your doctor should take into account the following factors:

- **Your particular social anxiety symptoms**. For example, beta-blockers are thought to be useful for discrete performance fears (e.g., public speaking, performing music), but not for more generalized forms of social anxiety.

- **Side effect profile of the medication**. For example, if you are already struggling with your weight, you might want to choose a medication for which weight gain is not a likely side effect.

- **Previous response to medications**. If you or a family member have previously responded to a particular medication, that drug might be a good choice to try again. On the other hand, if there is a drug that didn't work for you in the past (despite a long enough trial, at an adequate dose), this might be the time to try something new.

- **Additional psychological disorders that are present**. For example, if you are experiencing depression, it might make more sense to try an antidepressant than an anti-anxiety drug. The antidepressant would likely lead to an improvement in both problems.

- **Cost**. Older medications tend to be less expensive than newer medications, often because older drugs are available in generic forms.

- **Interactions with other medications and herbal remedies**. If you are already taking certain medications or herbal preparations, you should choose a drug that will not interact with what you are already taking.

- **Interactions with certain foods**. Medications such as phenelzine can be dangerous if taken with certain foods (those containing tyramine, such as aged cheese, draft beer). Other medications may also interact with foods. For example, grapefruit juice appears to decrease the metabolism of certain selective serotonin reuptake inhibitors (e.g., sertraline, fluvoxamine) so they accumulate in the body.

- **Interactions with medical conditions**. If you have a particular medical condition, you should choose a drug that will not interact with the symptoms of your medical problem.

- **Substance use issues**. If you enjoy drinking alcohol or if you use other drugs, you should choose a medication that is unlikely to interact with these substances.

- **Discontinuation issues**. Medications that leave the body quickly (i.e., those that have a short half-life) are more likely to cause withdrawal symptoms and are therefore more difficult to discontinue. If you or your doctor are concerned about your ability to discontinue a medication, this should be factored into your decision regarding which drug to take.

# Treatment with Antidepressants

Antidepressants are the most frequently recommended medications for social phobia. These drugs are called "antidepressants" because they were initially developed to treat depression. However, don't be fooled by their name. These drugs are useful for a broad range of psychological problems, including social phobia. In fact, they appear to work for this problem regardless of whether an individual is depressed. There are five main classes of antidepressant medications that are thought to be useful for treating social phobia. Each of these is described below. In addition, a table of recommended dosages is included at the end of this section.

## Selective Serotonin Reuptake Inhibitors (SSRIs)

The SSRIs are often the first choice for treating social phobia. In fact, one of these medications (paroxetine) has become the first drug to receive an "indication" (i.e., official approval) from the Food and Drug Association (FDA) for the treatment of social phobia. Despite this official FDA indication, however, there is no evidence that paroxetine works any better or worse than any other SSRI for the treatment of social phobia. They are all thought to be about equally effective. The SSRIs include: paroxetine (Paxil), sertraline (Zoloft), fluoxetine (Prozac), fluvoxamine (Lovox), and citalopram (Celexa). Note that citalopram has only recently become available in North America. Although it has been shown to be useful in treating depression and a number of different anxiety disorders, it is still less well researched for the treatment of social phobia, compared to the other SSRIs. However, it is likely that citalopram will soon be found to be an effective option for treating social anxiety as well.

Although the side effects vary slightly across the SSRIs, some of the most common ones include: nausea, diarrhea, headache, sweating, anxiety, tremor, sexual dysfunction, weight gain, dry mouth, palpitations, chest pain, dizziness, twitching, constipation, increased appetite, fatigue, thirst, and insomnia. Don't be discouraged by the long list of side effects. Most people experience only a very small number of side effects, which are usually quite manageable. In fact, some individuals experience no side effects at all. Generally, side effects are worse during the first few weeks of treatment and can be managed by keeping the dosage low until the person becomes used to the medication.

Selective serotonin reuptake inhibitors must be taken daily for about four weeks or more before they start working. They appear to affect *serotonin* levels in the brain. Serotonin is a chemical (called a neurotransmitter) that is involved in the transmission of information from one brain cell to the next. It is thought to be involved in the regulation of emotion and other aspects of psychological functioning.

Selective serotonin reuptake inhibitors are relatively easy to discontinue, although paroxetine, because it is metabolized more quickly by the body, is more likely than the others to cause withdrawal symptoms during discontinuation. Therefore, paroxetine should be stopped more gradually than the other SSRIs. Common withdrawal symptoms during discontinuation of paroxetine include: sleep disturbances, agitation, tremor, anxiety, nausea, diarrhea, dry mouth, vomiting, sexual disturbances, and sweating.

## Selective Serotonin and Norepinephrine Reuptake Inhibitors (SNRIs)

Venlafaxine (Effexor) is currently the only available SNRI. Unlike the SSRIs, venlafaxine acts both on the serotonin and norepinephrine neurotransmitter systems, both of which appear to be related to problems with anxiety and depression. Preliminary studies suggest that venlafaxine is useful for treating social phobia, although, like the SSRIs, it takes several weeks to have an effect. Controlled studies are currently underway and within a few years, we should have a greater understanding of how well this new medication works for social phobia.

The most commonly reported side effects of venlafaxine include: sweating, nausea, constipation, anorexia, vomiting, somnolence, dry mouth, dizziness, nervousness, anxiety, and sexual disturbances. When discontinued too quickly, the most common withdrawal symptoms include: sleep disturbances, dizziness, nervousness, dry mouth, anxiety, nausea, headache, sweating, and sexual problems.

## Serotonin-2 Antagonists/Reuptake Inhibitors (SARIs)

The SARIs include drugs such as nefazodone (Serzone) and trazodone (Desyrel). Preliminary studies with nefazodone suggest that this drug may be useful for treating social phobia, although further studies are needed. These drugs takes several weeks to work, and the exact mechanism of action is unknown. Typical side effects include: sleepiness, dry mouth, nausea, dizziness, constipation, visual disturbances, lightheadedness, and confusion. Abrupt withdrawal may lead to flu-like symptoms.

## Monoamine Oxidase Inhibitors (MAOIs)

MAOIs affect three neurotransmitter systems in the brain: serotonin, norepinephrine, and dopamine. The most commonly used MAOI for treating social phobia is phenelzine (Nardil). This drug has consistently been found to alleviate the symptoms of social phobia. Like the other antidepressants, phenelzine takes several weeks to have a therapeutic effect.

Despite their effectiveness, MAOIs are rarely used in clinical practice because the side effects tend to be worse than those from other medications, and because of necessary dietary restrictions. When taking MAOIs, foods containing a substance called tyramine must be avoided. These include aged cheeses, meat extracts, overripe bananas, sausage, tofu, soy sauce, draft beer, and many other foods. MAOIs are also dangerous in combination with certain other medications, including SSRIs. The most commonly reported side effects of MAOIs include: dizziness, headache, drowsiness, sleep disturbances, fatigue, weakness, tremors, twitching, constipation, dry mouth, weight gain, low blood pressure, and sexual disturbances.

## Reversible Inhibitors of Monoamine Oxidase (RIMAs)

Reversible inhibitors of monoamine oxidase are a type of MAOI that tend to have fewer side effects than traditional MAOIs. In addition, they are less likely than traditional MAOIs to interact with other medications and with foods containing tyramine. The only RIMA that is available now is moclobemide (Manerix). Findings from studies on moclobemide for social phobia have been mixed. Early studies found that this medication was helpful for treating social phobia, whereas more recent studies have found only modest effects. In some studies, moclobemide was no better than placebo (Antony and Swinson 2000).

The most commonly reported side effects for people taking moclobemide include: fatigue, constipation, low blood pressure, decreased sex drive, dry mouth, difficulties ejaculating, insomnia, vertigo, and headache. Like the other antidepressants, moclobemide takes several weeks to have a therapeutic effect.

# Dose Ranges for Antidepressants in the Treatment of Social Phobia

| Generic Name | Brand Name | Starting Dose | Daily Dose |
|---|---|---|---|
| **SSRIs** | | | |
| Paroxetine | Paxil | 10 mg | 40–60 mg |
| Fluvoxamine | Luvox | 50 mg | 150–300 mg |
| Sertraline | Zoloft | 50 mg | 100–200 mg |
| Fluoxetine | Prozac | 10–20 mg | 20–60 mg |
| Citalopram | Celexa | 10 mg | 20–60 mg |
| **Other Antidepressants** | | | |
| Phenelzine | Nardil | 15–30 mg | 30–75 mg |
| Moclobemide | Manerix | 200–300 mg | 450–600 mg |
| Venlafaxine | Effexor | 37.5–75 mg | 150–225 mg |
| Nefazodone | Serzone | 100–200 mg | 300–500 mg |

Adapted from M. M. Antony and R. P. Swinson. 2000. *Phobic Disorders and Panic in Adults: A Guide to Assessment and Treatment*. Washington, DC: American Psychological Association. Used with permission.

# Treatment with Anti-Anxiety Medications

The most frequently prescribed anti-anxiety medications are the benzodiazepines. These are sedatives from the same family as drugs such as diazepam (Valium) and lorazepam (Ativan). To date, only clonazepam (Klonapin in the USA, and Rivotril in Canada) (Davidson, Potts, Richichi, Krishnan, et al. 1993) and alprazolam (Xanax) (Gelernter, Uhde, Cimbolic, Arnkoff, et al. 1991) have been investigated in controlled studies for the treatment of social phobia. The typical starting dosage for alprazolam and clonazepam is .5 mg per day, with a maximum daily dose of 4 to 6 mg.

When taken on a regular basis, these medications tend to be effective for treating social phobia. The most common side effects include drowsiness, lightheadedness, depression, headache, confusion, dizziness, unsteadiness, insomnia, and nervousness. These drugs may affect a person's ability to drive safely and tend to interact strongly with alcohol. In addition, they should be used with caution by older people, because higher dosages have been associated with a greater likelihood of falling.

There are several advantages to taking benzodiazepines compared to antidepressant medications. First, they work very quickly (within a half hour) and therefore can be used on an "as needed" basis to deal with particularly stressful situations. They also may be used during the first few weeks of antidepressant treatment, while the individual waits for the antidepressant to take effect. In addition, the side effect profile of benzodiazepines is quite different from antidepressants, and it may be better for some individuals.

Despite these benefits, benzodiazepines have fallen out of favor in recent years because they can be difficult to discontinue. Discontinuation from these medications can cause temporary (but sometimes intense) feelings of anxiety, arousal, and insomnia. In rare cases, abrupt discontinuation can cause seizures. Given that discontinuation from these medications can cause intense anxiety, it is not surprising that some individuals have difficulty stopping these drugs. The symptoms of withdrawal can be minimized by discontinuing these drugs very gradually.

## Treatment with Beta-Adrenergic Blockers

Beta-blockers are normally used for treating high blood pressure. In addition, they are effective for decreasing some of the physical symptoms of fear such as palpitations and shakiness. A number of early studies suggest that beta-blockers are useful for managing intense fear in certain performance situations (Hartley, Ungapen, Dovie, and Spencer 1983; James, Burgoyne, and Savage 1983). In particular, they are often used by actors, musicians, and other performers to manage stage fright. However, beta-blockers are ineffective for treating more generalized forms of social anxiety and shyness.

The most commonly used beta-blocker for treating performance fears is propanolol (Inderal). This medication is normally taken in a single dose of 5 to 10 mg, about twenty to thirty minutes before a performance.

## Stages in Medication Treatment

Treatment with medication involves the following five different stages:

1. The first stage is the *assessment*. During this phase, your doctor will ask you the necessary questions to help choose the best medication for your needs.

2. The second stage is *initiation* of the drug. In most cases, medications are started at relatively low dosages, to give your body a chance to adapt gradually to the new drug.

3. The third stage is *dose escalation*. During this stage of treatment, the dosage is gradually increased until the individual's symptoms start to improve. The goal of dose escalation is to find the lowest dosage that is effective for a particular person. Throughout the process, care is taken to minimize any side effects that may be present.

4. The fourth stage is called *maintenance*. During maintenance, the individual continues to take the medication for an extended period of time. For the antidepressants, it is usually recommended that treatment continue for at least six months to a year, minimizing the chances of symptoms returning following discontinuation.

5. The fifth and final stage of medication treatment is *discontinuation*. Typically, some time after a person has improved on a medication, the individual is encouraged to decrease the amount of the medication to assess whether he or she is ready either to lower the dosage or to stop the medication completely. If a person is also receiving CBT, it may be helpful to have regular CBT sessions during the discontinuation phase.

# Combining Medications

Your doctor may recommend combining several medications for treating your social phobia. For example, a frequently prescribed combination treatment for social phobia is an antidepressant with a benzodiazepine. As discussed earlier, a benzodiazepine can be used to manage anxiety symptoms during the early weeks of treatment with an antidepressant, while a person waits for the antidepressant to start working. Despite this practice, there are no studies evaluating the effectiveness of combining medications for social phobia. Nevertheless, combining medications may be clinically useful in some cases, and this approach may be worth considering if your doctor recommends it.

# Combining Medication with Psychological Treatments

Studies comparing medications to CBT have generally found both approaches to be very effective (Gould, Buckminster, Pollack, Otto, et al. 1997; Heimberg, Liebowitz, Hope, Schneier, et al. 1998). Although studies have examined the relative effects of medications *versus* cognitive-behavior therapy, there are no published studies examining the combined effects of these two approaches (i.e., medication *plus* cognitive-behavior therapy administered together). Several studies on combined treatment are currently underway and results should be available in the next few years. In the meantime, there is no reason not to think that for some individuals, combined treatment is the most appropriate strategy for managing social phobia. If you decide to try this route, it is helpful if both treatments are delivered by the same person, or that the professionals providing you with CBT and medication are in contact with one another. Clearly, it can be most helpful when multiple treatments are delivered in a coordinated fashion.

# Natural and Herbal Remedies for Social Anxiety

In recent years, herbal preparations have been increasing in popularity for treating a wide range of health problems. For the treatment of anxiety and related problems, commonly used herbal preparations include St.-John's-wort, kava, ginkgo, Valerian root, and ginseng. With very few exceptions (such as the use of St.-John's-wort for depression), evidence supporting the use of herbal remedies for social anxiety, or other psychological disorders for that matter, is almost nonexistent (Wong, Smith, and Boon 1998). There is currently no evidence that any herbal remedies work better than (or even as well as) conventional medications for social phobia.

Furthermore, very little is known about the safety of these remedies or the extent to which they interact with conventional medications. However, because St.-John's-wort is thought to act on the serotonin system, we recommend against using this product in combination with other medications that affect serotonin levels. Make certain that your doctor knows if you are taking any herbal products. Controlled trials using herbal treatments for anxiety disorders are currently underway. In the coming years, more information regarding the safety, interactions, and effectiveness of these treatments will be available. For more information on the use of herbal remedies and psychological functioning, we recommend a new book called *Herbs for the Mind: What Science Tells Us About Nature's Remedies for Depression, Stress, Memory Loss and Insomnia* (Davidson and Connor 2000).

# Common Questions about Medication

*Question:*    Who can prescribe medication for social phobia?

*Answer:*    Any physician can prescribe medications. In some jurisdictions, psychologists may also have limited prescription privileges.

*Question:*    Is taking medication a sign of weakness?

*Answer:*    Taking medication for social phobia is no more a sign of weakness than taking medication for any other problem, including physical illness.

*Question:*    What level of improvement can I expect?

*Answer:*    A small percentage of people obtain no benefit at all from medications for social phobia. Another small group of people obtain almost complete improvement. However, most people with social phobia experience moderate improvements with medications. They tend to feel less anxious overall, and are more comfortable in a broader range of situations. However, there may still be areas in which the social anxiety is a problem for them.

*Question:*    Are medications for social anxiety dangerous?

*Answer:*    When taken as prescribed, medications for social phobia are generally safe. When side effects cause problems, as a rule they are easy to manage by decreasing the dosage or switching to a different drug.

*Question:*    Is it dangerous for me to stop taking my medication?

*Answer:*    Medications should always be stopped gradually, and in close consultation with your doctor. If done properly, discontinuation is generally safe.

*Question:*    What happens if my medication doesn't work for me?

*Answer:*    If your medication doesn't work (despite an adequately long trial, at a high enough dosage), you may still benefit from trying a different medication or from receiving CBT.

*Question:*    How long should I try a medication before assuming that it isn't going to work?

*Answer:*    Most antidepressants will work within four to six weeks. If you haven't experienced any benefit after eight weeks at a high enough dosage, it may be worth discussing the possibility of trying a different treatment with your doctor.

*Question:*    If I go off my medication and my anxiety returns, am I likely to benefit again if I resume taking the same medication?

*Answer:*    Often, when a previously effective medication is tried for a second time (following a break), it will work again. However, sometimes a particular medication is less effective the second time, and a different medication may be prescribed.

In summary, medications can be an effective method of managing severe social anxiety. Certain anti-anxiety medications (e.g., clonazepam) and a number of different antidepressants (e.g., paroxetine, phenelzine) have consistently been shown to help reduce symptoms of social anxiety. If you decide that you would like to try medication, the first step is to contact your family doctor or psychiatrist. Your doctor will be able to recommend a specific medication that is likely to work for you.

# Chapter 6

# Changing Your Anxious
# Thoughts and Expectations

The word *cognition* refers to the ways in which we process information, including activities such as thought, perception, interpretation, attention, memory, and knowledge. The word *cognitive* is simply the adjectival form of the term cognition. For example, *cognitive science* is the science concerned with the ways in which we think. *Cognitive therapy* is a type of psychotherapy that is designed to alter negative and unrealistic beliefs, thoughts, and interpretations.

This chapter provides an overview of strategies that have been shown to be useful for decreasing social anxiety by changing negative or unrealistic patterns of thinking. Many of the cognitive techniques and principles discussed in this book have been presented and expanded upon elsewhere by authors such as Aaron T. Beck (e.g., Beck, Emery, and Greenberg 1985), David Burns (1999), Richard Heimberg (e.g., Hope, Heimberg, Juster, and Turk 2000), and Christine Padesky (e.g., Greenberger and Padesky 1995). Over the years, strategies similar to those discussed in this chapter have been adopted by the majority of therapists who practice cognitive therapy.

## The Origins of Cognitive Therapy

Cognitive therapy was proposed in the 1960s and 1970s as an alternative to traditional psychodynamic psychotherapies, which were the most prevalent forms of therapy at the time. *Psychodynamic psychotherapies* are concerned with helping individuals understand the deep-rooted unconscious conflicts that supposedly cause or contribute to their psychological problems. Often, the focus of these therapies is on recounting early childhood experiences, interpreting dreams and other forms of unconscious experience, as well as on helping the individuals to understand the unconscious motivations for their behavior.

The earliest and most influential form of psychodynamic psychotherapy was undoubtedly *psychoanalysis*, which was developed by Sigmund Freud in the early 1900s. According to Freud, people's behaviors are influenced by conflicts among three competing forces that make up the personality: the id, ego, and superego. The *id* is that part of the personality present from birth and is concerned only with meeting a person's immediate needs and desires. In particular, its function is to satisfy primitive biological needs for sex and aggression, which Freud believed drove much of human behavior. The *ego* is the part of the personality that develops shortly after birth and it has the function of keeping the id under control. According to Freud, the ego helps us to determine what is safe and practical so we don't continually give in to our id impulses. Finally, the *superego*, which develops during childhood, is that part of the personality concerned with behaving morally, according to society's rules. In other words, the superego is our conscience.

Freud believed that specific types of problems are determined by interactions and conflicts among the id, ego, and superego. For example, people with relatively weak egos and superegos were believed to be prone to impulsive behaviors, whereas those with "overdeveloped" superegos were thought to be more anxious, controlling, and rigid in their behaviors.

Freud hypothesized that most of our thinking is unconscious and that people are often unaware of their motivations. In addition, he assumed that people engage in various strategies (called *defense mechanisms*) designed to keep uncomfortable feelings and thoughts from entering consciousness. For example, Freud proposed that depression can occur as a response to having unconscious aggressive thoughts or feelings toward a loved one. Because such feelings are usually believed to be unacceptable, an individual may do whatever is possible to keep such thoughts and feelings outside of conscious awareness. According to Freud, rather than allowing the aggressive thoughts to surface, the individual may turn those angry feelings inward, leading to feelings of self-hatred and worthlessness, which are often features of depression.

Although psychodynamic psychotherapies are still very popular, they have been criticized extensively and, increasingly, are losing ground to newer forms of therapy. Some reasons for the decline of psychodynamic psychotherapies are as follows:

- Little evidence supports the theoretical assumptions of psychodynamic psychotherapies. For example, there is no clinical research that supports the view that depression is caused by aggressive feelings toward others that have been turned inward.

- Most of the theoretical assumptions of psychodynamic psychotherapies cannot be tested, because they are based on unconscious motivations that cannot be measured. In addition, the theoretical foundations of psychodynamic therapy has been criticized as being logically flawed and based on circular reasoning.

- Compared to cognitive and behavioral treatments, there is little evidence supporting the effectiveness of psychodynamic psychotherapies for specific psychological problems, including anxiety and depression.

- The goals of psychodynamic treatments are often not well defined. Therapy is designed to help an individual to develop insight into the apparently unconscious causes of his or her problems. However, because "insight" is hard to define and measure, it is very difficult to assess whether the therapy is working.

- Psychodynamic psychotherapy tends to be expensive and impractical. Although briefer and less intensive forms exist, traditional forms of this therapy often involve several visits per week over the course of many years.

- Psychodynamic psychotherapies are relatively unconcerned with treating specific features of a condition (e.g., fear, avoidance, panic attacks, etc.) because these are viewed as merely symptoms of a deeper underlying problem.

- Psychodynamic psychotherapies (especially psychoanalysis) take a dark view of human nature—assuming that human behavior is driven by primitive drives, including aggressive impulses and the drive for sex. According to this view, little room exists for the role of individual choice in determining behavior.

- In psychodynamic psychotherapies, the therapist is seen as the "expert" regarding the client's behavior and motivations. Because the therapist's role is to interpret what the client says during therapy sessions, there is a risk of these interpretations being biased by the therapist's subjective viewpoint.

Despite these criticisms, psychoanalysis and the psychodynamic psychotherapies have made considerable contributions to the understanding and treatment of psychological problems. For example, these were the first treatments based on the assumption that simply talking to another person can lead to psychological changes. In addition, these treatments highlighted the importance of nonconscious information processing. Although there is little evidence to prove the existence many of the unconscious motivations proposed by Freud, there is evidence that suggests people are frequently unaware of the perceptions and interpretations that contribute to their understanding of their environment.

Finally, although many specific aspects of his theory were probably misguided, Freud highlighted the importance of early experience in determining psychological functioning later in life.

### The Birth of Cognitive Therapy

In the 1960s and 1970s, a number of psychologists and psychiatrists disenchanted with psychodynamic psychotherapies began to explore other ways of helping their patients and clients. Working independently, psychiatrist Aaron Beck (1963; 1964; 1967; 1976) and psychologists Albert Ellis (1962; 1989) and Donald Meichenbaum (1977) each developed new forms of therapy, based on the premise that people's difficulties with depression, anxiety, anger, and related problems stem from the ways in which they think about themselves, their environment, and the future.

For example, fear was assumed to stem from a belief that a particular situation was threatening or dangerous. Beck, Ellis, and Meichenbaum each developed treatments designed to help individuals recognize how their beliefs and assumptions contribute to their negative emotions, and to overcome psychological suffering by changing these negative thoughts. Ellis called his form of treatment rational emotive therapy and later renamed it *rational emotive behavior therapy* (1993). Meichenbaum referred to his form of treatment as *cognitive-behavior modification* (CBM). It was Aaron Beck, however, who first used the term *cognitive therapy* to describe his treatment. Each of these three new treatments was developed at about the same time and they were quite similar with respect to their underlying assumptions and some of the treatment strategies used.

Over the years, Beck's form of treatment has become more popular and prominent than either Ellis' or Meichenbaum's approaches. Furthermore, Beck's cognitive therapy has been subjected to more rigorous study than either REBT or CBM for the treatment of social anxiety. Therefore, the methods discussed in this chapter are based on those proposed by Beck and his collaborators, as well as others who adapted and expanded upon Beck's methods for treating social anxiety and related problems.

## Assumptions of Cognitive Therapy for Social Anxiety

Here are some of the basic assumptions of cognitive therapy, particularly as related to the treatment of shyness, social anxiety, and performance fears.

1. Negative emotions are caused by negative interpretations and beliefs. People who interpret a given situation in different ways are likely to experience different emotions. For example, imagine that a friend of yours has cancelled a dinner date at the last minute, without providing a reason. Below is a list of possible emotional reactions you might have depending on your beliefs and interpretations.

**Situation:** A friend cancels a dinner date with you at the last minute, and gives you no reason for the cancellation.

| Interpretation | Emotion |
| --- | --- |
| "My friend has been hurt or is ill." | Anxiety or Worry |
| "My friend isn't treating me with the respect I deserve." | Anger |
| "My friend doesn't care about me." | Sadness |
| "Thank goodness the dinner has been cancelled; I am always so nervous when I have to eat with others." | Relief |
| "I guess something else came up. Everyone changes plans from time to time, including me." | Neutral |

2. Anxiety and fear result when a person interprets a situation as threatening or dangerous. Although fearful predictions and interpretations are sometimes accurate, they are often exaggerated or inaccurate. Chapter 1 provided a list of thoughts and assumptions that can contribute to social anxiety. These include beliefs about one's performance (e.g., "People will think that I am an idiot"), as well as beliefs about the anxiety itself (e.g., "It is important for me not to appear anxious in front of other people"). Beliefs such as these help to maintain a person's anxiety in social and performance situations.

3. You are the expert regarding your own thoughts and feelings. Unlike other forms of therapy, which assume that the therapist is the expert, cognitive therapy assumes that the patient and therapist each has unique areas of expertise, and the best way to work on a problem is to take advantage of the skills and expertise that each brings to the therapeutic situation. The therapist is assumed to be an expert on the principles and methods of cognitive therapy. The patient is assumed to be an expert regarding his or her own experiences, assumptions, and beliefs. In most cases, the therapist and patient decide together whether a particular belief is exaggerated or unrealistic and together they generate strategies for changing negative patterns of thinking.

4. The goal of cognitive therapy is to be able to think more realistically, rather than simply to think positively. There are occasions where your anxious beliefs are realistic and are quite consistent with the actual threat in a given situation. In these cases, anxiety may be a good thing because it helps you stay on guard and protect yourself from possible danger. For example, being a bit nervous while interacting with an authority figure (e.g., your boss, a police officer) may protect you from seeming overly confident, demanding, or aggressive. Cognitive therapy focuses on situations where your beliefs, predictions, and interpretations are exaggerated when compared to the actual level of danger in the situation.

5. People naturally tend to seek out and pay attention to information that confirms their beliefs. In the case of social anxiety, people pay more attention and give more weight to evidence that others are judging them negatively (e.g., a history of being teased in high school) than to evidence that contradicts the anxious beliefs (e.g., a history of very positive performance appraisals at work). Cognitive therapy aims to help people to consider all the evidence before making any assumptions.

# Types of Anxious Thinking

Anxious thinking begins and persists when people make incorrect assumptions about what is likely to happen in a given situation, about the quality of their own performance, and about what other people are thinking of them. This section includes descriptions of some of the most common styles of thinking that often seem to play a role in social and performance anxiety. Note that there are additional examples of negative and exaggerated thinking that other authors have highlighted (see, e.g., Burns 1999), but that we have chosen not to include in this section. In most cases, these were omitted either because they were not especially relevant to social anxiety or because they were very similar and overlapped considerably with those examples that we have included. In fact, even the various thinking styles on this list overlap to some extent. As you may notice, a particular anxious thought (e.g., "Other people will think that I am boring") may easily fit into more than one category (i.e., probability overestimation, mind reading).

future forcast

## Probability Overestimations

A probability overestimation is a prediction that a person believes is likely to come true, even though the actual likelihood is relatively low. For example, someone who is fearful of giving presentations might predict that the next presentation is likely to go poorly, even though her presentations usually go well. Similarly, a person who is nervous about dating might assume that other people will find him unattractive, even though many people have found him to be attractive in the past. If your thoughts are similar to those listed below, you may have a tendency to overestimate the likelihood of negative events.

### Examples of Probability Overestimations

- I will be overwhelmed with panic.

- Everyone at the party will think I am stupid.

- My presentation will be a disaster.

- I will never be in an intimate relationship again.

- I will have nothing to say if I phone my cousin.

- I will lose my job if I make a mistake.

- If I go out, everyone will stare at me.

Can you think of recent instances when you assumed that things were going to work out badly, without any evidence for that assumption? If so, list your own examples of probability overestimations below:

_____

_____

_____

## Mind Reading

Mind reading involves making negative assumptions about what other people are thinking, particularly what they might be thinking about you. If social anxiety is a problem for you, it is likely that you assume that others think negatively about you. Although it is true that people sometimes make negative judgments about others, chances are this occurs much less often than you think. In most cases, your assumptions about what others are thinking are probably exaggerated or even completely untrue. Each of the following kinds of thoughts are examples of mind reading.

### Examples of Mind Reading

- People find me boring.

- My boss will think I'm an idiot if he sees my hands shaking.

- When people look at me, they are thinking I am strange or weird.

- Most people see anxiety as a sign of weakness.

- My friends think I am awkward or stupid when I lose my train of thought.

- People always know when I am feeling anxious.

Can you think of recent examples of times when you have made assumptions about what other people are thinking about you? If so, list your own examples of mind reading below:

_____

_____

_____

## Personalization

Personalization is the tendency to take more responsibility for a negative situation than you should, rather than acknowledging all of the different factors that may have contributed to the situation. Below are some examples of personalization, followed by examples of other factors that in reality may have contributed to the situation.

### Examples of Personalization

- At a friend's birthday party, I was talking to another guest and we ran out of things to talk about awfully soon. I was convinced that the conversation ended this way because I am so boring. In reality, other factors that may have contributed to the situation include (1) the other guest couldn't think of anything to talk about, (2) I had nothing in common with the other guest, even though neither of us is actually boring, and (3) it is normal for many conversations at parties to end fairly quickly. Nobody was at fault.

- The fact that my boss became angry at me for making a mistake is proof that I am incompetent. In reality, other factors that may have contributed to the situation include (1) my boss is always getting angry at people, so I shouldn't feel singled out, (2) my boss's expectations are too high (I know that not every boss in the world would have yelled at me for making a mistake. Part of why my boss became angry had to do with his own expectations, rather than me making a mistake), and (3) there are many reasons why people make mistakes besides incompetence.

- People were falling asleep during my presentation, proving once again that I am a really boring speaker. In reality, other factors that may have contributed to the situation include (1) the topic was somewhat dry and would have been difficult for any speaker to make exciting, (2) the presentation was late in the day, and the audience was feeling tired, and (3) it is normal for some people to feel bored at a talk; some people probably found it interesting.

- I was in an elevator and this woman was looking at me. She was probably thinking that I looked strange. In reality, other factors that may have contributed to the situation include (1) she liked my coat and was noticing it, (2) she was looking in my direction but wasn't really looking at me (e.g., she was staring into space, day dreaming), and (3) she noticed me but was thinking of other things.

Can you think of recent examples of times when you engaged in personalization? If so, list your own examples of personalization in the spaces below:

_____

_____

_____

## Should Statements

"Should" statements are incorrect or exaggerated assumptions about the way things *should* be. Statements that include words like "always," "never," "should," and "must" are often should statements. Sometimes, the tendency to use words such as these is a sign of having overly rigid and perfectionistic expectations for oneself or for others. Here are some examples:

### Examples of Should Statements

- I should never feel nervous around other people.

- I must never let my anxiety show.

- I should never make mistakes.

- I must never inconvenience other people.

- Others should never think badly about me.

- I should never do anything to draw attention to myself.

- Others must never tease me or laugh at something that I have done.

- I should always be interesting and entertaining to others.

- I must do things perfectly so everything is just right.

In the space below, list examples from your own life of unreasonable expectations (i.e., "shoulds") that you hold for yourself or others:

_____

_____

_____

## Catastrophic Thinking

Catastrophic thinking (also known as catastrophizing) is the tendency to assume that if a negative event were to occur, it would be absolutely terrible and unmanageable. From time to time, we all make mistakes, offend others, or look foolish. One difference between people who are socially anxious and those who are not particularly anxious is how they deal with these unfortunate social events. People who have very little social anxiety are often able to say to themselves, "Who cares what this person thinks? I have the right to make a mistake from time to time." In contrast, people who feel anxious around others are more likely to think, "It would be a disaster to have others think badly of me." Below are more examples of catastrophic thinking:

### Examples of Catastrophic Thinking

- It would be terrible if my anxiety showed during my presentation.

- I would not be able to handle making a fool of myself.

- It would be completely unacceptable to be unable to think of things to say during my date on Saturday night.

- If someone shows signs of not liking me, it feels like the end of the world.

- It would be terrible to lose my train of thought during a presentation.

- It would be a disaster if I blushed while answering a question in class.

In the space below, list examples of times when you have catastrophized or exaggerated how bad a particular outcome would be if it actually were to occur:

_____

_____

_____

## All-or-Nothing Thinking

All-or-nothing thinking (also called black-and-white thinking) is the tendency to judge any performance that falls short of perfection as being absolutely terrible. People who engage in this style of thinking tend to categorize their behavior as being either completely acceptable or awful, without acknowledging all of the possibilities that lie between these two extremes. As with "should" statements, all-or-nothing thinking is associated with excessive perfectionism and a tendency to hold unrealistic standards. Below are several examples of all-or-nothing thinking:

### Examples of All-or-Nothing Thinking

- If I lose my train of thought even once, I will blow the entire presentation.
- Even one person thinking I look nervous is too many.
- If I don't get an A on my exam, my teacher will think I am stupid.
- It is unacceptable if my boss makes any negative comments or suggests even one area for improvement during my annual performance review.
- Showing any signs of anxiety is almost as bad as falling completely apart.

In the space below, list examples of the times when you engaged in all-or-nothing thinking:

_____

_____

_____

## Selective Attention and Memory

Selective *attention* is the tendency to pay more attention to certain types of information than to other types. Selective *memory* is the tendency to remember certain types of information more easily than other types. As discussed earlier, people are more likely to attend to and remember information that is consistent with their beliefs. Therefore, people with social anxiety are more likely than others to remember times when they were criticized or teased by another person or when they performed poorly in a social situation. When performing in social situations or interacting with other people, individuals with social phobia are more likely to notice other people who appear to be bored or disapproving. Some other examples of selective memory and attention are given below:

### Examples of Selective Attention and Memory

- Ignoring positive feedback from a teacher or boss (i.e., discounting it as if it doesn't matter), yet taking negative feedback very seriously (i.e., letting it ruin your day).

- Focusing on the one low grade on your report card and ignoring all the high grades.

- Remembering being teased in high school, while forgetting about the good times spent with friends after school.

- Focusing on audience members who seem bored during your presentation and ignoring those in the crowd who appear to be enjoying your talk.

- Focusing on the moment during a conversation when you stumbled over your words and lost your train of thought, while ignoring the fact that the rest of the conversation was fairly smooth.

Can you think of ways in which you selectively pay attention to events or information that confirm your anxious beliefs and selectively ignore information that is inconsistent with those beliefs? In the space below, list examples of times when you have engaged in selective attention or memory:

_____

_____

_____

## Negative Core Beliefs

In recent years, cognitive therapists have begun to focus on the deepest, most central, and long-standing assumptions that contribute to a person's feelings of anxiety and depression. These types of thoughts are called core beliefs and they include negative assumptions that people hold regarding themselves (e.g., "I am incompetent"), other people (e.g., "Other people cannot be trusted."), and the world (e.g., "The world is a dangerous place"). The more strongly held these core beliefs, the more difficult they may be to change.

One technique for uncovering core beliefs involves continually asking about the meaning of each fearful belief you have until the core beliefs underlying your anxious interpretations are revealed. This process is illustrated in the following conversation between a therapist and client:

*Client:*     I am terrified to ask my coworker Cindy out on a date.

*Therapist:*  What are you afraid might happen if you ask her out?

*Client:*     Mostly, I'm afraid she will say "no."

*Therapist:*  Why would that be a problem?

*Client:*     If she rejects me, it will probably mean that she doesn't find me attractive.

*Therapist:*  What would be so bad about that?

| | |
|---|---|
| *Client:* | It will confirm my own belief that I am unattractive. |
| *Therapist:* | What if that is true? |
| *Client:* | Well, if I really am unattractive, that means nobody will ever think I am attractive or want to date me. It would mean that I am unlovable. |
| *Therapist:* | What would be bad about being unlovable? |
| *Client:* | If I am unlovable, I am bound to be alone forever. |
| *Therapist:* | Okay. You have mentioned a few basic core beliefs that may be contributing to your anxiety. You seem to be saying that (1) if another person turns down your invitation for a date, it means that she finds you unattractive, (2) if another person finds you unattractive, then everyone will find you unattractive, (3) being turned down for a date means that you are unlovable and destined to be alone forever. |
| *Client:* | I guess part of me knows that isn't true, but much of the time I just can't shake those beliefs. |

## How to Identify Your Anxious Thoughts and Predictions

In chapter 3, we discussed strategies for identifying your anxious thoughts. We suggest that you review the relevant passages in chapter 3 on identifying anxious thoughts before trying to use the techniques discussed in the remainder of this chapter. There is no point trying to change your anxious beliefs unless you are clear about the content of these beliefs. In addition to reviewing the anxious thoughts recorded in chapter 3, identifying your anxious beliefs, predictions, and assumptions should be an ongoing process. Whenever you find yourself in an anxiety-provoking situation, try to identify the specific thoughts and beliefs that are contributing to your discomfort. In most cases, you can identify your anxious predictions and assumptions by asking yourself a series of questions such as the following:

- What am I afraid will happen in this situation?

- What do I fear that the other person will think about me?

- What will happen if my anxious thoughts are true?

Sometimes, it may be difficult to pinpoint your fearful thoughts. Your fear may have been a part of your life for so long that the negative thoughts are well-rehearsed, very quick to rise to the surface of your mind, and almost automatic. Also, the fact that you probably avoid the situations you fear makes it that much more difficult to remember exactly what thoughts tend to occur when you are actually in the situation.

If you have difficulty identifying your anxious beliefs, we suggest that you try to engage with the situations you fear and attempt to identify your assumptions and predictions while you are still in the situation. With practice, it should get easier to recognize your anxious beliefs. In fact, even if you are unable to identify the specific thoughts that contribute to your anxiety, practicing being in the situation will likely lead to a decrease in your fear, as discussed in chapters 7 and 8.

# Strategies for Changing Anxious Thinking

This section provides an overview of seven different techniques for changing the beliefs and predictions that contribute to your social anxiety. These include (1) examining the evidence regarding your beliefs, (2) challenging catastrophic thinking, (3) remembering to consider your strengths and positive attributes, (4) taking the perspective of another person, (5) performing a cost-benefit analysis, (6) creating rational coping statements, and (7) doing some behavioral experiments. Along with a description of each strategy, we include exercises to provide opportunities to try each technique. Near the end of the chapter, we offer some suggestions for tying together all the pieces and for integrating the cognitive therapy techniques into a larger treatment plan.

## *Examining the Evidence*

The fact that you are anxious about being judged by others in a particular situation does not mean that your fearful predictions and thoughts are true. In fact, what we assume others are thinking is often completely different than what other people actually think of us. How many times have you heard someone say, "My hair looks awful" or "I am such a loser" and thought to yourself that, as far as you were concerned, the individual was just fine? ? If you are consistently assuming you are inferior in the eyes of others, the chances are that you are exaggerating or misinterpreting other people's reactions to your appearance, behavior, or performance.

The first step toward changing your thoughts is to recognize that your beliefs are not *facts*. Rather than assuming that your beliefs are true, it is important to treat your anxious thoughts as *guesses* or *hypotheses*. By examining the evidence, you will be able to assess the extent to which your beliefs are true. Remember, your natural tendency may be to seek out only information that confirms your negative beliefs about yourself. Examining the evidence involves trying to achieve a more balanced view by looking at *all* the evidence, especially information that contradicts or disproves your anxious thoughts and predictions.

In order to examine the evidence for your beliefs, we recommend you get into the habit of asking yourself questions such as the following:

- How do I know for sure that my prediction will come true?

- What does my past experience tell me about the likelihood of my thoughts coming true?

- Have there been times when I have experienced anxious thoughts that didn't come true?

- Are there facts or statistics that can help me to decide whether my prediction is likely to come true?

- Are there other possible interpretations for this situation?

- How might another person interpret this situation?

You may find it useful to type these questions on a small index card and to carry that card as a reminder in your pocket or wallet.

Essentially, examining the evidence involves four basic steps: identifying your anxious beliefs, generating alternative beliefs, weighing the evidence supporting and contradicting your beliefs, and choosing more realistic beliefs. Asking questions similar to those listed above will help you to identify alternative beliefs and to evaluate the evidence concerning your anxious and alternative beliefs. An illustration of how to use this strategy to combat a fear of blushing in front of coworkers at a meeting appears below:

### Steps for Examining the Evidence

#### 1. Identify the Anxious Thought

- My coworkers will think that I am weak or incompetent if they notice me blushing at the meeting.

#### 2. Generate Alternative Beliefs

- Nobody will notice my blushing.

- Only a small number of people will notice my blushing.

- People who notice my blushing will think I am feeling hot.

- People who notice my blushing will think I am feeling ill.

- People who notice my blushing will think I am feeling a bit anxious.

- It is normal to blush sometimes, so people will think nothing of it if they notice me blushing.

#### 3. Examine the Evidence

*Evidence Supporting Your Anxious Belief*

- I believe that my blushing is very extreme.

# Form for Examining the Evidence

**Situation**

_____

_____

_____

**Anxious Beliefs, Predictions, and Interpretations**

_____

_____

_____

**Alternative (Nonanxious) Beliefs, Predictions, and Interpretations**

_____

_____

_____

**Evidence Supporting My Anxious Beliefs, Predictions, and Interpretations**

_____

_____

_____

**Evidence Contradicting My Anxious Beliefs, Predictions, and Interpretations**

_____

_____

_____

**Choosing a More Realistic Way of Thinking**

_____

_____

_____

- In high school, people teased me for blushing on several occasions.

- I tend to notice when other people blush.

*Evidence Supporting Your Alternative Beliefs*

- I know a lot of people who blush easily and people don't seem to think they are strange.

- When I notice other people blushing, I don't think they are strange.

- Often people seem not to have noticed me blush when I asked them if it was noticeable.

- When people have noticed my blushing, they haven't tended to treat me differently.

- The people in the audience know me well. I can't imagine that their opinions of me would change dramatically based on whether I blush during a single presentation.

4. **Choose a More Realistic Belief**

- Some people may notice my blushing, but it's unlikely that they will think I'm strange.

---

Adapted from M. M. Antony and R. P. Swinson. 2000. *Phobic Disorders and Panic in Adults: A Guide to Assessment and Treatment.* Washington, DC: American Psychological Association. Used with permission.

The previous form can be used as you begin to work on examining the evidence supporting and contradicting your anxious beliefs. You may want to make copies of this form so that you can continue to use it whenever you encounter a feared situation.

To further illustrate the process of examining the evidence, here is an example of a discussion between a therapist and client demonstrating how to first identify anxious beliefs and then challenge those beliefs based on the client's past experiences.

*Therapist:*  What are you afraid will happen if you attend your company picnic next week?

*Client:*  I am nervous that I won't be able to come up with anything to say to anyone. Everyone else will be talking about their children. I am not in a relationship, and I have no kids, so I will have nothing in common with any of them.

*Therapist:*  How sure are you that you will have nothing to say?

*Client:*  Probably about 90 percent.

| *Therapist:* | What that means is that nine out of ten times that you attend an event such as this one, you have nothing to say. Is this really true? What happened at last year's company picnic? |
|---|---|
| *Client:* | When I first arrived, it was difficult. I stood off to the side and didn't say much to others. After a while, people started to include me in their conversations and it got easier. I think it was especially difficult last year, because I had just started at the company and didn't know anyone very well. |
| *Therapist:* | Were you able to think of things to say? |
| *Client:* | At first, I struggled. I think it was harder for me than it was for the others, but I was able to think of a few things to talk about, especially later in the afternoon. |
| *Therapist:* | Did everyone at last year's picnic bring a partner or spouse? Did they all talk about their children? |
| *Client:* | No. In fact, there are a few other single people at work. Last year, lots of people ended up talking about work. |
| *Therapist* | Thinking back to last year's company picnic, do you still think that you won't have anything to say at this year's picnic? |
| *Client* | Well, I may not be as talkative as some other people, but I suppose I will probably find something to talk about. Perhaps it will be easier this year because I have worked with these people for over a year, so I know them much better. |

## Challenging Catastrophic Thinking

To challenge catastrophic thinking requires shifting the focus of your thoughts from how terrible a particular outcome would be to how you might manage or cope with the situation if it were to occur. One of the most effective ways of overcoming your catastrophic thoughts is to ask yourself questions like the following:

- So what?

- What if my fears actually come true?

- How can I cope with _____ if it were to occur?

- Would _____ really be as terrible as I think?

- Does this really matter in the big scheme of things?

- Will I care about this a month from now? A year from now?

In many cases, you will realize that even if your fear does come true, it won't be the end of the world. You will cope with the situation and your discomfort will pass. Below you will see a therapy vignette illustrating how to use this technique to challenge catastrophic thoughts related to asking someone out on a date.

*Client:*        I am terrified of asking anyone out on a date for fear of rejection.

*Therapist:*    Is there a particular person whom you have considered asking out?

*Client:*        There is a guy in one of my classes. I have sat with him a few times. The class ends just before lunch, so I have often thought of asking him to have lunch with me.

*Therapist:*    What's stopping you? What do you think might happen if you ask him to join you for lunch?

*Client:*        Mostly, I am afraid he won't be interested in me. I will put him on the spot and he will have to come up with an excuse for rejecting my offer. I'm afraid he'll think I'm stupid, or even worse, he'll feel sorry for me.

*Therapist:*    As we've discussed previously, there are many different possible reactions that he could have. Thinking you're stupid or feeling sorry for you are just two of many possibilities. Nevertheless, let's assume for a moment that your fears actually are true. What if he does think you are foolish and pathetic?

*Client:*        I don't know. I hadn't really thought beyond that. I would feel terrible.

*Therapist:*    Would it mean that you really are pathetic and stupid?

*Client:*        I suppose not.

*Therapist:*    Would it mean that all other people also think you are stupid and pathetic?

*Client:*        Not really.

*Therapist:*    Why not?

*Client:*        Well, his opinion doesn't reflect that of other people. I know my friends don't think I'm pathetic. At least I hope not.

*Therapist:*    If you are not stupid or pathetic, why else would he reject you?

*Client:*        Perhaps he might have other lunch plans. Or, maybe he already has a girlfriend.

*Therapist:*    Those are both possibilities, but let's come back to your original thoughts. What if he really thinks you're pathetic and that's why he isn't interested in spending time with you.

*Client:*    I guess it wouldn't matter. Over the past few weeks, I have come to recognize that not everyone has to like me. Perhaps it would mean that we just aren't a good match.

*Therapist:*    If he declines your offer for lunch, do you think you will be able to cope with the feelings of rejection?

*Client:*    I think so. It will feel bad at first, but I think I can stop myself from getting too down on myself.

Overcoming catastrophic thinking also involves combating the tendency to concentrate only on the immediate consequences of some negative experience (e.g., "People will think badly about me during my presentation") and to forget that your discomfort will pass after a short time. In reality, the consequences of making a mistake or of embarrassing yourself are usually minimal and almost never last very long. Even if people notice that you have made a mistake or that you appear to be anxious, they are likely to forget about it after a few minutes. We have included a Decatastrophizing Form after this section to help you challenge your catastrophic thoughts in social situations. The form includes three columns. In the first column, you should describe the situation that led you to feel anxious. In the second column, describe your anxious thoughts and predictions. Now, ask the questions provided above in the bulleted list (e.g., "So what?") and record your noncatastrophic responses in the third column. Here are some examples.

*Column 1 (examples of situations)*

- Giving a presentation

- Having difficulty thinking of things to say during a conversation

- Attending a party

- Asking someone out on a date

- Walking through a busy mall

*Column 2 (examples of anxious thoughts)*

- _____ will think I am stupid.

- My hands will shake.

- I will look weak or incompetent.

- _____ will feel sorry for me.

- My anxiety will be noticed by _____.

*Column 3 (examples of noncatastrophic responses)*

- Even if _____ thinks I am an idiot, it doesn't mean I really am one. His opinion doesn't reflect that of everyone else.

- It wouldn't be the end of the world if _____ noticed my anxiety. Everyone feels anxious from time to time.

- Who cares if my hands shake? I have the right to have shaky hands. Probably no one will even notice. Even if they notice, they probably won't care. My boss has shaky hands and nobody seems to care.

- If I got ridiculed or laughed at, it would be manageable. Most people get teased and ridiculed from time to time. I certainly laugh at other people sometimes. Other than the temporary discomfort or embarrassment, it wouldn't really matter in the big scheme of things.

### Decatastrophizing Form

| Situation | Anxious Thoughts and Predictions (What do I think will happen?) | Noncatastrophic Responses (What if my thoughts come true?) |
|-----------|------------------------------------------------------------------|--------------------------------------------------------------|
|           |                                                                  |                                                              |
|           |                                                                  |                                                              |
|           |                                                                  |                                                              |
|           |                                                                  |                                                              |
|           |                                                                  |                                                              |
|           |                                                                  |                                                              |
|           |                                                                  |                                                              |

## *Remembering Your Strengths and Positive Attributes*

If you tend to focus on small mistakes and perceived flaws in your personality or appearance, you will likely continue to feel anxious. For example, if you assume that everyone is judging you based on whether your hands shake, you are more likely to be nervous when your hands are shaking. Similarly, if you assume that everyone else is criticizing you based on the ten seconds during your presentation when you lost your train of thought, you may continue to be nervous when giving presentations. Although it is true that we all judge and criticize other people from time to time, it is unlikely that people are noticing and judging the specific behaviors that you assume are being criticized.

People's judgments of one another are based on many different dimensions, including appearance (e.g., height, weight, hair color and style, facial features, clothing, shoes, etc.), intelligence (e.g., verbal abilities, problem-solving skills, knowledge of trivia, etc.), competence (e.g., abilities to do one's job well, skills at fixing things around the house), work habits (e.g., arrives on time, hard working, doesn't take long breaks), athletic abilities (e.g., tennis skills, fitness level, strength), creativity (e.g., musical or artistic skills), health habits (e.g., diet, exercise, smoking, drinking), health status (e.g., does the person have any medical problems?), social status (e.g., type of home, income, type of job), mood (happy, excited, sad, angry, fearful), personality (e.g., generosity, empathy, confidence, politeness, arrogance), to name just a few.

Most of us are far above average on some dimensions, far below average on some other dimensions, and well within average range on most dimensions. The extent to which a person criticizes you on a particular dimension probably depends on whether that person believes that particular domain is important. Although some people may criticize you for appearing nervous, it is likely that most people couldn't care less. If you assume others are focusing only on those dimensions in which you judge yourself to be inferior, you will continue to feel anxious and fearful around other people.

Because your natural tendency may be to focus on those areas in which you feel you don't measure up to others, it may take some practice to recognize dimensions in which you excel or in which you are similar to most other people. As a start, it may be helpful to list some of your strengths in the space provided below.

## Areas of Strength

_____

_____

_____

## Seeing with Another Person's Perspective

One powerful method for challenging the overly harsh standards that you may hold for yourself is to try to see the issue through another person's perspective. What if the tables were turned and a close friend came to you for advice and support after giving a presentation? What if your friend expressed many of the same thoughts that you experience when you are in a feared social or performance situation?

For example, what if your friend said to you, "I feel as if I totally blew it. My voice was trembling and at one point I even lost my train of thought. I'm sure I looked like a perfect idiot." How would you respond to your friend? Most likely you would say, "You probably did better than you think. Even if you did look anxious, people probably didn't care." Or, perhaps you would say something like this: "I also feel very anxious during presentations. It feels very uncomfortable in the moment, but eventually it passes."

It is often much easier to challenge someone else's anxious thoughts than it is to challenge your own. Therefore, we suggest that you try coping with your own anxious thoughts by mentally "stepping out" of the situation for a moment. Imagine that it is someone else (perhaps a close friend or family member) who is experiencing the anxiety. What might you tell him or her? Taking the perspective of a close friend may help you to challenge your own anxious thoughts.

Another helpful method involving using another perspective to look at your own situation is to imagine how you might judge someone else who exhibits the same anxious behaviors that you do. For example, if you are worried that others might criticize you if your voice become shaky, you might ask yourself, "Am I critical of other people when I notice their voice shaking?" Most likely, you would not assume someone else to be incompetent, stupid, or weak just because he or she seems a bit shy or anxious in a particular situation. Well, the same is true of other people. It is unlikely that they will make such harsh judgments of you, even if they do notice you are anxious.

Actually, in our experience, there is a good chance that others won't even notice when you are anxious or when you do something embarrassing. Here are two true stories from our own lives that illustrate just how oblivious people can be to what you (or anyone else, for that matter) are experiencing.

> It was my wedding day and the ceremony had just finished. At the reception, people were congratulating me. A couple of people told me that I looked very nervous during the ceremony. Interestingly, at least two other people mentioned how calm I seemed during the ceremony. The truth was that I had experienced both calm and anxious moments during the ceremony. I found it quite intriguing that different people watching the same event would have such different impressions of how I came across.          M.M.A.

> I was sitting on a crowded subway in Toronto when another passenger sat down rather hard beside me. The seat broke and we both hit the floor of the subway car. After rolling around the floor for a half minute or so, we both got up, fixed the seat, and sat down. When I looked up, I expected to see people staring, laughing, or maybe offering to help I noticed that no one was even looking our way. What I thought was a spectacle ended up not even being noticed by the others on the train.
>          R.P.S.

## Cost-Benefit Analysis

Here is an analogy that has little to do with social anxiety, but does illustrate the main point of this section. Most of us grow up believing that it is important to keep clean. So, we wash and shower, brush our teeth, change our clothes, and clean our homes. This belief protects us from looking unsightly, smelling bad, and from contracting various diseases. In other words, it is helpful for most of us to believe in the importance of keeping clean.

Some people, however, are overly concerned about being clean. We all know people who must have their homes spotless. They spend many hours each day cleaning and may become angry if anything is out of place. There are also individuals who are so terrified of becoming contaminated by germs or dirt that they wash their hands excessively. Some people with a condition known as obsessive compulsive disorder wash their hands several hundred times per day, to the point that their hands are red, have cuts, and are actually more susceptible to contamination and infection. For these individuals, the belief that "it is important to be clean" is not useful. Although this belief is useful for most people, it is not helpful when it is interpreted in an overly exaggerated or inflexible way. If anything, the belief leads to unhappiness and impaired day-to-day functioning. It's like having too much of a good thing. Even too many carrots can be unhealthy and turn your skin orange!

The same can be said of the thoughts that underlie social anxiety. As we have discussed throughout this chapter, anxious thoughts regarding social and performance situations are often untrue. However, sometimes they may be true (at least to some extent), but still be a problem. In addition to establishing whether your thoughts are true, it is useful to consider whether your thoughts and behaviors are helping you. If they are helpful, then they may be worth holding on to. If not, it may be time to let them go.

Almost everyone wants to make a good impression and probably no one would choose to be thought of as incompetent, stupid, boring, or weak. In fact, many of the anxious beliefs held by individuals with social phobia are similar in content to those held by people who don't have problems with social anxiety. Beliefs such as "It is important to be liked by other people" and "It is important to make a positive impression" are often helpful beliefs that most of us develop early in life. Making a good impression on others helps us to develop friendships, get promoted at work, and impress our teachers. In fact, many rewards in life depend on being able to influence others in a positive way.

However, excessive social anxiety is usually associated with a tendency to be overly concerned with the opinions of others . . . so much so that it interferes with your life and may actually lead to a more negative impression on others, particularly if you avoid important social events. The problem with the beliefs and thoughts associated with social anxiety is not necessarily that they are untrue (although sometimes they are), but rather that they are held in an exaggerated and inflexible way. In other words, beliefs such as "I should always make a good impression" may be helpful for some people but may not be helpful for you. Like washing your hands hundreds of times per day, being overly concerned about the impression you make on others may be too much of a good thing.

In addition to establishing the accuracy of your anxious beliefs and predictions, it may also be helpful to consider whether your thoughts and behaviors are helping you. Below is a form that you can use for this exercise. If you are unsure about whether a particular anxious thought is true or false, try examining the costs and benefits of constantly dwelling on the thought. How would the quality of your life improve if you didn't have the thought?

**Describe Your Anxious Thought or Prediction**

_____

_____

_____

**List the Benefits of Having That Anxious Thought or Prediction**

_____

_____

_____

**List the Costs of Having That Anxious Thought or Prediction**

_____

_____

_____

## Rational Coping Statements

At the height of your fear, it may be difficult to challenge your anxious thoughts using some of the techniques described in this chapter. You may find that your attention is completely focused on trying to get through the situation and it may seem impossible to think logically. _Rational coping statements_ are relatively easy to use and don't require the same level of logical analysis as other techniques, such as examining the evidence and evaluating the costs and benefits of your anxious thoughts. Rational coping statements are short nonanxious sentences that may help to combat your anxious thinking. Examples include the following:

- It would be manageable if _____ didn't like me.

- It's okay to blush in front of others.

- Panic attacks are uncomfortable but not dangerous.

- It is okay to look anxious during a presentation.

- People don't seem to notice my shaky hands.

You may find it helpful to write or type several coping statements on an index card and to carry the card with you as a reminder. When you are in an anxiety-provoking situation, you can take the card out of your wallet or purse and read and repeat one or more of these statements to yourself to combat your anxious thoughts. Choose statements that are most relevant to you. Also, choose statements that are believable. For example, there is no point telling yourself, "I am not going to be anxious" if you always feel anxious when giving speeches and you are about to give a speech. A more credible alternative is "It is not the end of the world if I become anxious."

The space below is to record five rational coping statements that are relevant to your own particular anxious beliefs.

1. _____

2. _____

3. _____

4. _____

5. _____

## Behavioral Experiments

Cognitive therapy involves examining the validity of your beliefs and thoughts in the same way that a scientist examines the validity of theories and hypotheses. The experiment is the most powerful strategy scientists use to test their own beliefs. In cognitive therapy for social anxiety, experiments involve challenging the client's anxious beliefs by setting up small behavioral tests to see whether a belief is in fact valid. Through a series of repeated behavioral experiments, it is likely that you will disprove many of the beliefs and predictions that contribute to your fear and anxiety. Some examples of specific experiments that can be used to test the validity of various anxious thoughts are listed below.

| Anxious Thought | Behavioral Experiment |
| --- | --- |
| It would be terrible to have my hand shake while I hold a glass of water. | Purposely shake your hand while you hold a glass of water. For a true test of your beliefs, let the water spill all over you! Then see if it really is so terrible. |
| I will make a fool of myself at my job interview tomorrow, so why bother going? | Go to the job interview and see what happens. |
| I can't cope with being the center of attention. | Do something to draw attention to yourself. For example, arrive to class late, drop your keys, wear your shirt inside out, or knock over some unbreakable items in a supermarket. |
| It would be terrible to seem stupid or incompetent. | Line up at a store and after your items have been rung up, explain to the cashier that you have forgotten your money. |

| | |
|---|---|
| I will be rejected if I ask a coworker to have dinner with me. | Invite your coworker for dinner and check out his or her reaction. |

When selecting possible experiments, try to choose practices in which you have little to lose. For example, don't tell your boss how much you hate him or her, just to see what happens! Try to select experiments in which the worst that will happen is possible discomfort or temporary embarrassment. Remember that the more social risks you take, the more often they will pay off. Along the way, however, you will also experience rejection from time to time. If you don't take risks, you will never be rejected, but you will also never experience the benefits of taking social risks, including improved relationships, a better job, and other possible rewards.

In the spaces below, try to imagine some experiments you could try in order to test out your particular anxious thoughts. In the first column, write down your anxious belief. In the second column, try to design a small experiment that will provide a good test of whether your belief is true.

**Anxious Thought**                      **Behavioral Experiment**

_____          _____

_____          _____

_____          _____

_____          _____

_____          _____

The next few chapters discuss strategies for confronting the very situations and feelings that you fear. As you will see, exposure to feared situations is actually a type of behavioral experiment. By repeatedly exposing yourself to situations that make you anxious, you will learn that your fears often do not materialize.

# Using a Thought Record or Cognitive Diary

Throughout this chapter, we have included various forms and diaries to be used for challenging anxious thoughts. In this section, we now provide a more generic Cognitive Record Form that can be used whenever you experience anxiety in a social situation. Unlike the other forms in this chapter, which are each designed for use with a particular technique (e.g., examining the evidence, overcoming catastrophic thinking, cost-benefit analysis), the Cognitive Record Form is designed to be used with any of the cognitive strategies. A blank version of the form is included, as well as a completed sample.

It really doesn't matter which form you use to record and change your thoughts. You can use these forms or design your own. The diaries in this chapter are only suggestions. The main point of these diaries is to get you into the habit of paying attention to your thoughts and actively trying to change them. Once the new patterns of thinking become second nature, it will no longer be necessary to record your thoughts on paper. In the meantime, we recommend that you use some type of diary or form several times per week after encountering a feared social or performance situation. The best times to complete the form are either before entering the situation (as a way of preparing for the encounter) or immediately afterwards (as a way of challenging any anxious thoughts that occurred while you were in the situation).

## Instructions for Completing the Cognitive Record Form

### Column 1: Situation

Record the date and time. Describe the situation and the triggers for your fear. Typical examples include the following:

- Went to a meeting

- Person was watching me on the subway

- Ate lunch with a coworker

- I was blushing

- My hands shook in front of my boss

- Went to a party

- Had to do an oral book report for class

- Was introduced to my sister's new boyfriend

- Went on a blind date

### Column 2: Initial Fear

Rate your fear level before countering your fearful thoughts. Use a 0 to 100 point scale, where 0 = no anxiety and 100 = extreme anxiety.

### Column 3: Fearful Thoughts and Predictions

In the third column, list any anxious thoughts that occur in response to the situation and triggers reported in column 1. Usually these thoughts will be predictions of danger, embarrassment, etc. Often these thoughts will be automatic or almost unconscious. It will take practice to identify them. Try to come up with very specific thoughts. A thought such as "Something bad will happen" is too vague. Typical examples of specific anxious thoughts include the following:

- People will notice that I am nervous

- I will make a fool of myself

- People will think I am stupid

- People will see me for the idiot I really am

- People will think I am ugly

- I will have to leave the situation

- I am incompetent and clumsy

- I need to drink alcohol to feel comfortable

- People can always tell how I am feeling

- Anxiety is a sign of weakness

- I will be viewed as boring

- People will not like me

- I will have nothing to say

## Column 4: Rational Responses and Countering

Use countering strategies to challenge your anxious thinking. For example, if you believe that other people will think you are incompetent if your hands shake, examine the evidence and try to identify other possible interpretations of the situation. You might ask yourself, "What else might people think?" or "Is it possible that people might not even notice?" or "What would I think of someone else if I saw his or her hands shaking?" As you realize that your predictions are unlikely to come true, your fear will likely decrease.

Note that in some cases, your predictions may be realistic (e.g., "I will get anxious when I give a presentation" is probably a realistic prediction for someone who usually becomes anxious in this situation). If this is the case, there are still a number of questions that you can ask yourself to challenge your anxious beliefs. For example, "What is the worst that can happen?" or "If my prediction were true, why would that be a problem?" or "What might it mean about me if my beliefs were true?" or "How can I cope with the possibility of my prediction being true?" By asking yourself questions such as these, it is likely you will conclude that even if your belief is true, it will be manageable.

## Column 5: Outcome

In the fifth column, describe the outcome of your attempts to challenge your anxious thoughts. Did the challenging work? What did you conclude regarding the accuracy of your anxious predictions?

---

Adapted from M. M. Antony and R. P. Swinson. 2000. *Phobic Disorders and Panic in Adults: A Guide to Assessment and Treatment.* Washington, DC: American Psychological Association. Used with permission.

# Cognitive Record Form

| Situation | Initial Fear (0-100) | Fearful Thoughts and Predictions | Rational Responses and Countering | Outcome |
|---|---|---|---|---|
|  |  |  |  |  |
|  |  |  |  |  |
|  |  |  |  |  |
|  |  |  |  |  |
|  |  |  |  |  |

Adapted from M. M. Antony and R. P. Swinson. 2000. *Phobic Disorders and Panic in Adults: A Guide to Assessment and Treatment*. Washington, DC: American Psychological Association. Used with permission.

# Sample Cognitive Record Form for Social and Performance Anxiety

| Situation | Initial Fear (0–100) | Fearful Thoughts and Predictions | Rational Responses and Countering | Outcome |
|---|---|---|---|---|
| Oct. 15— at work, giving a presentation | 85 | I will look incompetent. | I know the presentation material quite well, so I know what I am talking about. Even if people ask me about something I don't know, it's okay to say that I don't know. People will not judge how competent I am based on a single presentation. | My fear gradually decreased over a period of 15 minutes or so. People seemed to be interested during the presentation. I was able to answer their questions. |
| | | My boss will notice that I'm anxious. | It is possible that my boss will not notice. There are over 50 people in the room. My boss is not even looking my way. Besides, even if my boss did notice, she would be understanding. Everyone gets anxious sometimes . . . even my boss. | I'm not sure whether my boss noticed my fear. She didn't say anything to indicate that she noticed. |

Adapted from M. M. Antony and R. P. Swinson. 2000. *Phobic Disorders and Panic in Adults: A Guide to Assessment and Treatment.* Washington, DC: American Psychological Association. Used with permission.

# Trouble Shooting

*Problem:*    I have difficulty identifying my anxious thoughts.

*Solution:*   Ask yourself questions such as, "What might _____ think about me?" and "What do I think will happen in this situation?" If, after trying to answer these questions, you are still unable to identify your anxious beliefs, try to detect your thoughts while you are actually in the situation you fear. If you are unable to identify specific thoughts and predictions, don't worry. You can still benefit from the exposure-based strategies discussed in chapters 7 through 9.

*Problem:*    I have difficulty believing the alternative, nonanxious, rational thoughts.

*Solution:*   Sometimes the cognitive techniques seem superficial when a person first starts to use them. Over time, the new nonanxious thoughts should become more believable. If not, the exposure-based strategies (chapters 7 through 9) are among the most powerful methods for changing anxious thoughts and likely will help. Sometimes, changing thoughts through firsthand experience in a feared situation is more effective than trying to change thoughts by simply trying to think differently.

*Problem:*    When I am in a social situation, I am too anxious to think clearly, so I can't use the cognitive strategies.

*Solution:*   Try using the cognitive strategies before you enter the situation. If this is not practical, try using them after you have been in the situation for a while (your fear should decrease over time) or even after leaving the situation.

*Problem:*    I can't be bothered completing the monitoring forms. They are confusing and they take too long to complete.

*Solution:*   There are many different ways to learn the techniques described in this chapter. The forms and diaries are designed to make the process easier. However, if they are getting in the way of using the strategies, try developing a simpler form (for example, you may want to use a two-column form—with one column for recording your anxious thoughts and another column for recording your new nonanxious thoughts). Alternatively, you can even forget about the forms and diaries and simply use the techniques in your head.

# A Summary Guide to Challenging Thoughts

This chapter includes a large number of suggestions and strategies for identifying and changing your anxious thoughts. Now that you have had a chance to read through the chapter and complete some of the exercises, we encourage you to continue using the cognitive techniques to cope with your social and performance anxiety. Generally, using the cognitive strategies will involve the following steps:

1. Identify your anxious thoughts, predictions, and interpretations.

2. Examine the validity of your anxious predictions, using some of the techniques described in this chapter (e.g., examining the evidence, taking the perspective of another person, conducting a cost-benefit analysis, using rational coping statements). Are your predictions realistic? For example, will others really think _____ about you?

3. Examine the validity of your catastrophic thoughts by asking the question, "So what if my anxious thoughts are true?" For example, "What if a few people in the audience really think my presentation is awful? How might I cope with that?"

4. Use the Cognitive Record Form to identify and challenge your anxious thoughts on paper.

## Integrating Cognitive Strategies into Your Treatment Plan

The cognitive techniques described in this chapter are not meant to be used on their own. Rather they should be used as part of a comprehensive treatment plan that includes exposure to feared situations. Exposure-based treatments are discussed in chapters 7 through 9. We recommend that you first practice the cognitive techniques for a few weeks before formally beginning exposure practices. Learning to control your anxiety by managing your anxious thoughts will help you when confronting the situations that you fear. In addition to exposure and cognitive therapy, your treatment may also include medication (see chapter 5) and social skills practices (see chapter 10), depending on your own personal needs and preferences.

# Chapter 7

# Confronting Your Fears Through Exposure

Chapter 6 provided a detailed overview of cognitive strategies that have been shown to be useful for changing anxious patterns of thinking. Almost all of the cognitive techniques involve learning to think differently about social and performance situations by (1) broadening the possible range of interpretations and beliefs that you can hold regarding a particular social situation, and (2) considering all the evidence before assuming that a specific thought is true.

This chapter provides an introduction to a number of techniques that are useful for changing the behaviors that maintain your anxious beliefs and feelings. Essentially, these strategies involve confronting your fears directly by exposing yourself to the situations and the feelings that you currently fear and avoid. This chapter starts with a review of the behaviors that contribute to social anxiety and a summary of the strategies that can be used to change these behaviors. The remainder of the chapter provides more detailed descriptions of the underlying principles of exposure and the best ways to conduct exposure-based therapy.

Chapters 8 and 9 build directly on the content of this introductory chapter by providing more in-depth instructions regarding exposure to social *situations* (chapter 8) and exposure to feared *sensations* (chapter 9). The exercises described in chapters 7 through 9 should be used after you have had a chance to practice some of the cognitive methods described in chapter 6. We recommend that you begin to learn about exposure by reading chapters 7 and 8 and that you practice the situational exposure exercises for at least three to five weeks before moving on to chapter 9. Then, we suggest that you read chapter 9 and make some attempts to expose yourself to feared sensations, if these exercises are relevant to you. As reviewed in chapter 9, exposure to physical sensations may be useful if you are fearful of experiencing particular feelings (e.g., sweating, shaking, blushing, racing heart) associated with being anxious or nervous.

# Behaviors That Contribute to Social Anxiety

All organisms try to avoid situations that cause fear, pain, or discomfort. Avoidance is a method of protecting oneself from possible danger. In the short term, staying away from perceived threats is a very effective way of decreasing or preventing these uncomfortable feelings. Your experience has probably taught you that confronting feared situations causes you to feel overwhelmed, and that avoiding or escaping from feared situations leads to a sense of relief. However, avoiding the situations, objects, and feelings that make you anxious is also a guaranteed way to ensure that your fear will continue over the long term. The likelihood of threat in the social situations that you probably avoid is actually quite remote or even nonexistent. Under such circumstances, avoidance can do more harm than good, particularly in the long term.

By avoiding the situations that make you uncomfortable, it may seem as though you prevent your feared negative consequences from occurring. Just as a person who fears flying may believe that avoiding a flight has protected him or her from experiencing a possible plane crash, you may believe that avoiding social or performance situations protects you from experiencing various social catastrophes, such as being humiliated or criticized by others. Of course, statistically, the risk of dying in a plane crash is close to zero (about one in ten million, according to some sources). In other words, the risk of being in a plane crash is *almost* identical (i.e., close to zero) whether you fly or not! The same may be said of public speaking, attending parties, and other social situations. The risk of actual threat or danger is significantly less than socially anxious individuals usually assume. In fact, the long-term consequences of avoiding social situations are often far greater than the risks of confronting these situations.

Exposure to feared situations and feelings is a very powerful method of learning that avoidance is neither necessary nor helpful in the long run. By confronting your fears, you will discover that many of your anxious beliefs and interpretations are untrue or exaggerated. In addition, your interpersonal skills will improve as you will have more opportunities to engage in various types of social interaction and performance. In other words, not only will you become more comfortable making small talk, giving speeches, or dealing with conflict situations, you will also become more effective and competent at mastering these challenging situations.

There are three main types of anxious behaviors that we will review here. Each of these is a potentially harmful habit because it prevents your fear from decreasing over the long term. These behaviors include (1) avoiding feared social and performance situations, (2) avoiding feared sensations and feelings, and (3) subtle avoidance strategies.

## Avoidance of Social Situations

Avoiding social situations such as public speaking, making conversations, attending meetings, dating, and working out at the gym prevents you from learning that these situations are safe and that your fears are generally unwarranted. Escaping early from these situations (e.g., leaving a party after a few minutes) can also have a negative impact on your fear by reinforcing your belief that being in the situation makes you uncomfortable, whereas leaving the situation provides relief and a reduction in fear. In reality, staying in a situation despite the fear that it arouses also leads to a reduction in fear. Fear may take longer to decrease when you stay in the situation, but the long-term benefits will be greater. By staying until your fear decreases, you will learn that you can be right in the middle of the situation and feel relatively comfortable. Strategies for overcoming avoidance of feared situations are discussed throughout this chapter, as well as in chapter 8.

## Avoidance of Feared Sensations

As discussed previously, in addition to avoiding certain situations, you may also avoid feeling certain sensations or feelings, particularly in social situations. Perhaps you avoid eating hot foods that cause you to feel flushed when you are dining with friends or relatives. Alternatively, you may avoid wearing warm clothes while speaking in public, in case they cause you to sweat. Avoiding sensations such as sweating and blushing reinforces your beliefs that these sensations and feelings are dangerous. If you are fearful of experiencing particular symptoms in the presence of others, you will likely find that exposing yourself to these feelings can help you to become more comfortable with them. The goal is to reach a point at which sensations, like shaking or a racing heartbeat, are, at worst, mildly uncomfortable, but not frightening. The general principles discussed throughout this chapter will be relevant to overcoming your fear of physical symptoms. However, specific exercises for overcoming these fears are discussed more thoroughly in chapter 9.

## Subtle Avoidance Strategies

Subtle avoidance behaviors are not-so-obvious strategies that people often use to cope with anxiety-provoking situations. Unlike completely avoiding a feared situation, subtle avoidance strategies involve *partial* avoidance of the situation. Often these behaviors are not noticeable to others. In fact, they may be so subtle that even you are not aware of them. As is the case with more obvious types of avoidance, learning to let go of your subtle forms of escape will help you to overcome your fear, just as removing training wheels is an important step in learning to ride a bicycle, and letting go of crutches is an important step in relearning to walk after an injury. Some examples of subtle avoidance strategies are discussed below:

**Distraction**. Distraction involves escaping from anxious thoughts and feelings by focusing on thoughts or images that are more pleasant, or by keeping yourself busy with distracting activities. For example, while attending a party, you might offer to help serve food or drinks so that you are constantly busy with some activity and your mind is distracted from the anxious feelings that you might otherwise be experiencing. Or, while traveling on a bus or train, you might always be sure to bring a book or portable radio to distract yourself from feeling anxious about making eye contact with others, or from thinking about what others might be thinking about you. Such distractions may help you to feel comfortable while in social or performance situations, but in the long term, it prevents you from learning that you can manage the situation without having to rely on subtle avoidance.

**Overprotective behaviors**. Overprotective behaviors are small things that you may do to feel safer in the situations that you fear. Examples may include the following:

- Wearing makeup or a turtleneck sweater to hide blushing

- Finding out who else will be at a party before deciding whether to attend

- Wearing gloves to hide shaking hands

- Sitting down or leaning against a podium while giving a presentation

- Eating in a dimly lit restaurant, so your date won't notice your anxiety

- Wearing sunglasses to help avoid making eye contact

- Always attending social events with a friend so that you can avoid talking to people who you don't know well

When designing exposure practices, it is important that you also try to eliminate these subtle overprotective behaviors.

**Overcompensating for perceived deficits**. Overcompensating involves working extra hard to make sure that your fearful predictions don't come true. For example, if you are afraid of looking foolish during a presentation, you may spend many more hours than necessary rehearsing and memorizing what you will say. If you are fearful of making small talk, you may spend a large amount of time preparing topics of conversation and rehearsing what you might talk about. If you are afraid of looking unattractive, you may put too much effort into fixing your hair, choosing your clothes, or building your muscles at the gym. In many cases, these situations might be managed with less effort, leaving time and energy for other things. Exposure practices should be designed to eliminate any tendencies to overprepare or overcompensate for flaws that may not even be present.

For example, instead of spending hours memorizing a presentation, try giving your talk with only minimal (but still adequate) preparation.

**Excessive checking and reassurance seeking.** Excessive checking involves spending too much time and effort trying to find out whether you are perceived by others in a positive light. We all engage in occasional checking (e.g., looking in the mirror at a party, asking a coworker whether he or she enjoyed your presentation). In fact, we recommend that you *occasionally* continue to check on other people's reactions to you and your actions. Checking and receiving reassurance are helpful ways of testing out your beliefs. However, if you ask for reassurance or check too frequently, this may be a behavior you want to decrease.

The key here is moderation. Occasional checking is helpful, but constant checking can be a problem. Constantly obtaining reassurance about your performance is like constantly checking with your doctor whenever you experience an unusual sensation. Never going to the doctor may cause you serious health problems that might otherwise have been detected early or prevented. But going to the doctor several times a week to check out every ache and pain can backfire; your doctor may stop taking your concerns and complaints seriously.

**Substance use.** Substance use can undermine the effects of exposure by artificially lowering your level of fear in social and performance situations. For exposure to be effective, it is important for you to experience some degree of fear. It is also important for you to learn that your fear decreases naturally if you stay in the situation. Drinking alcohol or using other drugs whenever you are in a situation that makes you anxious will prevent you from ever learning that your anxiety will decrease, even if you don't use the drug or alcohol. When designing exposure practices, we recommend that you not drink alcohol or use drugs during the practice. If you want to have a glass of wine or a beer at a party, try to wait until after your fear has decreased somewhat.

# A Step-by-Step Overview for Conducting Exposure-Based Treatments

The main steps involved in any exposure-based treatment program are initial assessment, planning appropriate exercises, carrying out the practices, and taking steps to maintain the improvements over the long term.

## Initial Assessment

The issue of assessment was discussed in chapter 3. To plan effective exposure practices you will need to know the situations and sensations that you fear and avoid as well as becoming aware of the different variables that affect your fear level. When you completed the exercises in chapter 3, you probably identified a number of variables that affect your fear level when you are in a social or performance situation that causes you to feel uncomfortable. You should review the relevant sections of chapter 3 before beginning your exposure practices.

## *Planning Appropriate Practices*

Planning your exposure practices starts with developing a *hierarchy* of situations you fear. Such a hierarchy is a list of situations ranked in order of difficulty, from most fear-provoking to least fear-provoking. Chapter 8 provides examples of hierarchies and includes instructions on how to develop your own hierarchy for situational exposure. Chapter 9 provides sample hierarchies and instructions for developing your own hierarchy for exposing yourself to feared sensations. Developing a hierarchy of exercises will provide you with a structure that will allow you to begin with easier exercises and work your way up to more difficult ones.

## *Carrying Out the Practices*

Once you have identified some practices likely to be helpful, the next step is to begin carrying them out. Generally, exposure begins with more manageable situations and works up to more and more difficult situations. As confronting the situations becomes easier, you should begin to let go of the subtle forms of avoidance that were discussed earlier. Later, after practicing situational exposure for several weeks (as described in chapter 8), it may be useful to add exercises involving exposure to feared feelings and sensations (as described in chapter 9).

Exposure practices should be structured, planned in advance, and carried out frequently. The ways in which exposure practices are carried out affect whether the practices are helpful or not. Exposure can actually increase your fear if not done properly. The remaining sections of this chapter provide suggestions as to the best ways to conduct exposure to maximize the chances of decreasing your fear.

## *Maintaining Your Improvements*

In order to maintain your improvements, it is important that you continue occasional practices even after your fear has decreased. These strategies are explored in greater detail in chapter 11.

# Types of Exposure

This section discusses three different dimensions that should be taken into account when planning exposure practices. They are (1) exposure to social situations versus feared sensations; (2) imagined versus live exposures; and (3) gradual versus rapid exposure.

## Exposure to Social Situations versus Feared Sensations

*Situational exposure* involves exposing oneself to places and situations that produce anxiety. Overcoming social and performance anxiety almost always includes situational exposure as a component. In other words, to become more comfortable with public speaking, meeting strangers, or lunching with your coworkers, you will need to practice these activities.

Some people with social and performance anxiety may also benefit from exposure to sensations. This form of exposure is called *interoceptive exposure* and it involves practicing a number of exercises that trigger particular physical sensations. For example, spinning in a chair can be used to induce dizziness. Running up and down the stairs will make your heart race. Interoceptive exposure is useful for people who are fearful of experiencing uncomfortable physical sensations.

If you are not afraid of the feelings, i.e., the physical sensations, that you experience when you are anxious, there is no need to practice these exercises. However, if you are frightened by the physical sensations you experience in social situations, you may find it helpful to practice experiencing these feelings purposely until they no longer frighten you. Interoceptive exposure can be combined with situational exposure so that feared physical sensations are purposefully brought on during the course of the exposure to feared situations. Chapter 9 provides a detailed description of how to use interoceptive exposure to reduce your fear of sensations.

## Imagined versus Live Exposure

Exposure can be conducted in your imagination (picturing yourself in a feared situation) or in real life (actually entering the feared situation). Generally, whenever possible, we recommend that live exposure (also called *in vivo exposure*) be used rather than imagined exposure. Although both approaches can lead to a reduction of fear, live exposure has two big advantages. First, some people have difficulty imagining feared situations in a way that actually arouses their fear. And, second, there is evidence that live exposure is more effective at reducing fear (Emmelkamp and Wessels 1975).

Nevertheless, under certain circumstances, imagined exposure may be helpful. If you are too fearful to enter a situation in real life, you can use imagined exposure as a stepping-stone to the real situation. For example, if you are planning to ask someone out on a date, you might consider using an imagined exposure to the situation at first. Once you have become more comfortable at imagining the situation, trying the real thing might become easier. Also, imagined exposure can be helpful when the situation is impractical or impossible to practice in real life. For example, if you must give a presentation to a group of 200 people, you may not be able to practice it in front of a large group. Instead, imagining a large group in your mind's eye might be a good way to practice for the actual presentation when you are preparing your talk.

*Situational role-play* is a compromise between imagined exposure and live exposure. Role-play involves rehearsing being in a particular situation with the help of a friend, family member, or therapist. For example, before exposing yourself to a real job interview, you could practice mock interviews with other individuals posing as the interviewers. Or, you could ask your family or friends to act as the audience while you practice a presentation. These various forms of situational exposure (imagined, in vivo, and role-plays) are discussed more thoroughly in chapter 8.

## Gradual versus Rapid Exposure

Exposure may be conducted gradually or rapidly. *Rapid exposure* involves taking steps very quickly, skipping steps, and sometimes trying more difficult situations before you have completely mastered easier situations. For example, rapid exposure to public speaking might have you start off with talking in front of large groups of unfamiliar people instead of to small groups of familiar people.

*Gradual exposure* tends to begin with easier practices and progresses to the more difficult practices much more slowly. Compared to rapid exposure, a person who is working with gradual exposure may spend more time practicing each step before moving on to the next level of difficulty. In addition, gradual exposure is less likely to leave out intermediate steps, compared to rapid exposure. With gradual exposure, by the time you get to the top steps of your hierarchy, you will be better prepared and less likely to feel overwhelmed by the practice.

Gradual exposure is similar to progressing through school one grade at a time. If you had to jump from ninth grade to twelfth grade, it is likely you would find the increase in difficulty overwhelming. By progressing through high school one grade at a time, each grade seems to be just slightly more difficult than the previous grade. By the time you get to twelfth grade, the increase in difficulty is only a small step, compared to what you have been doing in eleventh grade.

Gradual exposure to public speaking might begin by presenting small speeches in front of a close friend or family member or by asking questions at meetings. After those practice situations become easier, you might try speaking for longer periods of time during meetings, or practicing a speech in front of a small group of friends or family members. This could then progress to practicing your speech in front of several coworkers. With gradual exposure, you might not actually speak in front of large groups of unfamiliar people until many earlier steps have been mastered.

Gradual and rapid exposure are both effective ways of reducing fear, and the end result of each is usually the same. However, each approach has advantages and disadvantages over the other. Rapid exposure works quicker than gradual exposure. Therefore, with rapid exposure it is likely you will see changes more quickly, which will save you time. Also, quick results may motivate you to work even harder at overcoming your fear. However, compared to gradual exposure, rapid exposure is associated with higher levels of discomfort and fear. Rapid exposure requires a strong commitment from you to tolerate higher levels of discomfort.

The differences between these two forms of exposure can be compared to the difference between jumping into a cold swimming pool and entering the pool slowly. Jumping into the pool quickly causes more initial discomfort, but you get used to the water more quickly. On the other hand, getting into the pool slowly and gradually may be less shocking to your system, but it will take you longer to get used to the water.

We recommend that you practice exposures as slowly or as quickly as you want to . If you prefer to try things more quickly, that's fine. If you prefer a more gradual approach, that's fine, too. Sometimes, you may find it difficult to judge whether a particular step is too difficult. Remember, there is no harm in taking steps too quickly. If an exercise ends up becoming too overwhelming, you have the option of continuing to practice it until it becomes easier, or stepping back, trying a less difficult exercise, and working your way up to the difficult practice more gradually. Either approach is likely to be helpful. The decision is a matter of personal preference and how much discomfort you are willing to tolerate.

# How Exposure Works

Most cognitive-behavioral researchers and therapists believe that exposure works by providing individuals with an opportunity to test the validity of their fearful thoughts, assumptions, and interpretations. In chapter 6, we discussed the use of *behavioral experiments* for challenging anxious beliefs and predictions. Repeated exposure may be thought of as a form of behavioral experiment. By entering feared situations and exposing yourself to feared sensations repeatedly, you will discover whether your beliefs about social and performance situations are true or false.

## *Why Exposure May Not Have Worked in the Past*

People who are about to begin exposure-based treatments often wonder why they should expect exposure to work now if it hasn't worked in the past. In all likelihood, you have already been exposed to certain anxiety-provoking social situations from time to time and, in many cases, your fear has probably not decreased. In fact, your anxiety may have increased with repeated exposures. Given such previous experiences with exposure, you may be skeptical about whether simply exposing yourself again to feared social situations will lead to a decrease in your fear.

It is important to acknowledge that exposure is not effective under all circumstances. For example, unpredictable exposure can lead to an increase in fear, particularly if it involves a negative event or consequence. Imagine this situation: You are afraid of dogs and a dog unexpectedly runs out from behind a tree and starts growling at you. That kind of exposure would only make your fear worse.

On the other hand, if you are gradually exposed to your neighbor's friendly dog, at your own pace, your fear of dogs might decrease.

In everyday life, exposure to feared situations is often unpredictable. In addition, such everyday exposures tend to be brief and infrequent. All of these factors make exposure in everyday life less likely to lead to a decrease in fear, compared to the type of exposure that is used in cognitive-behavioral therapy. A summary of the main differences between the type of exposure you may have experienced in the past (previous exposure) and the type that has been shown as useful for helping people overcome fear (therapeutic exposure) appears below.

**Typical Previous Exposures**

These are often *unpredictable and uncontrollable* (e.g., you "end up" in the middle of an unexpected conversation; you are "forced" to go to a party that you would rather not attend).

These have a *brief duration* (e.g., you get into the situation, feel anxious, then leave. This teaches you that, "When I am in the situation I feel frightened, but when I leave I feel better").

These are *infrequent* (e.g., because you usually avoid anxiety-provoking situations, you are not in them very often. Each time you are in the situation, it's like starting over).

These usually involve *anxious thinking* (e.g., "People think I'm an idiot," "People will think I'm terrified if they notice my shaky hands").

These include *subtle ways of avoiding* the situation (e.g., by distracting yourself, using alcohol or drugs, bringing someone with you, or sitting in a certain "safe" location).

**Typical Therapeutic Exposures**

These are *predictable and under your control* (e.g., you make a decision to enter an anxiety-provoking situation specifically so that you can learn to be more comfortable in that situation).

These are *prolonged* (e.g., you decide to stay in a situation until the anxiety diminishes on its own. This teaches you that you can be in the situation and your anxiety eventually will subside without anything bad happening).

These are *frequent* (e.g., you practice your exposures over and over again and close together. The benefits of repeated exposures start to add up to diminished anxiety).

These include *countering your anxious thoughts* (e.g., you ask yourself questions to counter or challenge your anxious beliefs and predictions).

These *do not include subtle avoidance strategies* (e.g., you make a decision to not use these strategies, so that you to teach yourself to master the situation on your own).

Adapted from M. M. Antony and R. P. Swinson. 2000. *Phobic Disorders and Panic in Adults: A Guide to Assessment and Treatment.* Washington, DC: American Psychological Association. Used with permission.

# Obstacles to Completing Exposure Practices

There are many different reasons why people sometimes don't follow through on exposure practices. We suggest that you anticipate the possible obstacles in advance and try to think of ways to overcome them. There are always going to be reasons not to practice. To combat the excuses you will undoubtedly come up with, you will need to remind yourself of your reasons to continue to practice despite lack of desire, lack of time, or being overwhelmed with the idea of confronting situations that make you anxious and uncomfortable. Here is a listing of some of the most common reasons why people procrastinate when it comes to doing exposure exercises. Possible solutions to these problems are also given.

*Obstacle:*    My practices are never planned in enough detail, so I am not sure exactly what I am supposed to do.

*Solutions:*   • At the beginning of each week, plan your exposure practices thoroughly. You should know exactly what you are going to do, where you are going to do it, and when you are going to practice (e.g., dates and times).

*Obstacle:*    Although I have good intentions, my plans never seem to work out. For example, when I plan to have lunch with a friend, I often find that my friend isn't available when I call.

*Solutions:*   • Make sure you make plans early. Leaving things for the last minute will make it much more likely that your plans won't work out.

               • Be sure to have a backup plan. For example, if you're planning to have lunch with a coworker, make sure you have an alternative second plan and, sometimes, even a third plan, just in case your friend isn't available for lunch.

*Obstacle:*    I always forget to practice.

*Solutions:*   • Plan your practices the way you would any other activity in your day. Set aside blocks of time to practice and record them in your appointment calendar just as you would for any other appointments, so you don't forget.

               • Set an alarm (e.g., on your wristwatch or a small clock) as a reminder to practice.

               • Ask other people to remind you, if necessary.

*Obstacle:*    The idea of doing therapeutic exposure work seems overwhelming. I am just too scared.

*Solutions:*    • Start with an easier practice. The activity that you choose should be challenging, but not completely overwhelming. If a particular task seems impossible, start with an easier task that does seem possible.

• Use the cognitive strategies discussed in chapter 6 to challenge your anxious thoughts before entering a feared situation.

*Obstacle:*    I am too busy. There never seems to be enough time to do the work.

*Solutions:*    • Put aside small blocks of time to be used exclusively for your social anxiety exposure practices. If time is reserved just for this purpose, you will be less likely to feel as if your practices are getting in the way of your other important activities. This is something you want to do for yourself. If you really want to deal with your social anxiety, you know you can find the small blocks of time to reserve for the practices. Think of practice times as taking a class. You may not always want to go to a class, but if you want to learn what is being taught there, you find the time to go.

• Choose practices that can be completed during the course of your regular routine. For example, you need to eat every day—you might as well eat some of your meals with other people instead of always eating alone.

• Set aside a large block of time (e.g., clear a week-long vacation from work) and spend the whole time practicing exposure full time.

*Obstacle:*    I am not convinced that exposure practices will be helpful.

*Solutions:*    • Begin with a smaller exposure practice in which you have little to lose, but in which you can still test whether exposing yourself to the situation leads to a decrease in your fear. The belief that exposure won't work is probably just another example of a negative thought that isn't necessarily true.

• Examine the validity of your beliefs regarding exposure. For example, are there reasons why exposure may not have worked in the past? After you finish reading this chapter, you may have some new ideas about how to ensure that exposure will be more likely to work now.

*Obstacle:*    My feared situations are difficult to create. For example, I can't think of any places to practice public speaking.

*Solutions:*      • Chapter 8 contains a large number of possible situations in which to practice exposure. Reading chapter 8 should help you to generate ideas.

• Talk to family members and friends. They may be able to help you to come up with some ideas for practices.

# How to Conduct Exposure Practices

This section provides suggestions for getting the most out of your exposure practices. These include instructions regarding how to prepare for practices, variables to keep in mind when planning practices, what to do during a particular practice, and what to do following the practice. Some of the most important suggestions are summarized in a checklist at the end of this section.

## Preparing for Exposure Practices

As much as possible, it is important to plan your exposure practices in advance. As discussed earlier, planning involves making decisions at the beginning of the week regarding particular practices that you intend to try as well as coming up with backup practices in case your original plans don't work out. It is very likely that planning will involve setting aside particular times during which to practice. You should also have an idea of how a practice fits in with your short-term and long-term goals. For example, if your long-term goal is to be able to give a presentation to a large group of coworkers, practicing speaking to smaller groups may be an important step in your plan.

Before beginning any particular practice, we suggest that you make some very specific predictions regarding what might happen during the practice. Once you are aware of your anxious thoughts and predictions, use the cognitive strategies described in chapter 6 to challenge your thoughts. Challenging your anxious thoughts before entering into the situation will help you to manage your fear and discomfort.

## Importance of Predictability and Control

As discussed earlier, exposure works better if it is predictable and if you have a sense of control over what is happening in the situation. Therefore, it is best to start with exposure practices in which you have a pretty good idea of what is likely to happen. Some situations, however, are inherently unpredictable. For example, if you decide to ask another person out on a date, it may be difficult to know how the other person will respond. In these cases, you can make the situation somewhat more predictable by considering in advance all of the possible outcomes that could occur. For example, the person might accept your invitation, turn it down, or put off responding for the time being (e.g., by not returning your call, saying "I'm not sure, let me get back to you"). By anticipating as many outcomes as possible (as well as how you might cope with each outcome), you will be less likely to be surprised.

## Duration of Exposure

Exposure works better if it lasts long enough for your fear to decrease. We suggest that you try to stay in the situation for as long as possible. For example, if you are at a party, try to stay for at least a couple of hours. If you are giving a presentation and have the option of making it longer, try to take advantage of the opportunity to speak for a longer time.

If you are practicing being in a situation that is naturally very brief (e.g., asking a stranger for the time or directions), you can prolong the anxiety-provoking situation by repeating the exposure over and over for a longer period. For example, instead of asking one person for information while walking through a shopping mall, (e.g., "Where is The Gap?"), you can ask twenty or thirty different people for the same information over the course of an hour or more. The chances are good that your fear will decrease over time.

## Frequency of Exposure

Exposure works better if practices are repeated close together. For example, giving a speech once a week is more effective than giving a speech once a month. Daily speeches will decrease your fear more effectively than once a week, even if the number of practices is the same. In other words, giving a presentation five days in a row will likely lead to a greater decrease in fear than giving a presentation once per week, for five consecutive weeks. So, try to schedule practices as frequently as possible. We recommend that you set aside at least an hour to practice exposure on most days. Once your fear has begun to decrease considerably, it is a good idea to gradually spread out the practices to every few weeks or even to every few months, depending on the situation and how often it arises in your day-to-day life. Occasional practices will help to maintain the improvements you have made in decreasing your fear.

## Practice in a Variety of Situations

To some extent, working on decreasing your fear in a particular social or performance situation will help you to feel more comfortable in other social situations as well. For example, if you learn to feel comfortable asking questions in class, some of that success may "spread" to other situations, such as speaking up in meetings at work. To get the most out of exposure, however, it is best to practice in a variety of different contexts, places, and situations. For example, if you want to be more comfortable making small talk, we recommend that you practice with your coworkers, family members, strangers in the elevator, at parties, and in as many other situations as possible.

## Choose Practices That Are Challenging But Not Impossible

You may feel discouraged if while trying a particular practice, you become anxious or uncomfortable. There is no need to feel discouraged. In fact, you *should* feel uncomfortable during exposure practices. That's why you are doing the practices in the first place. Over time, you will begin to feel less anxious. A successful practice is *not* one in which you don't become anxious. Rather, a successful practice is one that you complete, regardless of how anxious you feel.

On the other hand, it is not necessary to choose practices that are completely terrifying or in which you find it impossible to stay in the situation. If a situation seems too difficult, we encourage you to try something easier. But try something.

## Choose Practices with Minimal Risk

Choose practices in which the likely consequences are minimal, except for a period of feeling anxious. For example, if you want to be more comfortable with the possibility of seeming foolish or being the center of attention, there are lots of *safe* practices that you can try (e.g., walking around with your shirt inside out, telling the cashier that you have forgotten your wallet when you reach the front of the grocery line). There is no need to take unnecessary risks, such as telling your boss what a jerk he is or yelling out a dirty joke at your best friend's wedding. If you are not sure about the realistic risks associated with a particular practice, ask someone whose judgment you trust (perhaps a friend or family member).

## Measuring Your Improvement

It will be helpful to assess your anxiety from time to time using the forms and suggestions in chapter 3. Evaluating your improvement periodically will remind you of how far you have come and will also let you know when it is time to move on to new situations.

## Including a Helper or Coach

Consider including a friend, coworker, or therapist to act as a coach during exposure practices. This individual can help you with role-play practices (e.g., mock job interviews, practicing making small talk) and can provide you with feedback following your practices. If you choose to include a helper during some exposure exercises, that person should be familiar with the basic principles of exposure. Either you should instruct the person regarding a helper or coach's role, or you should have the person read the relevant sections of this book. In fact, some combination of both approaches may work best. In addition, the man or woman whom you choose to work with should be supportive and unlikely to become frustrated if things don't work out as planned.

## Keep Your Expectations Realistic

Don't expect your anxiety to change overnight. It will likely take weeks or months for it to improve. Also, you won't be able to follow your improvement like a straight line on a graph. You may find that in some situations your anxiety decreases fairly quickly, whereas in other situations success may take longer. Also, you may find that some exposure practices don't lead to any improvement in your fear. You may even have weeks during which your fear and anxiety worsen. A good rule of thumb is to expect one step back for every two or three steps forward.

## Don't Fight Your Fear

When you feel anxious or uncomfortable, fighting your fear and trying to make it go away will likely cause your discomfort to increase. Instead, we recommend that you let the fear happen and, if anything, try to welcome it. Your fear will likely pass more quickly if you are not trying so hard to get rid of it. Remember, the worst thing that can happen is just a feeling of anxiety and some uncomfortable sensations that eventually will pass. Being anxious is not dangerous.

Fighting your fear is like lying in bed trying to fall asleep (e.g., telling yourself, "I must fall asleep"). Often, the more you try to sleep, the harder it becomes. In fact, for some people who have trouble sleeping, trying to stay awake is a productive strategy. As soon as they stop trying to sleep, they fall asleep quite quickly. When you can allow yourself to become truly anxious, eventually you will become much more comfortable in social and performance situations. This sounds contradictory, but it really works this way.

## Eliminate Subtle Avoidance Behaviors

As discussed earlier in this chapter, it is important that you stop doing the subtle avoidance strategies you use to feel safer in social and performance situations. For example, if you tend to sit on your hands so that people won't notice them shaking, try letting your hands show. If you prefer to avoid talking about yourself when conversing with others, purposely try to talk about your own interests and opinions. For example, mention a book that you've recently read or a movie that you've seen, and share your opinions. If it's a best-seller or a big hit, and you liked it, try to convey your enthusiasm to the person with whom you are talking; if you didn't like it, don't hide your opinion. Express yourself and take a chance on engaging in an exciting dialogue.

Eliminating safety behaviors such as overpreparing for presentations, drinking alcohol at parties, and wearing makeup to hide blushing will help you to learn that social situations can be managed, even without using these strategies and behaviors.

## Ending a Practice and Moving On to the Next One

Ideally, an exposure practice should not end before your fear has decreased to a mild or moderate level (e.g., 20 to 40 on a 0 to 100 point scale). Sometimes, this will take a few minutes; other times, it may take several hours. If possible, try to stay in the situation until you feel more comfortable.

In reality, you may not always have control over when an exposure practice ends. For example, if you are practicing eating lunch with coworkers during a half hour lunch break, you may not have the option of stretching the lunch into two hours just to give your anxiety a chance to decrease. If the situation ends before your anxiety has decreased, try to practice the same situation again, as soon as possible. Continue to repeat the practice until it does become easier. At that point, you can move on to another practice.

### Using Exposure Records and Diaries

To get the most out of your exposure practices, we suggest that you use the diaries and forms provided in chapters 8 and 9 to monitor your progress.

## The Aftermath of Exposure: Processing What Happened

Chances are that you will feel good following your exposure practices. Although you may be tired, you likely will also feel relieved to have completed the practice and proud of your accomplishments. Nevertheless, some individuals tend to analyze their every move and criticize their performances during the practice (e.g., "People surely noticed my anxiety," "I came across like a bumbling idiot"). If you tend to dwell on what happened during your practices, we suggest that you try to put a more positive spin on the experience.

Remember that the main reason you are practicing exposure is to eventually feel more comfortable in social and performance situations. However, for now, expect to feel uncomfortable during practices. Expect that your performance won't be perfect. Rather than dwelling on what happened or didn't happen, try to use the cognitive techniques from chapter 6 to challenge your negative thinking. Also, try to take something positive from the experience. Even if things didn't go the way that you had hoped they would, you can still use the experience to plan future practices and to generate ideas for what you might do differently the next time.

## Exposure Checklist

This section included a long list of guidelines for how to get the most out of your exposure practices. Here is a checklist of the most important suggestions, in summary form:

- Plan practices in advance. Set aside time to practice exposure.

- Exposure practices should be predictable and under your control (particularly early in the process).

- Exposure should be frequent (almost daily), especially at the start.

- Exposure should be prolonged. Try to stay in the situation until your fear has decreased.

- Use cognitive strategies to challenge anxious thoughts *before* entering the situation.

- Use cognitive strategies to challenge anxious thoughts *during* the practice.

- Use cognitive strategies to challenge anxious thoughts *after* leaving the situation.

- Don't fight your anxious feelings in the situation. Just let the feelings happen.

- Eliminate subtle avoidance strategies, like distraction, alcohol use, and overprotective behaviors.

- Practice in a number of different situations.

- Choose practices in which the actual risk is minimal, especially at first.

- Choose practices that are challenging, but not impossible.

- Complete exposure records (see chapters 8 and 9) with each practice.

## Trouble Shooting

*Problem:*     My fear does not decrease during my exposure practices.

*Solution:*     This is normal to some extent. Although anxiety and fear usually decrease during the course of a particular exposure practice, most people experience occasional practices where their anxiety doesn't decrease. Here are some suggestions for dealing with this situation.

> - Make sure that you are staying in the situation long enough. Sometimes it can take several hours for a person's fear to diminish.

- Make sure that you are not using subtle avoidance strategies. The normal pattern during exposure is for fear to increase and then gradually to decrease. Using subtle avoidance strategies such as distraction may cause the fear to go up and down repeatedly over the course of the practice, because most people are not very good at distracting themselves for long periods.

- Negative thinking can sometimes interfere with the effects of exposure. If your fear does not decrease during a particular exposure practice, try to challenge your anxious thoughts using the techniques described in chapter 6.

- If all else fails, just keep practicing. Sometimes, it takes repeated exposure practices before a person's fear begins to lessen.

*Problem:* My fear returns between exposure practices.

*Solution:* This is normal for most people. With more and more practice, your fear will decrease more quickly during practices and will not return as intensely between them. One way of preventing your fear from returning between exposures is to increase the frequency of your practices, particularly early in treatment.

*Problem:* My physical symptoms (e.g., stuttering, shaking, sweating) are very noticeable.

*Solution:* Remember that, despite how it seems to you, the chances are good that your symptoms are not as noticeable to others as you think they are. Furthermore, as your anxiety decreases, the intensity of these symptoms will likely decrease. If you are concerned about people noticing your symptoms, use the cognitive techniques from chapter 6 to challenge your anxious thinking. Remember that there are lots of people who blush, shake, or lose their train of thought and couldn't care less about what other people think. The problem is not that you experience these symptoms, but rather your beliefs about the consequences of having these symptoms.

*Problem:* I am just not good at _____ (e.g., making small talk, public speaking, etc.).

*Solution:* Your social skills are likely much better than you think they are. As discussed in earlier chapters, people who are socially anxious tend to be overly critical of their social and performance skills. Nevertheless, there may be ways in which certain skills can be improved. It is likely that exposure alone will contribute to an improvement of your skills. For example, practicing making small talk will help you to learn what works during a casual conversation and what doesn't. In addition, we suggest that you read chapter 10, which includes specific strategies for improving social and communication skills.

*Problem:*    My fear is too high to benefit from exposure.

*Solution:*    Ideally, you should choose practices that arouse a fear level of 70 to 80 out of 100, although it is also okay if your fear reaches even higher levels. One method for keeping your fear in check is to use the cognitive strategies from chapter 6 to challenge your anxious thoughts before entering the situation. At times, however, even using the cognitive techniques beforehand will not prevent your fear from becoming very intense. If you find that your fear is completely overwhelming, you have three options. First, you can try to wait a while longer to see if your fear decreases. Alternatively, you may consider taking a short break and then trying the same exercise again. Finally, you can try switching to a less difficult practice. Any of these approaches is usually fine. The main point is not to give up completely.

*Problem:*    The situations that I fear are very brief in duration, so there isn't enough time for my fear to decrease.

*Solution:*    This issue was discussed earlier in the chapter, but is worth highlighting again here. Ideally, if an exposure practice is brief, you should try to find creative ways to lengthen the duration of the practice if possible. For example, if you are fearful of chatting with the cashier at the front of a supermarket line, try lining up repeatedly over the course of an hour or two and buying only a few items at a time. This approach will give you more opportunities to talk to the cashiers, compared to paying for all your groceries at once.

*Problem:*    I just had something terrible happen during an exposure practice (e.g., my boss criticized my presentation). How can I ever try exposure again?

*Solution:*    Although rare, it is possible that an unexpected negative event will occur during an exposure practice. For example, you could experience a bad panic attack during a job interview, or you may be laughed at during a presentation. If something bad does happen during an exposure practice, it is natural for some of your fear to return. It may be helpful to "rethink" the negative event using the cognitive techniques described in chapter 6. In addition, we recommend that you resume your exposure practices. If necessary, you can return to a previous item in your hierarchy and work your way back to where you were when the unfortunate incident took place.

*Problem:*    I don't avoid the situation, and yet my fear persists.

*Solution:*    Although exposure usually leads to a decrease in fear, occasionally people report having intense fear in social situations despite almost never avoiding these situations. For example, a person may eat with others on a regular basis, but still experience this situation as an anxiety-provoking one. Or, someone may give presentations several times per week, without ever experiencing a decrease in fear. If you continue to experience fear, despite never avoiding the feared situation, you may find it difficult to come up with appropriate exposure exercises. In such a case, generally, there are three strategies to consider. First, if you are fearful of experiencing symptoms of arousal while in social situations, try using the interoceptive exposure exercises discussed in chapter 9. Second, assess whether you are engaging in subtle avoidance strategies, overprotective behaviors, alcohol or drug use, or other strategies that may be undermining the effects of the exposure. If so, you must try to discontinue these behaviors. Finally, a special effort should be used to identify and challenge the anxious predictions and beliefs that continue to maintain your fear (see chapter 6).

# Chapter 8

# Exposure to Social Situations

In chapter 7, we provided an overview of the basic principles underlying exposure-based treatments for social anxiety. This chapter presents additional information and exercises about how to use these strategies to confront the social and performance situations that make you anxious or uncomfortable. Note that you should become very familiar with the material in chapter 7 before moving on to this chapter.

As noted previously, we suggest that you use the cognitive strategies described in chapter 6 to combat anxious thinking before, during, and after exposure practices. During practices, you should refrain from using subtle avoidance techniques such as distraction, drug or alcohol use, and overprotective behaviors (e.g., eating in a dimly lit restaurant, so people don't notice your blushing). Finally, exposure works best when practices are conducted in the following ways:

- Frequent (daily, if possible)

- Prolonged (until the anxiety decreases)

- Predictable and controllable

- Planned in advance

- Conducted in a variety of different situations

# Situational Exposure Practices

This section provides suggestions for exposure practices involving different types of social and performance situations including the following: public speaking, making small talk, dealing with conflicts, being the center of attention, eating and drinking in public, writing in front of others, job interviews, being in public, and talking to people in authority. Space is included in each section for you to record additional ideas for practices that might be relevant to your own social and performance anxiety. At first, many of the items suggested in this section may seem overwhelming. However, as suggested in chapter 7, you should begin with challenging but *manageable* practices. Over time, you will become more comfortable and most likely you will be able to try some of the more difficult practices.

Furthermore, some of these practices may seem very easy to you. If you have no trouble with a particular type of social or performance situation, there is no need to practice confronting that situation. Instead, focus on the situations that are anxiety-provoking for you.

## Practices for Public Speaking

To overcome a fear of speaking in front of others, it is helpful to take advantage of opportunities that come up during the course of your job or other activities in your day-to-day life. If public speaking opportunities don't normally arise in your life, there are many different ways of creating these situations. Some of these include the following:

- **Speak up in meetings at work**. For example, share your opinions about the issues that are being discussed. Ask and answer questions. If the opportunity to make a brief presentation arises, take advantage of it.

- **Offer to give a presentation at work or at some other organization to which you belong**. For example, if you belong to a book club or reading group, offer to present a summary of the book that your group is reading. If you have some special expertise, offer to share it with your coworkers by giving a formal presentation.

- **Go to a public lecture and ask questions**. Public lectures are often advertised in the newspaper and also may be promoted on television (e.g., your local cable access channel) or on the radio. Also, check out advertisements on community bulletin boards and posters at the library, supermarket, local colleges, or other public places.

- **Take a course at a college, university, or any school that offers adult education courses**. Try to choose courses that provide the opportunity to give presentations. If these are not available, make a point of asking questions several times during each class. If you are unable to enroll in a course, another option is to simply audit or sit in on a large class at a local university. Professors will sometimes give guests permission to audit a course or observe a class without formally enrolling. Often, undergraduate classes contain hundreds of students, so no one would notice an extra person. Auditing a large class will save you money and provide you with an opportunity to ask questions in a public space.

- **Make an impromptu speech or toast at a wedding or other celebration**. If you are invited to a party or are planning to have a party of your own, offer to make a short speech in front of the other guests.

- **Take a public speaking course**. There are numerous companies that offer public speaking courses (especially for businesspeople). These classes are sometimes expensive, but it may be worth finding out more about the available options (perhaps your workplace would help to cover the costs). Check your local yellow pages.

- **Join Toastmasters**. Toastmasters is an organization that sponsors weekly meetings, in many different locations, for individuals who are interested in overcoming a fear of public speaking or in learning to speak more effectively. Typically, groups include twenty to thirty individuals and annual membership is quite inexpensive. Check your local telephone book to contact a group near you or visit the Toastmasters web page (www.toastmasters.org) for more information.

- **Take a drama or music class**. Taking a theater, drama, or music class will provide you with opportunities to perform in front of others. Check whether classes are available at local high schools, colleges, the YMCA, or through other agencies.

- **Give a lecture at a local elementary school, high school, or college about your work**. Often, schools will hold career days, on which students have opportunities to learn about particular jobs or careers. Additionally, teachers sometimes will invite guests to speak to their classes about particular types of careers or jobs. Call a local school principal to find out about opportunities in your neighborhood school.

Now, can you think of other possible practices that involve public speaking? If so, record them in the space below:

## Other Practices

## Practices for Making Small Talk, Casual Conversation, and Informal Socializing

Casual conversation and small talk can take place anywhere. The list below provides a few examples of situations where you might have the opportunity to practice these skills. In addition to planning several large practices per week, you should try to engage in several mini-practices throughout the day.

- **Have friends over for a get-together**. For example, invite several coworkers over for dinner, or to watch a movie or sports event on TV. Or, have a birthday party for a friend or family member. Make sure that you interact with your guests! Don't come up with excuses to avoid them (e.g., serving food and drinks to the exclusion of conversation, cleaning up, or washing the dishes).

- **Speak to strangers on elevators, in waiting lines, at bus stops, or at other public locations**. With repeated practice, making small talk will become easier. Prolonged exposure works best, so try to talk to many different people over the course of an hour or two, to get the most benefit. Smile, say hello, and use humor, if appropriate. Although you should be prepared for some people to react negatively (remember, other people may also be shy or they may be uninterested in making small talk), most people will probably react positively.

- **Ask for directions or for the time**. Walk up to a stranger in a mall or store and ask what time it is. Or, ask how to find a particular location. As mentioned earlier, prolonged exposure works best, so try to do this repeatedly over an hour or two, or until your anxiety decreases.

- **Go to a social event**. For example, attend your annual office holiday party, a class reunion, a community dance, or a local art gallery opening. Situations such as these will provide you with opportunities to mingle and make small talk.

- **Talk to coworkers or classmates**. Try arriving at school or work a bit early so that you will have the opportunity to chat with others. Make a point of saying hello to your coworkers or classmates during breaks. Simple questions such as, "How was your weekend?" are often a great way to get a conversation started.

- **Talk to your neighbors**. Go for walks in the neighborhood and say hello to your neighbors. If you have a new neighbor, consider asking him or her over for a drink or dessert. Invite some of your other neighbors as well.

- **Talk to dog owners who are walking their dogs**. Dog owners often love to talk about their dogs. If you have a dog, try going for walks in areas where other people walk their pets. Make comments or ask questions about other people's dogs (e.g., "nice dog" or "What kind of dog is that?)". If you return to the same routes frequently, you will likely see the same people over and over again. You may even make some new friends.

- **Talk to cashiers or other staff personnel in stores**. For example, comment on the weather, ask for advice or information (e.g., "Does this shirt go with these pants?"), or "special order" a book or CD.

- **Give or receive compliments**. Offer someone else a compliment. For example, tell a coworker that you like her sweater or new haircut, tell an artist that you like his work, or compliment a waiter on the quality of your food. If you are uncomfortable receiving compliments, just say "Thank you" when someone praises you. Don't discount the praise by telling the person all the reasons why you don't deserve it.

- **Express a controversial opinion**. If you have a controversial opinion about some issue, express it. For example, if you didn't like a movie that someone else is raving about, let them know what you didn't like about the film. If you disagree with someone else's political views, explain your perspective on the issue. Try not to put down the other person or to discount that person's views when you are expressing your own opinions.

- **Join an ongoing conversation**. In some circumstances, it is perfectly appropriate to join an ongoing conversation. For example, at parties people often walk about, moving in and out of different conversations. See if you can join in with a group of people who are discussing some issue that interests you.

- **Talk to parents of other children**. Just as pet owners enjoy talking to other pet owners, parents usually enjoy talking about their children with other parents. If you have children, get involved in situations where you might have the opportunity to talk to other parents. For example, attend parents' night at your children's school or enroll your children in a class (e.g., swimming, music) with other children. Take advantage of any opportunities to talk to the other parents.

- **Meet two or three friends at a café**. Invite several coworkers or friends to meet you after work or school for a coffee, drink, or snack. Alternatively, invite others to join you for lunch.

- **Join a club or organization**. Consider joining a bowling league, aerobics class, volleyball league, bingo group, self-help group, church group, or other organization. Ideally, the club or organization should meet frequently (e.g., weekly) for you to get the most benefit from attending it.

Can you think of other possible practices that involve informal socializing, casual conversation, or making small talk? If so, record them in the space below:

**Other Practices**

_____

_____

_____

## *Practices Involving Conflict Situations*

These practices should be planned carefully. Unlike the other practices recommended in this chapter, these are likely to cause another person to become angry or impatient with your behavior. If you think that the other individual is likely to have difficulty controlling his or her anger, you may want to save these practices for another time and place. You should try to choose practices in which the risks are minimal. Ask a friend or family member if you need a second opinion. You may also want to skip ahead to the sections on assertive communication in chapter 10 to prepare yourself for this kind of interaction. It is important that potential conflict situations be dealt with *assertively* rather than with *aggression*, which is likely to escalate the other person's anger.

It may seem rude to do things purposely that will inconvenience or anger others. On the other hand, as you continue to read this section, you will see that most of these practices involve only minor inconvenience to other people. Furthermore, many of these situations (e.g., having to wait longer in a line, etc.) are situations that people often encounter anyway. The substantial gains that you may obtain from these practices is likely to outweigh any inconvenience that you create for others.

Listed below are some examples of practices that others have found useful for becoming more comfortable with conflict situations.

- **Ask someone else to change his or her behavior**. For example, ask your roommate to wash his or her dishes rather than leaving dirty dishes lying around. Or, ask another person to stop talking in a movie theater.

- **Stay stopped in your car when the light turns green**. Pretend you are changing the radio station or that you didn't notice the light turn green. The drivers who are backed up behind you eventually may become frustrated and honk their horns. This should be your signal to drive away.

- **Say "No," when you don't want to do something**. If someone asks you do something that you don't want to do or something you think you should not do (e.g., donating money that you can't afford, doing more than your fair share of work, etc.), practice saying "No" in an assertive (but not aggressive) way. Again, we recommend that you read chapter 10 for suggestions regarding assertive communication.

- **Return an item to a store**. Try returning a book, an article of clothing, or some other item to a store. In most cases, the staff at the store will gladly take back the item. However, sometimes, you may encounter a negative response, which will provide you with the opportunity to get used to this uncomfortable situation. To really test yourself, try to return an item without a receipt, without the original packaging, or after the allowed period for returns has passed. You likely won't get your way, but you will get an opportunity to practice dealing with possible conflict.

- **Send food back in a restaurant**. Ask your server to take your food back (e.g., to change the dressing on your salad, make your soup hotter, cook your steak more thoroughly, or bring you a different drink).

- **Take an extra long time at a bank machine when there are people waiting behind you**. For example, rather than withdrawing $100, make five withdrawals of $20 each. There is a good likelihood that someone will react negatively to the longer wait. Again, this will be a good opportunity to deal with a conflict situation.

- **Pretend to forget your money when paying for an item in a store**. For example, when you reach the front of a supermarket line, tell the cashier that you have forgotten your wallet. Or, have more items in your cart than you can afford to purchase. The people behind you may begin to mutter with annoyance, but you will be testing yourself in an anxiety-provoking situation, so it will be worth it.

- **Ask a stranger to stop smoking**. If you are in a restaurant or bar, or even in a public place outdoors, try asking the person next to you to stop smoking. Use some discretion. For example, don't practice this if the other person seems dangerous, is much bigger than you are, or if you think he or she might become very angry.

Now, can you think of other possible practices that involve some risk of mild conflict? If so, record them in the space below:

**Other Practices**

_____

_____

_____

## Practices Involving Being the Center of Attention

- **Join a gym or take an aerobics class**. Rather than exercising alone, practice exercising in front of others. For example, join an aerobics class and take a spot near the front of the room. Or, lift weights near other people who are more experienced and stronger than you are.

- **Say something incorrectly**. Purposely answer a question incorrectly in class. Or, mispronounce a word.

- **Speak loudly**. Speak loudly in a public place (e.g., at a mall, in a bus, or on the subway), so that others around you can hear your conversation.

- **Have a mobile phone or pager go off in a public place**. Arrange for someone to page you or call you on your cell phone while you are at the dentist, eating at a restaurant, or walking through some other public place. Use some discretion here. For example, you may not want to try this practice during a college exam, job interview, or while watching a movie, unless your intention is to practice annoying the people around you.

- **Drop something**. Drop your keys or your books. Or, spill water all over your shirt.

- **Talk about yourself**. When engaging in conversations with other people, talk more freely about yourself. Talk about your family, your job, and your hobbies. Offer your opinions about political issues, books that you have read recently, or movies that you have seen.

- **Participate in a party game**. For example, play Pictionary, Trivial Pursuit, or some other game with friends, coworkers, or your family.

- **Wear your shirt or dress inside out or backwards**. Walk around a public place while making a fashion faux pas. The more outrageous the better. For example, wear shoes that don't match. Wear a plaid shirt with striped pants. Wear your dress or shirt inside out (this exercise is even better, if your dress or shirt has shoulder pads), or wear a formal evening gown during the day. With practice, you will become much less concerned about looking conspicuous.

- **Knock over a display in a store**. For example, knock over a few rolls of paper towels or toilet paper in the supermarket. Again, it is important to use good judgment. For example, don't knock over glass jars of tomato sauce. That would be going too far!

Now, can you think of other possible practices that involve being the center of attention? If so, record them in the space below:

**Other Practices**

_____

_____

_____

## Practices for Eating or Drinking with Others

People who fear drinking in front of others are often concerned about having shaky hands and spilling their drinks. Those who are fearful of eating in front of others may be nervous about making a mess, looking unattractive while eating, or feeling flushed from eating hot foods. You should choose to practice exposure in situations that will challenge your specific anxieties. For example, if you are more anxious when eating messy foods, you should order foods that are more likely to be messy. If you are nervous about blushing or sweating, order hot soup or a spicy meal. A list of situations offering an opportunity to eat or drink in front of others is provided below.

- **Eat a snack at your desk**. If your desk at work is in an open area, eat a snack at your desk. This may be easier than eating with your coworkers. When this exercise becomes easier, you can move to other practices, such as those described below.

- **Hold a drink at a party or gathering**. If you tend to be anxious when holding a glass of wine or a soft drink in front of others, try doing just that the next time you are at a party or other social gathering. Try *not* to hide your hands if they begin to shake. If alcohol tends to decrease your anxiety, make sure you don't drink significant amounts of wine, beer, or spirits, until after your anxiety has decreased on its own.

- **Have lunch with coworkers**. You probably eat lunch every day. You might as well try to eat with other people, if the opportunity arises. If your natural tendency is to eat at your desk or to eat lunch in restaurants alone, invite a coworker to join you for lunch once or twice every week.

- **Meet a friend at a restaurant for dinner**. If you tend to feel safer in dark restaurants, challenge yourself by choosing a more brightly lit location. Try to choose a seat where you are more likely to be observed by the other people in the restaurant.

- **Invite people over for a meal**. For example, invite two or three friends or neighbors over for dinner.

- **Dine at other people's homes**. After you have had guests to your own home, this situation is an appropriate step to try. You may find it more difficult to eat in another person's home if you are concerned about not being able to control the environment (e.g., the lighting), who the other guests are, and what types of food are served.

- **Dine alone in a restaurant, food court, or another public place**. If eating alone in public makes you anxious, having lunch alone in a restaurant or food court is an appropriate practice. You might also want to consider eating in other public places, such as a sitting on a bench in a park or in a shopping mall.

Can you think of other possible practices that involve eating or drinking in front of others? If so, record them in the space below:

**Other Practices**

_____

_____

_____

## Practices for Writing in Front of Others

As a rule, people who are uncomfortable writing in front of others are concerned about having shaky hands while they are writing. They also may be fearful of others judging their handwriting or noticing personal information that they may be recording. Examples of situations that can provide an opportunity to write in front of others include the following:

- **Pay for items using a check**. Instead of paying with cash, write a check when purchasing merchandise in a store. Be sure to complete the check in front of the cashier (don't write out the check before you get to the store: that's cheating). If you are concerned about having the cashier notice your shaky hands, try making your hands shake purposely. In fact, to really challenge your fear, let your hands shake so much that you have to write a whole new check.

- **Write a letter while seated in a public place**. Write a letter to a friend while sitting in a café, riding on a bus, or relaxing on a public bench. Make sure that there are others around who can see you writing.

- **Fill out forms or applications in front of other people**. For example, complete an application for a new credit card or loan at a bank, making sure that the bank officer is seated across from you and watching. Or, complete an application for a new video store membership. At work, be sure to sign documents when other people are watching.

Can you think of other possible practices that involve writing in front of other people? If so, record them in the space below:

**Other Practices**

_____

_____

_____

## *Practices for Job Interviews*

To become more comfortable with job interviews, the best exposure practices are those that provide experiences similar to real job interviews. Some examples are provided below:

- **Apply for a volunteer position.** Many volunteer opportunities (e.g., in hospitals, schools, and other organizations) begin with an interview process that is very similar to an interview for a paying job. You may feel less pressure if you know that you are applying for a nonpaying position. If so, this would be a good place to start. In addition to giving the employer the opportunity to meet you, another purpose of an interview is to give you a chance to evaluate the position. Applying for a volunteer position does not commit you to accepting it if it is offered. If you decide it is not for you, you can always turn it down. If you apply for several volunteer jobs, you will become more comfortable with the entire interview process.

- **Practice interviews with family members or friends**. Practicing job interviews with friends or family members is another good way to begin the process of overcoming anxiety over job interviews. You will need to coach your friend or family member about the nature of the interview and the role that he or she should take. You may also want to work up to having some of these role-play interviews become particularly challenging (e.g., with a hostile interviewer), so you can learn to be more comfortable with difficult interviews in real life.

- **Apply for jobs that are not particularly interesting to you**. A great way of learning to overcome a fear of job interviews is to practice interviewing for jobs that you wouldn't take even if they were offered to you. You might as well learn how to interview more effectively in situations in which you have nothing to lose. By practicing interviewing for jobs you don't want, you will be better prepared when it comes time to interview for a job that interests you.

- **Apply for jobs that do interest you.** If you are looking for a new job, eventually you must be able to interview for the job you want. The more jobs that you apply for, the more interviews you will be offered. The more interviews that you get, the more opportunities you will have to practice your interviewing skills and to overcome your fear of being interviewed. Although it is reasonable to start the process by interviewing for jobs that are not particularly interesting to you, you should also be applying for jobs that you might really be interested in accepting.

Can you think of other possible practices that involve interviewing for a job? If so, record them in the space below:

**Other Practices**

_____

_____

_____

## Practices for Being in Public

For some people, just being around other people is anxiety-provoking, even if there is no interaction or direct social contact. If being in a public place is difficult for you, here are some examples of public places where you may be able to practice exposure. Remember to practice frequently and to stay long enough for your fear to decrease. If you must leave the situation, try to return to it as soon as possible.

- **Go to a mall or supermarket.** Shopping is a good way of exposing yourself to other people in a public place. Try shopping when the stores are more crowded to challenge your fearful thoughts even more.

- **Make eye contact in a public place.** If appropriate, try making eye contact with other people while you walk down the street or while sitting on a bus or subway. Of course, for safety reasons, this may not be wise in some cities, particularly at night, or in dangerous parts of town.

- **Go to a concert or sporting event.** A guaranteed place to encounter lots of other people is at a large concert, sporting event, movie theater, or other entertainment venue. If you prefer to sit in an aisle seat or near the exit (for a quick "escape"), try sitting in the middle of the row and away from the exit.

- **Read in a public place.** Spend some time reading your favorite book, a newspaper, or a new novel at a coffee shop or library.

- **Join the YMCA or a health club**. This suggestion was recommended earlier, in the section on being the center of attention. We mention it again here because health clubs provide an excellent opportunity to be around other people.

Can you think of other possible practices that involve being in public? If so, record them in the space below:

**Other Practices**

_____

_____

_____

## Practices for Speaking to Authority Figures

Going out of your way for some form of contact with people in authority who make you feel uncomfortable is an effective way to learn how to be more comfortable with authority figures. Examples of relevant exposure practices are listed below. If any of these are situations in which you would like to feel more comfortable, they may be appropriate practices for you to try.

- **Have a meeting with your boss or teacher**. If you are a student, ask your teacher to meet with you to discuss some difficult homework. If you are working, ask your boss for an appointment to discuss your performance or some other aspect of your job.

- **Ask a pharmacist questions about a medication**. If you are taking any medications, ask a pharmacist to answer particular questions about the medication (e.g., side effects, drug-drug interactions, etc.). If you are not taking any medications, you can still ask questions, perhaps on behalf of a friend or family member.

- **Ask your doctor to explain a particular medical issue**. Make an appointment with your family doctor to ask questions about any symptoms that you may be experiencing. Don't leave until your all questions are answered.

- **Meet with your bank manager**. For example, arrange to meet with your bank's manager or loan officer to discuss the possibility of obtaining a loan or mortgage.

Can you think of other possible practices that involve interacting with people in authority? If so, record them in the space below:

**Other Practices**

_____

_____

_____

# Challenging Your Worst Fears

By repeatedly exposing yourself to anxiety-provoking situations, you will continue to challenge most of your deeply held beliefs and predictions regarding your ability to cope with social and performance situations. Ideally, exposure practices should be designed to test the validity of your anxious assumptions. For example, if you are fearful of saying something foolish during a conversation at a party, it is not enough simply to attend parties, although just attending may be a reasonable first step. To more thoroughly challenge such an anxious belief, you also would need to talk to other people at the party. By having numerous conversations with others, eventually you will learn that most of what you say is not foolish at all.

After reaching a certain level of comfort talking to other people at parties, the next step might be to practice saying something silly or foolish *purposely* and to evaluate the consequences. This exercise would help to challenge your anxious beliefs at an even deeper level. Chances are that even if you did say something foolish at a party, the consequences would be negligible. With the practice of exposure you would learn not only that you can engage in effective conversations with others, but that even if you make a mistake from time to time, it doesn't really matter.

The strategies discussed in this section are useful for increasing the intensity of your exposure practices, by testing out the validity of your "What if" thoughts. Rather than dwelling on questions like "What if I make a mistake?" or "What if I draw attention to myself?" we suggest that you try to answer these questions by purposely making a mistake or purposely drawing attention to your behavior. In all likelihood, you will discover that nothing terrible happens.

## *Purposely Making Mistakes*
## *(Try to Look Stupid)*

When you have begun feeling more comfortable in some of your feared situations, a reasonable next step is to make some small mistakes *purposely* or to do things that make you look foolish or stupid. Examples of this kind of purposeful behavior include the following: pronouncing a word incorrectly while speaking to your boss, asking an obvious question in class, or bumping into a door. There is no need to make big mistakes (e.g., purposely failing an exam, crashing your car). Small mistakes will work just fine and the consequences will be minimal.

### *Purposely Drawing Attention to Yourself*

If being the center of attention is difficult for you, your exposure practices should include attempts to draw the attention of others to your behavior. For example, rather than arriving early or on time for a movie or a class, try arriving a few minutes late, so that everyone is aware of you when you enter the room. Although you may feel embarrassed momentarily, you will learn from the practice that the whole experience doesn't matter, even minutes later. You embarrassment will be temporary. Also, people probably will forget about your late arrival almost instantly, and soon will be thinking about other things.

### *Purposely Increasing Your Anxiety Symptoms*

In addition to entering the situations that you fear, a more complete test of your anxious beliefs is to deliberately arouse some of the symptoms that frighten you in social or performance situations. Chapter 9 discusses these strategies in some detail. Some examples of possible exposure exercises include the following: wetting your forehead (to simulate sweating) before giving a presentation, purposely appearing to lose your train of thought during a meeting or presentation, and purposely allowing your hands to shake while writing or holding a drink. By deliberately bringing on the symptoms you fear (in a predictable and controlled way), you will learn to be less frightened of having these symptoms show in front of others.

### *Expressing Personal Opinions*

Finally, if you are afraid to express personal opinions during a conversation, just engaging in conversations (i.e., while avoiding the expression of personal opinions) will not be enough to test the validity of your fearful beliefs. Conversation alone will not teach you that your fears are unfounded. Instead, you should make sure that you express your feelings or opinions during your exposure practices.

# Developing a Situational Exposure Hierarchy

Before beginning exposure therapy, it is helpful to generate a list of very specific situations that range in difficulty from mildly anxiety-producing to extremely anxiety-producing. This list of situations, called a *situational exposure hierarchy*, will help to guide your exposure practices.

Usually, the situations on the hierarchy are generated based on particular *themes* that contribute to how much fear you are likely to experience. These themes may include the size of the group or audience (e.g., one person may be easier to talk to than five people; five people may be easier to handle than fifty), the length of time involved (e.g., a five-minute conversation versus a thirty-minute conversation), your relationship with the other person (e.g., a family member versus a stranger), and so forth.

Two examples of situational exposure hierarchies are provided below. The first hierarchy is for a person with the fear of public speaking, whereas the second is for someone who experiences social anxiety in many different situations (generalized social anxiety). Note that the hierarchy items are very specific with respect to the duration of the practice, the types of people present, and other relevant variables. Developing specific items is important because it is difficult to develop practices based on overly vague or generalized hierarchy items. Fear and avoidance ratings are based on a scale ranging from 0 (no fear, no avoidance) to 100 (maximum fear, complete avoidance).

### Sample Situational Exposure Hierarchy: Public Speaking

| Situation | Fear | Avoidance |
|---|---|---|
| 1. Give a one-hour formal lecture to 200 strangers, about a topic that I don't know well. | 100 | 100 |
| 2. Give a one-hour formal lecture to 30 strangers, about a topic that I don't know well. | 99 | 100 |
| 3. Give a one-hour formal lecture to 200 strangers, about a familiar topic. | 90 | 100 |
| 4. Give a one-hour formal lecture to 30 strangers, about a familiar topic. | 85 | 100 |
| 5. Give a one-hour informal presentation to 20 coworkers about an unfamiliar topic. | 85 | 90 |
| 6. Give a one-hour informal presentation to 20 coworkers about a familiar topic. | 70 | 70 |
| 7. Give a one-hour informal presentation to 20 young children about my work. | 65 | 65 |
| 8. Make comments or ask questions in a large meeting (more than 15 people). | 50 | 60 |
| 9. Make comments or ask questions in a small meeting (e.g., 5 or 6 people). | 40 | 40 |

10. Offer to make a toast at a family dinner.      35     35

### Sample Situational Exposure Hierarchy: Generalized Social Anxiety

| Situation | Fear | Avoidance |
|---|---|---|
| 1. Give a one-hour formal lecture to 30 coworkers, about a familiar topic. | 100 | 100 |
| 2. Have a party at my home for my coworkers. | 95 | 95 |
| 3. Ask Pat out for a movie date. | 90 | 100 |
| 4. Answer a personal ad in the newspaper. | 85 | 100 |
| 5. Attend the annual holiday party at work without drinking alcohol. | 85 | 85 |
| 6. Attend a retirement tea for a coworker who is retiring. | 70 | 70 |
| 7. Have a formal dinner with Rita (a friend). | 70 | 75 |
| 8. Talk about personal feelings or opinions with my coworkers. | 60 | 60 |
| 9. Have a fast food lunch with Rita (a friend). | 60 | 50 |
| 10. Have a conversation with the person sitting next to me on a bus. | 50 | 50 |
| 11. Ask someone for directions or for the time. | 45 | 45 |
| 12. Call Rita on the telephone. | 40 | 40 |
| 13. Eat alone in a crowded food court at the mall. | 40 | 40 |
| 14. Walk around at a crowded mall. | 35 | 35 |
| 15. Answer the telephone without checking my "call display window." | 30 | 50 |

To generate your own hierarchy, refer back to the suggested exposure practices in this chapter as well as to the results of your self-assessment in chapter 3. Choose situations that range in difficulty from slightly anxiety-provoking to completely overwhelming.

Record these situations in order of difficulty (starting at the most anxiety-provoking) in the spaces provided on the blank Situational Exposure Hierarchy Form below. Next, rate each situation to describe the level of fear you would feel if you were in that situation right now (use a 0 to 100 point scale, where 0 = no fear; 25 = mild fear; 50 = moderate fear; 75 = intense fear; 100 = very intense fear). Finally, using a 0 to 100 point scale, indicate how much you would tend to avoid each situation on your hierarchy (0 = do not avoid the situation; 25 = hesitate to enter situation, but rarely avoid it; 50 = sometimes avoid the situation; 75 = usually avoid the situation; 100 = always avoid the situation).

### Situational Exposure Hierarchy Form

| Situation | Fear (0–100) | Avoidance (0–100) |
|---|---|---|
| 1. _____ | ____ | ____ |
| 2. _____ | ____ | ____ |
| 3. _____ | ____ | ____ |
| 4. _____ | ____ | ____ |
| 5. _____ | ____ | ____ |
| 6. _____ | ____ | ____ |
| 7. _____ | ____ | ____ |
| 8. _____ | ____ | ____ |
| 9. _____ | ____ | ____ |
| 10. _____ | ____ | ____ |
| 11. _____ | ____ | ____ |
| 12. _____ | ____ | ____ |
| 13. _____ | ____ | ____ |
| 14. _____ | ____ | ____ |
| 15. _____ | ____ | ____ |

# Imagined Exposure to Social Situations

Whenever possible, *in vivo* exposure (actual exposure to feared situations) is preferable to exposure in imagination. In fact, imagined exposure is rarely used in a systematic way for treating social anxiety. Still, exposure in imagination may be useful either when the real situation is too overwhelming for you to enter or when you are unable to confront the actual situation for practical reasons (e.g., you have an upcoming college exam, and no earlier opportunities to practice taking exams).

Imagined exposure may be helpful to prepare you to enter the actual situation. When using imagined exposure, the guidelines are generally the same as for in vivo exposure. For example, practices should be frequent (e.g., daily) and should continue until your fear decreases (e.g., thirty to sixty minutes). Whenever possible, imagined exposure should be followed by in vivo exposure in the actual situation.

When conducting imagined exposure practices, close your eyes and try to imagine the situation as vividly as possible. Some people find it helpful to make a tape recording describing the situation in detail and then listen to the tape during subsequent practices. Other people find it helpful simply to imagine being in the situation, without the help of a recorded description. Either way, it is important to imagine the experience vividly, so that it feels as real as possible. Your imagined exposure practices should produce many of the same feelings that are produced by real exposure, although the intensity of these feelings may be lower during imagined exposure. We recommend that you ask yourself the following questions to help bring the experience to life:

- What do I see around me? What do my surroundings look like? Who else is here?

- What is happening in this situation?

- What emotions am I feeling?

- What thoughts am I thinking?

- What physical sensations am I experiencing? How intense are they?

- What is my environment like? Is it hot? Humid?

- What am I doing while in this situation?

- What sounds am I hearing?

- What odors am I sensing?

# Situational Role-Play

Situational role-play is simulated exposure practice in which you rehearse being in a specific social situation before actually entering the real situation. Role-play can provide you with exposure practice without creating the same social risks sometimes present in the actual situation. In other words, you have less to lose during simulated exposures, compared to real-life exposures. Below are some examples of how to use situational role-play to improve your level of comfort, as well as to improve your skills for dealing with particular social situations.

- Before giving a formal presentation at work, practice giving your talk to several friends and relatives. Ask your simulated audience for feedback. If possible, repeat this role-play practice several times.

- If you are nervous about making small talk with strangers at parties, ask your partner (or any close friend or relative) to pretend to be an unfamiliar person. Imagine that you have both arrived early for a party and are waiting in the living room while the host prepares food in the kitchen. Practice engaging in small talk, as if you have just met for the first time.

- If you have an upcoming job interview, you can prepare by having friends or relatives simulate interviewing you for a job.

- In order to practice asking another individual out on a date, you could rehearse what you might say with a close friend or relative.

In the spaces below, record several more simulated exposure role-plays you could use to begin confronting the situations that you fear.

1. _____

_____

_____

2. _____

_____

_____

3. _____

_____

_____

4. _____

_____

_____

5. _____

_____

_____

# Using Exposure Records and Diaries

Keeping good records during exposure practices will help you to monitor your progress over time. The Exposure Monitoring Form is an example of a diary that can be used to record your experiences during exposure practices. In addition, the Exposure Monitoring Form is designed to help you to challenge your anxious thoughts during exposure practices. Note that although this form may seem somewhat complex at first, with practice it will become easier to complete.

At the top of the Exposure Monitoring Form, you should describe the particular situation that you are practicing, as well as the date, time, and duration of the practice, and your fear level before and after the practice (use a 0 to 100 point scale, where 0 = no fear and 100 = maximum fear). The middle part of the form is used for testing the validity of your fearful beliefs and predictions regarding the exposure practice. The first three columns are completed before the practice and the last column is completed after the practice.

In the first column, record your emotional response to the upcoming practice (e.g., fear, nervousness). The second and third columns are used for recording your fearful beliefs and predictions and the evidence regarding the validity of these predictions. (Chapter 6 has many examples of possible fearful beliefs as well as instructions on how to evaluate the evidence concerning these thoughts.) After the practice is completed, you should record its outcome, as well as your updated impressions of the validity of your original predictions.

In the lower part of the form, there is space to record your fear level periodically during the practice, using a scale ranging from 0 (no fear) to 100 (maximum fear). The frequency with which you record your fear ratings will depend on the duration of the practice. For example, ratings might be recorded every minute for a practice lasting ten minutes, or every thirty minutes for a practice lasting all day. The last step in completing this form is to plan for your next practice by answering the question, "Based on this experience, what exposure will you do next?"

# A Step-by-Step Guide to Conducting Exposure to Social Situations

A comprehensive exposure-based treatment should include the following steps:

- Develop a situational exposure hierarchy. Although the hierarchy should be used to guide your exposure practices, you may be flexible. For example, feel free to work on situations that are not on your hierarchy. In addition, you may decide to revise your hierarchy as particular situations become less anxiety-provoking.

- Plan your exposure practices on a week-by-week basis. At the start of each week, you should have a good idea of the types of practices that you will conduct over the coming week, as well as the dates and times you will conduct these practices.

- Develop a long-term exposure plan. You should have an idea of the types of situations in which you are likely to conduct exposure practices over the coming months. Of course, this plan probably will change frequently, depending on the results of your practices each week.

# Exposure Monitoring Form

**Describe the Exposure Situation** _____    **Date and Time** _____

**Initial Fear Level (0–100)** _____    **Fear Level at End (0–100)** _____    **Duration of Exposure** _____

| COMPLETE BEFORE THE EXPOSURE PRACTICE | | COMPLETE AFTER THE EXPOSURE PRACTICE |
|---|---|---|
| What emotions and feelings (e.g., fear, anger) do I have about the exposure? | What anxious thoughts, predictions, and assumptions do I have about the exposure? What do I expect will happen during the exposure practice? | 1. What was the outcome of this practice? What actually happened? <br> 2. What evidence did I gain from this practice? How accurate were my original thoughts and predictions? |
| | What evidence do I have that my fearful thoughts are true? | 1. Outcome: <br> 2. Evidence: |

**Fear Levels (0–100) During the Exposure Practice (rate every _____ minutes)**

1. ___  2. ___  3. ___  4. ___  5. ___  6. ___  7. ___  8. ___  9. ___  10. ___  11. ___  12. ___  13. ___  14. ___  15. ___  16. ___

17. ___  18. ___  19. ___  20. ___  21. ___  22. ___  23. ___  24. ___  25. ___  26. ___  27. ___  28. ___  29. ___  30. ___

Based on this experience, what exposure will you do next? _____

© 2000 Peter J. Bieling, Ph.D., and Martin M. Antony, Ph.D. Used with permission.

- Start with exposure to situations that are near the bottom or middle of your hierarchy. If a situation is too difficult, try something easier. If a practice doesn't create anxiety, try something more difficult.

- As exposures to particular situations become easier, begin practicing exposure in situations that are more anxiety-provoking.

## *Integrating Situational Exposure Strategies into Your Treatment Plan*

Although exposure to feared situations is perhaps the most important technique for overcoming your fear, the exposure methods described in this chapter (and in chapter 7) are often most effective when they are used as part of a comprehensive treatment plan. In addition to situational exposure, your treatment should include the cognitive strategies described in chapter 6, which will help you to reinterpret your experiences during exposure to feared situations. As reviewed earlier in this book, we recommend that you first practice the cognitive techniques for several weeks before formally beginning exposure practices.

Also, your treatment program may include medication (chapter 5), exposure to feared sensations (chapter 9), and social skills practices (chapter 10), depending on your own personal needs and preferences. As you will see, these strategies are typically used in the context of your own situational exposure practices. Exposure is the foundation upon which the other treatment strategies are introduced.

# Chapter 9

# Exposure to Uncomfortable Sensations

*Interoceptive exposure*, the clinical name for the intentional, purposeful exposure to internal physical sensations, such as dizziness and sweating, was originally developed as a treatment for an anxiety-based condition known as panic disorder. *Panic disorder* is a problem in which people experience sudden rushes of panic, without any obvious trigger or cause. People with panic disorder tend to be very fearful of the physical sensations they experience during their panic attacks (e.g., racing heart, heavy sweating, dizziness) and they often interpret these symptoms as a sign of imminent danger or threat (e.g., an impending heart attack or complete loss of control). Interoceptive exposure was developed to teach those with panic disorder how to stop fearing the physical feelings associated with physical arousal and anxiety. With repeated exposure to these induced physical symptoms, people learn to be less frightened of their own internal feelings and sensations.

Anxiety over experiencing physical arousal symptoms is not unique to panic disorder. A number of studies (e.g., Chambless and Gracely 1989; Taylor, Koch, and McNally 1992) have found that people with other anxiety-related problems (including extreme social anxiety) also experience anxiety about feeling certain physical sensations. Given that social anxiety is often associated with a fear of experiencing anxiety symptoms (especially those that might be visible, such as blushing, sweating, shaking, and losing one's train of thought), it makes sense that deliberately exposing oneself to various feared symptoms (i.e., interoceptive exposure) while in social situations might lead to a greater decrease in fear, compared to exposing oneself to feared situations without interoceptive exposure. That is, if a person is particularly fearful of experiencing certain physical symptoms in social situations, adding interoceptive exposures to the situation can heighten the relevant sensations. In this way, the person learns not only that he or she can tolerate being in the situation (with the normal levels of arousal that may occur) but also that he or she can learn to tolerate the situation even when the feared sensation is particularly intense. By bringing on these sensations in a controlled and predicable way, eventually the person learns to be less anxious in the social situations.

Although there has not been much research on the use of interoceptive exposure in social anxiety, in our clinical practices we have found that this technique is often helpful for those who suffer from excessive social and performance fears (Antony and Swinson 2000). In fact, we have recently begun a formal study to confirm the usefulness of interoceptive exposure for individuals with social anxiety who are fearful of experiencing the feelings associated with their fear.

The techniques described in this chapter *are not meant to be used instead* of the strategies described in earlier chapters. To overcome your social anxiety, the most important strategies probably are the cognitive techniques described in chapter 6 and the situational exposure strategies described in chapters 7 and 8. You should not attempt to use interoceptive exposure until you have practiced the strategies described in chapters 6 through 8 and are thoroughly familiar with them. Furthermore, before attempting the interoceptive exposure techniques, you should be very familiar with the basic rules of exposure. As reviewed in chapter 7, exposure works best if (1) it is practiced frequently, (2) if each practice lasts until the fear has decreased, and (3) if practices are predictable and under your control. In addition, the cognitive strategies described in chapter 6 should be used to combat anxious thinking *before, during,* and *after* your exposure practices. Finally, during your exposure practices, you should not use subtle avoidance techniques such as distraction, drug or alcohol use, and overprotective behaviors (e.g., wearing makeup to hide blushing).

# Introduction to Interoceptive Exposure

Interoceptive exposure involves using specific exercises purposely to bring on physical sensations that make you uncomfortable or anxious. Initially, the exercises are practiced in "safe" situations, like your home. After you get used to the exercises, the next step is to try them in anxiety-provoking situations, such as immediately before entering a social or performance situation. Examples of interoceptive exposure exercises (as well as the main sensations that they trigger) are listed below. In addition to this list, there are many other possible exercises that can be used. For example, if you are afraid of a choking or gagging feeling in your throat, wearing a necktie or scarf may be a good way of creating this feeling for the purpose of exposure therapy. The exercises below should be thought of only as a partial list. At the end of the list, there is space for you to record additional exercises that might be useful for triggering symptoms that you fear.

| Interoceptive Exposure Exercises | Typical Sensations Experienced |
|---|---|
| 1. Shake head from side to side (30 seconds) | Dizziness or lightheadedness |
| 2. Spin around in a swivel chair (60 seconds) | Dizziness or lightheadedness, feeling unreal, nausea |
| 3. While sitting, bend over and place head between legs for 30 seconds, then sit up quickly | Dizziness or lightheadedness |
| 4. Hold breath (30 seconds or as long as possible) | Breathlessness or smothering feelings, racing or pounding heart, dizziness or lightheadedness, chest tightness |
| 5. Hyperventilate (shallow breathing at a rate of about 100–120 breaths per minute) (60 seconds) | Breathlessness or smothering feelings, dizziness or lightheadedness, racing or pounding heart, feeling unreal, trembling or shaking, numbness or tingling sensations |
| 6. Breathe through a small, narrow straw (plug your nose if necessary) (2 minutes) | Breathlessness or smothering feelings, racing or pounding heart, choking feelings, dizziness or lightheadedness, chest tightness, trembling or shaking |
| 7. Tense all the muscles in your body or hold a "push-up" position (60 seconds or as long as possible) | Trembling or shaking, breathlessness or smothering feelings, racing or pounding heart, dizziness or lightheadedness, blushing |
| 8. Carry heavy weights or bags (60 seconds or as long as possible) | Trembling or shaking, breathlessness or smothering feelings, racing or pounding heart, dizziness or lightheadedness, blushing |
| 9. Run in place (or run up and down stairs) (60 seconds) | Racing or pounding heart, breathlessness or smothering feelings, chest tightness, sweating, trembling or shaking, blushing |
| 10. Sit in a hot stuffy room (e.g., a sauna, hot car, or small room with a space heater) (5 to 10 minutes) | Sweating, breathlessness or smothering feelings, hot flushes, blushing |
| 11. Drink a hot drink or wear overly warm clothing | Sweating, blushing, hot flushes |

## Other Exercises to Trigger Feared Sensations

| Exercise | Symptoms Experienced |
| --- | --- |
| _____ | _____ |
| _____ | _____ |
| _____ | _____ |
| _____ | _____ |
| _____ | _____ |

Adapted from M. M. Antony and R. P. Swinson. 2000. *Phobic Disorders and Panic in Adults: A Guide to Assessment and Treatment.* Washington, DC: American Psychological Association. Used with permission.

## Is Interoceptive Exposure for You?

Although interoceptive exposure is helpful for many who suffer from social anxiety, it is usually unnecessary for overcoming the problem. Furthermore, for some people, there is virtually no benefit from doing these exercises. Interoceptive exposure *is* likely to be helpful to you if either of the following statements is true:

- You are generally afraid of experiencing anxiety symptoms such as a rapidly beating heart, dizziness, shaking, blushing, or sweating.

- You are afraid of experiencing anxiety symptoms in front of other people.

If you are fearful of experiencing physical arousal feelings in general or when in social or performance situations, we recommend trying the exercises described in this chapter. However, if you are not fearful of the sensations that you experience when anxious, and you are not concerned about others noticing your anxiety symptoms, then there is no need to practice these exercises. In fact, you can skip ahead to chapter 10.

## How Does Interoceptive Exposure Work?

Like situational exposure, interoceptive exposure is believed to decrease fear by disproving a person's fearful beliefs, assumptions, and predictions. By deliberately bringing on uncomfortable feelings in a controlled and predictable manner, you will learn that (1) you can control the sensations that normally appear to be uncontrollable and (2) even if you do experience noticeable physical feelings in front of other people, the consequences are likely to be minimal.

By learning to allow yourself to be anxious in front of other people, and to allow others to observe your anxiety symptoms, eventually you will become less concerned about your anxious reactions and about what people think when they notice your shaking, sweating, blushing, or other signs of anxiety. By becoming less concerned about experiencing these feelings, you will probably become less anxious when exposed to social and performance situations.

### A Warning About Interoceptive Exposure

If you are healthy, the exercises described in this chapter are not at all dangerous. However, if you have certain health problems, some of the exercises could worsen your condition. For example, if you have asthma or a bad cold, you should probably not practice hyperventilation or breathing through a straw. If you experience neck or back pain, we recommend against shaking your head from side to side or engaging in any other exercises that could aggravate your condition. To be safe, we recommend checking with your doctor to see if any of these exercises are likely to be dangerous or problematic for you.

# A Step-by-Step Guide to Interoceptive Exposure

This section describes the four main steps involved in using interoceptive exposure to overcome the fear of experiencing physical arousal sensations:

1. Finding out which interoceptive exposure exercises are most effective for bringing on *your* anxiety symptoms.

2. Developing an *interoceptive exposure hierarchy*.

3. Practicing the interoceptive exposure exercises in nonsocial situations until they are no longer anxiety-provoking.

4. Combining interoceptive exposure with situational exposure (i.e., purposely trying to arouse uncomfortable anxiety symptoms while you are in a social situation).

### Step 1: Symptom Induction Testing

Before beginning to practice interoceptive exposure exercises on a regular basis, you should first determine which exercises are most likely to be effective for you. This can be achieved by attempting each exercise at home and paying attention to the types of symptoms that you experience, the effect of the exercises on your fear level, and how similar the experience is to the fear that you normally experience in social situations. The Symptom Induction Testing Form below can be used to record your responses to each exercise. We have included space for additional exercises that you may have identified earlier in the chapter.

# Symptom Induction Testing Form

*Instructions*: For each symptom induction exercise: (1) list the physical *symptoms* that were experienced; (2) rate the intensity of *fear* using a scale of 0 (no fear) to 100 (maximum fear); and (3) record the *similarity* of the experience to typical episodes of anxiety and fear using a scale from 0 (not at all similar) to 100 (identical).

| Exercise | Symptoms | Fear (0–100) | Similarity (0–100) |
|---|---|---|---|
| Shake head from side to side (30 seconds | | | |
| Spin around in a swivel chair (60 seconds) | | | |
| While sitting, bend over and place head between legs for 30 seconds, then sit up quickly | | | |
| Hold breath (30 seconds or as long as possible) | | | |
| Hyperventilate (shallow breathing at a rate of about 100–120 breaths per minute) (60 seconds) | | | |
| Breathe through a narrow, small straw (plug nose if necessary) (2 minutes) | | | |
| Tense all the muscles in the body or hold a push-up position (60 seconds or as long as possible) | | | |
| Carry heavy weights or bags (60 seconds or as long as possible) | | | |
| Run in place (or run up and down stairs) (60 seconds) | | | |

| | | | |
|---|---|---|---|
| Sit in a hot stuffy room (e.g., a sauna, hot car, or small room with a spaceheater) (5 to 10 minutes.) | | | |
| Drink a hot drink or wear overly warm clothing | | | |
| Other | | | |
| Other | | | |

Adapted from M. M. Antony and R. P. Swinson. 2000. *Phobic Disorders and Panic in Adults: A Guide to Assessment and Treatment*. Washington, DC: American Psychological Association. Used with permission.

## Step 2: Developing Interoceptive Exposure Hierarchies

Just as the *situational exposure hierarchy* described in chapter 8 is used to guide your situational exposure practices, *interoceptive exposure hierarchies* are useful for choosing appropriate interoceptive exposure exercises. In most cases, we recommend that you develop two interoceptive exposure hierarchies: one for practicing the exercises outside of social situations (see Step 3) and a second hierarchy for practicing interoceptive exposure while in (or immediately before entering) social or performance situations (see Step 4). If you are not at all fearful of experiencing anxiety sensations outside of social situations, then developing a hierarchy for practicing interoceptive exposure in nonsocial situations is less important. Instead you should focus on exercises to practice while exposed to social and performance situations.

To develop a hierarchy for interoceptive exposure, first eliminate any exercises that you know will not make you anxious (based on the results of your symptom induction testing, completed in Step 1). For example, if the sensations created by physical exercise (e.g., jogging) are not frightening to you at all, eliminate this exercise from your list. Next, take the remaining exercises and put them in hierarchical order, starting with the most anxiety-provoking and ending with the least anxiety-provoking. Record your level of expected fear for each exercise, using a scale ranging from 0 (no fear) to 100 (maximum fear). Examples of interoceptive exposure hierarchies reflecting (1) practices outside of social situations and (2) practices in social situations are shown below. We have also included space to record your own hierarchies.

## Sample Interoceptive Exposure Hierarchy for Practices in Nonsocial Situations

| Exercise | Fear Rating (0–100) |
| --- | --- |
| 1. Hyperventilate at home alone (1 minute) | 60 |
| 2. Breathe through a straw at home alone (2 minutes) | 45 |
| 3. Spin in a chair at home alone (1 minute) | 35 |
| 4. Shake head from side to side at home alone (30 seconds) | 30 |

## My Interoceptive Exposure Hierarchy for Practices in Nonsocial Situations

| Exercise | Fear Rating (0–100) |
| --- | --- |
| 1. _____ | _____ |
| 2. _____ | _____ |
| 3. _____ | _____ |
| 4. _____ | _____ |
| 5. _____ | _____ |
| 6. _____ | _____ |
| 7. _____ | _____ |
| 8. _____ | _____ |
| 9. _____ | _____ |
| 10. _____ | _____ |

## Sample Interoceptive Exposure Hierarchy for Practices in Social Situations

| Exercise | Fear Rating (0–100) |
|---|---|
| 1. Hold a heavy bag for 60 seconds immediately before holding a filled glass of water in front of others (to induce shaky hands) | 100 |
| 2. Breathe through a straw for 2 minutes immediately before entering a cocktail party and making small talk | 80 |
| 3. Wear a warm sweater while giving a presentation | 80 |
| 4. Eat hot soup to induce flushing and sweating at a dinner party | 60 |
| 5. Run up and down stairs at a party | 40 |
| 6. Hyperventilate just before calling someone on the telephone | 35 |

### My Interoceptive Exposure Hierarchy for Practices in Social Situations

| Exercise | Fear Rating (0–100) |
|---|---|
| 1. _____ | _____ |
| 2. _____ | _____ |
| 3. _____ | _____ |
| 4. _____ | _____ |
| 5. _____ | _____ |
| 6. _____ | _____ |
| 7. _____ | _____ |
| 8. _____ | _____ |

9. _____    _____

10. _____    _____

### Step 3: Practicing Interoceptive Exposure in Nonsocial Situations

If you are not fearful of practicing the interoceptive exposure exercises in nonsocial situations, it is not necessary to spend a lot of time on step 3. However, if there are exercises that you intend to practice in social situations (step 4), we recommend that you first try them a few times in nonsocial situations to make sure that you are familiar with the exercise.

If there are exercises that are anxiety-provoking for you, even in nonsocial situations, we recommend that you practice them repeatedly in nonsocial situations (i.e., at home or another safe space) before practicing in social situations. Use your *interoceptive exposure hierarchy for nonsocial situations* to help you to choose which exercises to practice. Begin with exercises that are challenging but unlikely to be so overwhelming that you cannot complete them. After you have chosen an exercise, set aside about fifteen minutes, twice a day, to practice the exercise repeatedly. After each repetition of the exercise, take a short break (from thirty seconds to a few minutes) until the symptoms decrease. Continue to practice the exercise another five or six times, or until your fear has decreased. Later in this chapter, you will find a diary you can use to record the results of each practice and to challenge any anxious thoughts that arise during the practice.

Each time you do an exercise, you will continue to feel the physical symptoms associated with the exercise. However, your fear of the symptoms should decrease across individual practices and across days. For example, if you are practicing hyperventilation, you will likely continue to become hot and light-headed each time you do the exercise. However, over time, those feelings should become less frightening.

### Step 4: Practicing Interoceptive Exposure in Social Situations

After you have practiced situational exposure (chapter 8) and interoceptive exposure in nonsocial situations, the next step is to combine these two approaches. Combining interoceptive and situational exposure is one of the most challenging types of exposure that you can practice. However, this type of exposure can also provide you with the strongest possible evidence that your anxious predictions are exaggerated or untrue. By entering the social and performance situations that you fear, and purposely inducing arousal sensations to enhance your fear, you will learn that these situations are manageable even when you feel

extremely uncomfortable. To select possible exercises for combining interoceptive and situational exposure, refer back to your *interoceptive exposure hierarchy
for practices in social situations* (step 2).

# Integrating Interoceptive Exposure into Your Treatment Plan

As discussed earlier, we recommend that your psychological treatment program
(cognitive-behavioral therapy) begin with the cognitive strategies discussed in
chapter 6. After practicing the cognitive techniques for several weeks, situational
exposure should be practiced for several more weeks or months until you feel
more comfortable in social situations (chapters 7 and 8). Only then, do we recommend that you consider adding interoceptive exposure if you are still fearful of
experiencing anxiety symptoms in front of others. As your fear continues to
decrease through exposure and cognitive therapy, you may also consider working on your social and communication skills (chapter 10).

## *Using Interoceptive Exposure Records and Diaries*

Keeping good records during interoceptive exposure practices will help you
to monitor your progress over time. The Interoceptive Exposure Diary will help
you to measure changes in your fear across interoceptive exposure practices. Furthermore, this diary is designed to help you to challenge your anxious thoughts
during exposure practices. The first column indicates the trial number (1, 2, 3,
etc.). In the second column, you should record the specific sensations that you
experience. In the third column, record your fear level during each exercise trial.
Finally, the fourth and fifth columns are for recording your anxious thoughts during the exercise and for countering your thoughts with more realistic beliefs.

# Trouble Shooting

*Problem:*    The interoceptive exposure exercises don't frighten me.

*Solution:*    If the exercises don't cause anxiety when you practice them in
nonsocial situations, try practicing them immediately before
entering social situations. If they still do not increase your fear,
then discontinue the interoceptive exposure exercises. However,
you should continue to use the cognitive strategies (chapter 6)
and the situational exposure exercises (chapters 7 and 8).

*Problem:*    The interoceptive exposure exercises are too overwhelming for me
to complete.

*Solution:*    If an interoceptive exposure exercise is too overwhelming, even when conducted in a nonsocial situation, try an easier exercise from your hierarchy and don't move on to the more difficult exercises until the easier ones become manageable.If an interoceptive exposure exercise is overwhelming, but only when practiced in a the context of a social or performance situation, you can practice an easier exercise from your interoceptive exposure hierarchy and work your way up to the more difficult exercises. Or, you can continue to practice situational exposure without the interoceptive exposure exercises. Hold off on introducing interoceptive exposure practices in social situations until you are able to manage the situation on its own (without interoceptive exposure).

# Interoceptive Exposure Diary

*Instructions*: This form should be completed each time you practice interoceptive exposure. For each interoceptive exposure trial: (1) list the physical *symptoms* that you experienced; (2) rate the intensity of your *fear* using a scale of 0 (no fear) to 100 (maximum fear); (3) list your specific anxious predictions regarding the exercise (e.g., what might happen during the exercise?); and (4) list alternative nonanxious predictions and evidence to support these predictions (i.e., countering).

Describe the Exposure Exercise _____    Date and Time _____

| Trial No. | Symptoms Experienced | Fear (0-100) | Anxious Thoughts and Predictions | Countering |
|-----------|---------------------|--------------|----------------------------------|------------|
| 1. | | | | |
| 2. | | | | |
| 3. | | | | |
| 4 | | | | |
| 5.. | | | | |
| 6. | | | | |
| 7. | | | | |

Adapted from M. M. Antony and R. P. Swinson. 2000. *Phobic Disorders and Panic in Adults: A Guide to Assessment and Treatment.* Washington, DC: American Psychological Association. Used with permission.

# Chapter 10

# Communicating More Effectively

For some people, one consequence of avoiding social situations is never having the opportunity to master the communication skills that would help them deal effectively with others. For example, if your fear has prevented you from being interviewed for jobs or from asking other people out on dates, your lack of experience in these areas may make it even more difficult for you to know how to best deal with these situations (e.g., what to say, what to wear, how to behave, etc.). The ability to interact effectively with other people must be learned and it takes practice, just like learning to play the piano or training to run a marathon.

As discussed earlier, when you practice being in the situations you fear, your performance in these situations is likely to improve. This chapter provides some additional strategies for enhancing the quality of your interactions with other people. Most of these strategies can be used during the course of your situational exposure practices (chapters 7 and 8).

As you read this chapter, there are a few important points to keep in mind. First, our purpose in writing this chapter is not to suggest that you lack social skills. Rather, our aim is to help you increase your awareness of the different ways in which your behavior may impact on others. If anything, your social and communication skills are already much better than you think they are. Research consistently has shown that many people who are socially anxious assume that they make a much worse impression on others than they really do (Antony and Swinson 2000).

You should also bear in mind that there is no such thing as a perfect set of social skills. What works best in one situation or with one group of people, may not work at all well in another situation or with another group. For example, the best way of asking one person out on a date may cause a refusal with someone else. Although one set of interview skills may help you get one job, they may work against you when applying for another type of job. In other words, no matter how well-developed your social skills are, they can never be perfect. Like the rest of us, you will continue to stumble from time to time and occasionally you will make a bad impression on other people—we all do.

Finally, the strategies described in this chapter should not be thought of as rules to be followed by everyone. Rather, they are suggestions and guidelines that you may find helpful in some situations. For example, we suggest that certain types of body language (e.g., standing too far away from another individual during a conversation) may be interpreted as a sign of aloofness or that you are uninterested in talking. However, standing too close also may cause other people to feel uncomfortable. Unfortunately, it is very difficult to define the ideal amount of "personal space." What works well for one person may not work as well with another. Personal space requirements also vary across ethnic groups and subcultures. That is, among some groups standing quite close to the person with whom you are speaking is the norm. But in another group that norm might cause great discomfort. Given that it is often difficult to know how to behave in a particular situation, it is best not to get too caught up in whether you are using these strategies perfectly or whether you are making a perfect impression on others.

Improving social and communication skills can involve working on many different behaviors. A list of examples is provided below. As you read through the list, pay attention to the specific skills you are interested in improving. We recommend that you consult some of the recommended readings cited throughout this chapter and the Additional Recommended Reading at the back for more detailed suggestions. One of the most comprehensive books on improving communication is *Messages: The Communication Skills Book* (McKay, Davis, and Fanning 1995). Another excellent source is Robert Bolton's (1979) book, *People Skills*.

# Social Skills Training

- Eye contact (e.g., making appropriate eye contact when talking to other people)

- Body language (e.g., learning to have an "open" posture and to stand at an appropriately close distance to other people during conversations)

- Tone and volume of speech (e.g., not talking too quietly)

- Conversational skills (e.g., learning to stop apologizing unnecessarily, and to stop belittling yourself; learning to disclose information about yourself, and to use open-ended questions instead of closed-ended questions)

- Public speaking skills (e.g., learning to talk to an audience during a presentation instead of reading from a paper; using slides, overheads, and audiovisual aids; answering audience questions and criticisms clearly without boring or irritating the audience)

- Interview skills (e.g., preparing for an interview: what to wear, questions to ask, questions to expect)

- Dating skills (e.g., asking someone to lunch or dinner, manners, generating conversation topics, ending the date gracefully)

- Assertiveness skills (e.g., learning how to ask for things assertively, without being either too passive or too aggressive)

- Conflict skills (e.g., learning how to deal with other people with whom you disagree or who might be angry or hostile)

- Listening skills (e.g., truly listening to others when they are speaking instead of comparing yourself, ruminating about what to say next, etc.)

- Other interpersonal skills (e.g., learning the difference between imposing on others' time and privacy and making reasonable requests for help or social contact)

Adapted from M. M. Antony and R. P. Swinson. 2000. *Phobic Disorders and Panic in Adults: A Guide to Assessment and Treatment*. Washington, DC: American Psychological Association. Used with permission.

# Learning to Listen

Communication is a two-way street. Listening effectively is as important as what you say when you are engaging in a conversation, being interviewed, or participating in a meeting. When you feel anxious, your attention tends to shift from the situation itself to your experiences in the situation. In other words, you become aware of how you are feeling, and you begin to wonder whether your anxiety symptoms are noticeable to the other people in the room, and whether those people are judging you negatively. At the same time, you become less aware of other aspects of the situation, including what other people are saying. This lack of concentration on what others are saying may reinforce your uncertainty about whether your responses are appropriate. Often, even when you think you are listening, you may be only partially aware of what is being said.

There are several costs to not listening. First, you may miss important information that the other person is trying to communicate. You may hear only the parts of the message that are consistent with your anxious beliefs, thereby increasing your anxiety. For example, if you hear only your boss's negative comments and miss his or her praise during a performance appraisal, you will undoubtedly feel worse than if you had heard the entire appraisal. Not hearing the entire message also may lead you to respond inappropriately, sometimes to something completely different than what was actually said. Furthermore, the other person may sense that you are not listening to what is being said. As a result, you may be perceived by that person as aloof, distracted, or bored by the conversation.

## Blocks to Effective Listening

In *Messages: The Communications Skills Book* (McKay, Davis, and Fanning 1995) the authors list a number of different factors that frequently interfere with our ability to listen to others during conversations, meetings, arguments, and other types of social interactions. Of these, five are especially common when people are feeling anxious in a social situation. These listening blocks include the following:

- **Comparing yourself to the other person**. We all compare ourselves to others as a way to evaluate our own behavior and accomplishments. However, excessive social anxiety may be associated with the tendency to do this more often, to make unfavorable comparisons (e.g., comparisons with those who are more successful on a particular dimension), and to feel bad after making such comparisons. This tendency to make negative comparisons while conversing (e.g., criticizing yourself with unspoken comments such as, "I am not as smart as he is" or "She is more attractive than I am") interferes with your ability to listen to and hear what is being said.

- **Filtering what the other person says.** Filtering involves listening only to certain parts of what the other person is saying. In social anxiety, this could involve paying attention only to those parts of the conversation that seem to indicate that the other person is being critical or judgmental.

- **Rehearsing what to say next**. If you are overly concerned about saying the right thing during conversations or meetings, you may be mentally rehearsing how you will respond to other people's comments rather than truly listening to what is being said. Although you may engage in rehearsing to maximize your ability to say the right thing, this practice, if used too often, may have the opposite effect.

- **Derailing the conversation**. Derailing involves switching the topic of conversation when it becomes either boring or uncomfortable. In social anxiety, derailing may take place when the conversation moves into anxiety-provoking areas. For example, if a coworker asks you about your weekend, and you did not do anything special because you did not have a date, you might shift the conversation back to a work-related topic, rather than disclose what you perceive to be overly personal information. Derailing has the effect of making the other individual feel as though you are not listening or are not interested in the conversation.

- **Placating the other person**. Placating involves agreeing with the other individual regardless of what he or she says, to avoid potential conflict. Because social anxiety is associated with a fear of being disliked or negatively judged, people who are socially anxious often go out of their way to agree with others. However, most people don't expect to have others agree with them all the time. If you always agree with whatever is said, it may raise the other person's suspicions about whether you are really listening.

## Improving Your Listening Skills

The authors of *Messages* (McKay, Davis, and Fanning 1995) provide a number of suggestions for improving listening skills. First, they suggest that effective listening should involve *active* participation rather than just sitting quietly and absorbing the information. Active listening involves *maintaining appropriate eye contact*, *paraphrasing* what the person has said (e.g., "So, in other words, what you are saying . . .), asking for *clarification* (e.g., asking questions to help you understand what was said), and providing the other person with *feedback* (i.e., your reactions to what he/she said). Whenever possible, feedback should be immediate (as soon as you understand the communication), honest (reflecting your true feelings), and supportive (i.e., gentle, unlikely to be hurtful to the other person).

In addition, McKay, Davis, and Fanning recommend that people should try to listen with *empathy*. Being empathic means conveying to the person with whom you are speaking the idea that you genuinely understand his/her message as well as the feelings that person is experiencing. As discussed in chapter 6, there are many different ways of interpreting a given situation. By trying to understand another person's perspective, you will be better able to listen to that person, and to convey the fact that you are listening. Note that it is not necessary for you to agree with the other person's perspective—just to understand it. However, even when someone says something that you believe to be completely incorrect, you probably can identify at least a small part of the message that is true. Letting the person know that you understand his/her perspective conveys empathy even if you don't agree with the overall content of what was said.

Finally, effective listening requires listening with openness and awareness. *Openness* involves listening without trying to find fault. *Awareness* involves (1) being aware of how a communication fits in with your own knowledge and experiences, and (2) being aware of any inconsistencies in the verbal message itself and the nonverbal aspects of the communication, such as tone, posture, and facial expressions.

### Exercise

The next time you are in a conversation, try some of the effective listening skills described above.

1. Make eye contact during the conversation.

2. Paraphrase what the other person says, and ask for clarification if you are unsure about any aspect of the communication.

3. Give feedback when appropriate, making sure that your feedback is immediate, honest, and supportive.

4. Finally, make sure that you are listening with empathy, openness, and awareness.

After trying this exercise in a real-life situation, come back to this chapter and list on the lines below any ways in which the experience was different from your usual conversations. Did the conversation last longer? Was it more gratifying? Did the other person respond differently to you? Did you experience less anxiety than usual?

_____

_____

_____

# Nonverbal Communication

When you feel anxious in a social situation, you probably engage in behaviors designed to avoid communicating with others. These may include avoiding eye contact, speaking very quietly, or even avoiding the situation completely. Despite your efforts to avoid communication, however, it is virtually impossible not to communicate. In fact, what you actually say in words during a conversation makes up a very small component of the messages you communicate to others. Nonverbal aspects of communication, including eye contact, posture, tone of voice, and your physical distance (or closeness), communicate at least as much information as your verbal messages. In fact, even when you completely stay away from a feared social situation, you communicate a message to others. For example, by repeatedly avoiding meetings at work, others may assume that you are shy, uninterested, or even hostile.

Despite wanting others to respond positively, people who are shy or socially anxious often exhibit nonverbal behaviors that communicate to others, "Stay away from me." Examples of these closed nonverbal behaviors include leaning back or standing far away from other people, avoiding eye contact, speaking quietly, crossing your arms over your chest, clenching your fists, and maintaining a serious facial expression. Although you may believe that these behaviors serve as a form of protection in anxiety-provoking situations, they tend to have the opposite effect.

Instead of protecting you from potential threat or from being judged by others, these behaviors probably increase the likelihood that others will react negatively. For example, at a party, people are most likely to approach someone who is smiling, making eye contact, and talking at a reasonable volume. When someone stands far away, speaks quietly, and avoids eye contact, it is natural to assume that the individual is either uninterested in speaking, or difficult to get to know.

Of course, moderation is the key here. Too much eye contact can make people uncomfortable. In addition, someone who stands too close or smiles at inappropriate times may make others feel uneasy. The appropriate intensity for each of these behaviors is impossible to define. Furthermore, what is appropriate in one situation is not necessarily appropriate in another. For example, although it is okay to stand several inches away from a romantic partner during an intimate conversation, you might want to stand further back when talking to a coworker. With respect to nonverbal communication, there are differences across gender and across cultures. Therefore, we suggest that you experiment with using different nonverbal behaviors to find out what works best for you in the particular situations that you encounter from day to day.

### Exercise

Closed nonverbal behaviors are behaviors that close the channels of communication by sending the message that the opportunity for contact or communication with you is unavailable. A list of closed nonverbal behaviors often associated with social anxiety is provided below. Beside each example, to the right, is an alternative nonverbal behavior that indicates an openness to communication.

After reading this list, identify whether you tend to use any closed nonverbal behaviors excessively. Over the coming week, try to replace some of your closed behaviors with open behaviors during the course of your exposure practices. Record your experiences in the space provided. For example, record whether people react differently to you when you smile more, make eye contact, or speak more loudly.

| Closed Nonverbal Behaviors | Alternative Open Nonverbal Behaviors |
| --- | --- |
| Leaning back while sitting | Leaning forward while sitting |
| Standing far away from another person | Standing closer when talking to others |
| Avoiding eye contact | Maintaining eye contact |
| Speaking quietly | Speaking at a volume easily heard |
| Crossing your arms | Keeping your arms uncrossed |
| Clenching your fists | Keeping your hands relaxed and open |
| Maintaining a serious facial expression | Smiling warmly |

Speaking with a timid tone          Speaking with a confident tone

Sitting hunched over                 Sitting up straight

Adapted from M. M. Antony and R. P. Swinson. 2000. *Phobic Disorders and Panic in Adults: A Guide to Assessment and Treatment.* Washington, DC: American Psychological Association. Used with permission.

### Results of Changing My Nonverbal Behaviors

# Conversational Skills

Many people often must struggle to find things to say when making casual conversation or small talk, particularly in situations that make them anxious. For example, you may find it difficult to contribute to a conversation at a party or meeting, and, as a result, you may be relatively quiet. When you do get involved in a conversation, perhaps you find that the discussion fizzles quickly, as you and the other person run out of things to say. In this section, we discuss ways of starting and ending conversations, as well as methods of improving the quality of your conversations. These suggestions may be adapted for different types of conversations including talking to a coworker or classmate, conversing on a date, or speaking with a stranger while waiting in line.

Keep in mind that the suggestions in this section are not always going to work smoothly. For example, if you start talking to someone in an elevator, the person may respond positively or you may be ignored. If an individual responds negatively when you try to make contact, remember that it is not necessarily because you did something wrong. The other person may be shy or may be concerned about his or her safety (having been raised never to talk to strangers). Also, it is possible that your communication will be misunderstood. If things don't work out during a particular practice, try to understand why and to figure out what you can do differently next time. Learning from your experiences will help you to plan future practices that are more likely to work out satisfactorily.

Finally, if you want to learn more about making conversation, we recommend that you read the third edition of Alan Garner's (1997) book, *Conversationally Speaking: Testing New Ways to Increase Your Personal and Social Effectiveness.*

## Starting a Conversation

There are many different informal situations in which people start conversations with one another. For example, people often speak to strangers in grocery store lines and elevators, or on buses, subways, airplanes, and in other public places. You also may choose to speak to coworkers, both in the work setting and at social events related to work (e.g., a holiday party). If you are a student, make a point of always sitting in the same area of the classroom so that you can become familiar with some of the other students. Arrive at class early, to increase your opportunities to speak to others.

Although getting a conversation started is sometimes difficult, it can become easier with practice. Remember to pay attention to your nonverbal behaviors. Make eye contact and speak so the other person can hear you. If you are at a party, it is perfectly appropriate to walk up to a group of people who are already talking. After a few minutes of standing around with the group, you can join in the conversation.

The topic of conversation should usually begin with something genial and not too personal, particularly if you don't know the other individual very well. You may begin with a question (e.g., "How was your weekend?"), a compliment (e.g., "I like your new haircut"), an observation (e.g., "I notice that you are not driving your usual car"), or an introduction (e.g., "I don't believe we have met. My name is . . ."). Other appropriate topics include: hobbies, your job, a movie or TV show you recently saw, the weather, something you recently read, your vacation, a recent shopping trip or outing, and sports. After you have been talking for a while, particularly if you have known the person for some time, it may be appropriate to discuss more personal topics, such as your spiritual beliefs, politics, relationships, personal feelings, difficult family situations, and topics related to sexuality.

## Improving the Quality of Your Conversations

As stated earlier, a conversation typically is a two-way street. It is not enough to just listen to another person. Nor is it appropriate to talk only about yourself, without giving the other person a chance to speak. Of course, there are exceptions to this rule. There are some people who are very happy to have you do all the talking or allow them to do all the talking. However, for most of us, a conversation is far more interesting if we have the opportunity to express our own thoughts, feelings, and experiences, and also the chance to listen to another person's views and experiences.

The active listening skills described earlier in the chapter will enhance the quality of your conversations. In addition, we recommend that you go out of your way to disclose information about yourself when talking to others. As mentioned earlier, the information you disclose need not be overly personal at first. Instead, you can start by talking about your weekend's activities, your favorite football team, or a class that you are taking.

Asking the other person questions will communicate that you are interested in what he/she has to say. You can ask about their experiences (e.g., "How was that restaurant you dined at last night?") or you can ask for the other person's reaction to something you have said. If possible, try to use open-ended questions rather than close-ended questions. A *closed-ended question* is one that elicits a response of only one or two words. For example, the closed-ended question "Did you like the movie?" could easily lead to responses like "Yes" or "No," at which point you would be back at square one, trying to find another topic of conversation. Closed-ended questions usually begin with words like *are, do, who, when, where,* and *which.*

In contrast, open-ended questions usually elicit more detailed answers. Open-ended questions are more likely than closed-ended questions to generate longer and more interesting conversations. These types of question usually begin with words or phrases like *how, why,* and *in what way.* For example, the question "What did you think about the movie?" draws out a more thorough response than "Did you like the movie?"

Here are some examples of closed-ended and open-ended questions:

| Closed-Ended Questions | Open-Ended Questions |
|---|---|
| Did you have a good weekend? | What did you do this weekend? |
| Who is your favorite candidate? | What do you like about the different  candidates? |
| What do you do for a living? | How did you get into your line of work? |
| Do you like your psychology professor? | Why do you like your psychology professor? |

Note that a question can be too open-ended, so that it is responded to as if it were a closed-ended question. For example, questions like "How are you?" or "How was your day?" typically lead to a one-word response such as "Fine."

## Ending Conversations

All conversations eventually come to an end. Furthermore, in informal social situations (e.g., at a party, on a date, on the phone), conversations almost always end because one or both people lose interest in what is being talked about or they reach a point at which they would rather be doing something else or talking to someone else.

If you are especially sensitive to rejection, you may become more anxious as a conversation nears its end. Or you may be hurt if you think that the other person seems less interested in continuing to converse. Nevertheless, if you begin to pay attention to other people's conversations, you will notice that all discussions reach a point at which there is little more to be said. Sometimes this point is reached in a few seconds. Other times, it may take a few minutes or even an hour for a particularly interesting conversation to end. Running out of things to talk about is not a failure and does not mean that you are boring. It is a normal feature of all conversations.

Typically, people try to find graceful ways to get out of conversations that have run their course. At a party, you might excuse yourself to refill your drink or visit the bathroom. Or, it may be appropriate to mention politely that you need to catch up with another person at the party. In a work setting, people often end the conversation with a reference to work (e.g., "Well, I need to get back to work") or a pledge to continue the conversation later ("Perhaps we can have lunch together some time soon"). Often, simply saying something like, "It's been nice talking to you, but I need to run" is sufficient.

### Exercise

Try using some of these conversational strategies the next time you are having a conversation. If you rarely encounter situations that allow for conversation, you may need to go out of your way to seek out such a situation. During the practice, pay special attention to using the strategies for starting the conversation, improving the quality of the conversation, and ending the conversation. In the spaces below, record your experiences after using the relevant strategies for each phase of the conversation.

*Starting the conversation:*

_____

_____

_____

*Improving the quality of the conversation:*

_____

_____

_____

*Ending the conversation:*

_____

_____

_____

# Job Interviews

Most people feel somewhat nervous when being interviewed for a job. However, showing no signs of anxiety could work against you in some interview situations. In fact, not showing any signs of anxiety during an interview might be interpreted by the interviewer as a sign that you are overconfident. But if you are particularly anxious in social situations, interviews may be even more anxiety-provoking for you than they are for the average person. Chapter 6 reviewed strategies for changing the beliefs that contribute to your anxiety in situations such as interviews. Chapters 7 and 8 recommended practicing exposure to interviews (using both real interview practices and role-play simulations) as a strategy for learning to become less anxious. In this section, we provide additional suggestions for improving interview skills. These suggestions are meant to be used along with the cognitive and exposure-based techniques discussed in earlier chapters.

Essentially, being prepared for an interview involves knowing what to do before the interview, how to behave during the interview, and what to do when the interview is over. Suggestions are provided for each of these interview phases. For a more detailed discussion of this topic, we suggest reading *Messages: The Communication Skills Book* (McKay, Davis, and Fanning 1995).

## *Preparing for the Interview*

- Before the interview, practice interviewing with friends, family members, or for other jobs that are not really of interest to you. As discussed in chapters 7 and 8, practicing being interviewed will help to decrease your anxiety when you are in the actual situation.

- Keep the situation in perspective. Remember that it is only an interview. If it doesn't work out, there will be other opportunities. Think of the interview as a learning experience or an opportunity to improve your interviewing skills.

- Take time to understand the purpose of the interview, learn who will be interviewing you, what the structure of the interview will be, and how long the interview will run. If possible, find out the interviewer's name, and make sure you remember it. If that is not possible, when the interviewer introduces himself/herself to you, pay attention and try to use the name when you say good-bye.

- Try to learn as much as possible about the organization where you are being interviewed and about the person who is interviewing you. Perhaps the organization has a web site. If so, you may even be able to see a picture of the person who will be interviewing you beforehand. Being knowledgeable about the organization during the interview will provide a strong proof that you really are interested in the position.

- Take some time to identify your strengths and have a good idea of what you can contribute to the organization in case you are asked. You may want to take some notes with you, to prevent forgetting something that you want to mention.

- If you are asked about your weaknesses or limitations, there is no need to list every flaw that comes into your mind. Instead, you can mention one or two limitations, phrasing them in such a way that they are unlikely to be viewed as a problem. For example, you can choose to mention "limitations" that may be viewed as strengths by the interviewer (e.g., "I tend to work too hard, so I need to remind myself to take breaks"). Or, you can deflect the question by talking about a limitation that you had in the past that is no longer a problem (e.g., "When I first started my previous job, I didn't have much experience working with computers. However, over the past few years, I got a lot of computer experience so that's not an issue anymore").

- Prepare at least ten questions you can ask during the interview. Write them down so you won't forget. For example, you should consider asking questions about the types of responsibilities that you are likely to have, the hours you will be expected to work, who you will be working with, and the structure of a typical day. Questions about salary, vacations, and benefits generally should be asked after you have received an offer, although for certain positions it may be appropriate to ask these questions during the interview.

- Bring extra copies of your résumé and other supporting documents, in case the interviewer does not have easy access to these materials. Also, the interviewer may wish to consult someone else about your qualifications for the position or to recommend you to someone else in the firm.

## During the Interview

- Under no circumstances should you be late. Give yourself enough time to get to the interview and arrive a bit early.

- Your appearance is important. Make sure that you are dressed attractively and that your hair is neat. Note that appropriate attire for one job interview may be quite inappropriate for another type of job. If you are not sure what to wear, err on the side of dressing in a more conservative and professional manner.

- Remember to use some of the strategies discussed earlier in this chapter. For example, really listen to what the interviewer asks or tells you. Pay attention to your nonverbal communication and try to maintain eye contact.

- Be courteous, polite, and tactful. Remember to say "please" and "thank-you." Don't disparage the organization, the interview process, or the person interviewing you. In fact, try not to be overly negative about previous jobs and employers, even if you were unhappy in a previous position.

- Try to appear flexible and willing to compromise. For example, if the hours aren't perfect, let the interviewer know that you will do what you can to accommodate the schedule. After you get the offer, you can renegotiate the hours. If it doesn't work out to your satisfaction, you can always turn down the position.

- Ask questions. A job interview has two purposes: (1) to allow the interviewer to decide about you and (2) to give you an opportunity to decide whether you want to work for that particular organization. Make sure you ask questions during the interview. Not only will asking questions help you to find out more about the position, but it will also convey to the interviewer that you are serious about the job.

- In general, be yourself during the interview and answer questions honestly. However, try not to offer too much unnecessary personal information. For example, if the interviewer asks whether you are nervous, it is okay to say that you are feeling a bit anxious. On the other hand, there is no need to provide details about any personal difficulties or stresses that you may be experiencing, including frequent panic attacks, depression, or marital problems.

### After the Interview

- Ask the interviewer what the next step is. For example, if the organization will be interviewing other candidates, when can you expect to hear their decision? Is there likely to be a second or third interview for the finalists?

- After the interview, send a letter thanking the interviewer for his or her time.

- Take some time to think about what went well during the interview and what you might have preferred to do or say differently. This information will be helpful for planning your next set of interviews if you don't get the job.

## Assertive Communication

This section describes three ways of communicating: passively, aggressively, and assertively. Whereas passive and aggressive styles of communication rarely have the desired effect, assertive communication is more likely to get positive results. This section will teach you to understand the differences among these three types of communication, and will provide you with an introduction to methods for ensuring that you communicate assertively.

## Passive Communication

Generally, shyness and social anxiety are associated with a tendency to communicate passively. Passive communication involves expressing one's needs indirectly, often in a quiet voice, and perhaps with frequent pauses and hesitations. Passive communication places the other person's wants, needs, and desires ahead of your own. This style of communicating is often associated with a strong desire to avoid any possibility of offending or inconveniencing the other individual. However, because your message is not communicated directly, the other person may never receive the message that you intended to communicate. Therefore, passive communication closes the channels of communication and may cause you to feel hurt and resentful. In fact, this resentment eventually may put you at risk for communicating in an aggressive manner later on. For example, a passive way of inviting someone to socialize is the vague statement, "We should get together sometime."

## Aggressive Communication

Aggressive communication involves expressing your feelings, needs, or wants at the expense of another person's feelings, needs, and wants. Aggressive communication tends to be judgmental, critical, and accusatory, both in content and in tone. Like passive communication, this style of responding closes the channels of communication and can result in hurt feelings, grudges, anger, and alienation from the other person. An example of an aggressive way of asking someone to socialize is the statement, "If you cared about me and weren't so selfish, you would invite me to get together with you more often."

## ☀ Assertive Communication

Often, people assume that passive and aggressive styles of communicating are their only two options. However, a third option does exist. In contrast to aggressive and passive styles of communicating, assertive communication takes into account one's own feelings, needs, and wants, as well as those of the other person. Assertive communication has many of the features of good communication, including a tendency to be direct, clear, and immediate. An example of an assertive way to invite someone to socialize is the question, "Would you like to see a movie with me this weekend?"

In addition, assertive communication should include active listening to the other person's perspective (e.g., trying to hear and understand the other person's point of view, validating the other person's feelings, asking for clarification, etc.). Although assertive communication does not guarantee that you will get your way, compared to aggressive and passive styles of communication, assertive statements are more likely to keep the channels of communication open and to maximize the chances of reaching a mutually satisfactory resolution.

## *Dealing Assertively with Conflict Situations*

If your goal is to convince someone else to change his or her behavior, an appropriate way of doing that is to make sure that your message is neither passive nor aggressive. Instead, you should try to communicate your message in a way that is factual, direct, and empathic.

Begin by describing your observations regarding the situation. Observations reflect your perspective regarding the facts, rather than your interpretations of those facts. Observations should be based on reality, and therefore are usually very difficult to argue with. For example, "You arrived home too late" is not an observation because whether the person's arrival is "too" late is open to interpretation. However, the statement "You arrived home an hour later than you said you would" is an observation (assuming it is true) and is therefore less likely to lead to a defensive response from the other person.

After describing your observations, the next step is to describe you feelings about the situation. Feelings are emotions such as anger, anxiety, worry, and sadness. Feelings are not thoughts. For example, the statement "I feel that you should not be late" is not really a feeling statement. In contrast, "I feel hurt and worried when you arrive home later than you say you will" is a feeling statement. As is the case with communicating your observations, it is difficult to argue with a feeling statement. Only you know how you really feel.

Finally, it is important to communicate the ways in which you would like things to change. To follow the earlier example through, you might say, "I would like you to phone me if you are going to be more than thirty minutes late."

After you communicate your message in terms of these three components, you need to make sure that you give the other individual a chance to express his or her perspective on the situation. Make sure you take advantage of the active listening skills that were discussed earlier in this chapter.

In addition to the basic assertiveness skills described earlier, there are a number of other strategies that may help you to deal with conflict situations:

- Make sure that you choose an appropriate time to talk about the situation. Don't put it off indefinitely. On the other hand, don't talk about the issue during the height of your anger. Also, don't insist that the issue be discussed right away if the other person is busy or unwilling to discuss the issue. Sometimes it is best to schedule a meeting at a mutually convenient time and to discuss the matter then.

- Make sure that you challenge the beliefs that contribute to your anxiety, anger, or hurt feelings. As discussed in chapter 6, our feelings are influenced by our beliefs, and our beliefs may be exaggerated or unrealistic at times. In other words, the situation may not matter as much as you think it does. When discussing the situation with the other person, try to maintain your cool by thinking about the situation realistically.

- Before confronting a situation, decide whether it is worth it. Is it a situation that matters? Will it take care of itself, even if you don't say anything? For example, if your difficult neighbor is moving away next week, perhaps it is not important to complain about the way he or she maintains the lawn.

- Try bouncing your thoughts off a neutral third party. Hearing another person's views regarding the issue may help you to see things in a different way. This can be particularly useful to determine whether your expectations regarding the situation are distorted.

- Try to understand the other person's perspective. Like you, the other individual is just trying to survive the best way that he/she can. Hostility and anger often are triggered by feelings of threat or hurt. If you develop an empathic understanding of the other person's perspective and beliefs, you will have a greater chance of finding a compromise and resolving the conflict, particularly if the other person can see that you are genuinely trying to understand.

- Consider writing a letter to the other person. Sometimes it is easier to communicate your thoughts and feelings in writing. However, even in a letter, you should use an assertive communication style rather than a passive or aggressive one.

- If you want to learn more about dealing with difficult people, we recommend that you do some additional reading on how to deal with conflict situations. For example, the book *The Complete Idiot's Guide to Getting Along with Difficult People* (Toropov 1997) has hundreds of ideas for how to get along with difficult people in a broad range of contexts, including dealing with coworkers, a difficult boss, nasty neighbors, strangers in public places, and other people that you may encounter from day to day (e.g., store clerks, repair people, restaurant servers).

# Meeting New People, Making Friends, and Dating

This section describes ways of improving the skills that are important for meeting new people and developing new relationships. The topics covered include suggestions for where to meet new people and ways to deal with certain stresses associated with developing relationships, such as the possibility of being rejected.

## Places to Meet New People

In a survey of more than 3,000 Americans, Laumann, Gagnon, Michael, and Michaels (1994) studied the ways and places in which people meet. Among married people, the ways that individuals met their spouses are shown by percentages as follows:

| Way of Meeting | Percent* |
| --- | --- |
| Introduction by a friend | 35% |
| Introduction by self | 32% |
| Introduction by a family member | 15% |
| Introduction by a coworker | 6% |
| Introduction by a classmate | 6% |
| Introduction by someone else | 2% |
| Introduction by a neighbor | 1% |

*Note: the numbers do not add up to 100 percent because a small number of people gave multiple answers.

In the same survey, the places that married individuals met their spouses were broken down into percentages as follows:

| Location of Meeting | Percent |
| --- | --- |
| School | 23% |
| Work | 15% |
| Party | 10% |
| Place of worship (e.g., church) | 8% |
| Bar | 8% |
| Gym or social club | 4% |
| Personal ad | 1% |
| Vacation | 1% |
| Elsewhere | 30% |

The statistics were similar for people in unmarried partnerships (e.g., couples cohabiting, couples in long-term partnerships, and couples in short-term partnerships), although some of the numbers were different in these other groups. For example, compared to married people, unmarried individuals in short-term relationships were more likely to have met their partners at a bar (17%) or a party (25%), and less likely to have met them at a place of worship (1%).

In addition to these places, there are many other locations in which it is relatively easy to develop new friendships or to meet a potential partner. Some examples include the following: through a hobby (e.g., joining a photography club or a theater group), getting involved in a sport (joining a bowling league, a running club, or a hiking group), getting in shape (e.g., lifting weights in a gym, joining an aerobics class, taking swimming lessons), taking dance classes, volunteering for an organization, forming a book club or reading group, attending public lectures, taking a part-time job, enrolling in an adult education course, or traveling (e.g., with a group).

The best way to meet new people is to do the things that you enjoy doing. That way, you are likely to meet people who enjoy the same things you do. For example, if you don't enjoy drinking alcohol or spending time in bars, you should think twice about trying to meet people in bars. Clearly, at a bar, you are likely to meet those people who enjoy going to bars. You should also keep in mind the types of people you are likely to meet by getting involved in a particular activity. For example, if you want to meet people close to your own age, try to get involved in activities that attract people in your age group.

It is not enough just to be around other people. To *meet* other people, it will be necessary to take interpersonal risks in the situation. For openers, you should maintain eye contact, make a point of saying hello, and be sure to smile from time to time. Casual contact is more likely to develop into a friendship or relationship if you purposely engage in conversation. Furthermore, as you get to know someone, you must take bigger risks such as asking that person to meet you for coffee, go to a movie, or join you for a day's outing to a park or a museum.

## Dating Skills

There are several excellent published guides to dating, a number of which are listed in the recommended readings at the end of the book. One of our favorites is the *Unofficial Guide to Dating Again* by Tina Tessina (1998). Although the book is written for people who are just starting to date again after a long period of not dating (e.g., perhaps following a divorce or the breakup of a long-term relationship), the book is appropriate for anyone who is interested in suggestions regarding all aspects of dating.

Regardless of how it may seem, there are lots of available partners out there, regardless of whether you are old or young, male or female. Furthermore, the idea that there is only one person out there who is your soul mate, is a myth. There are many different people who are potentially excellent partners, each having very different qualities to bring to a relationship. Although it may sound like a cliché, it is often true that someone comes along when you least expect it, and often it occurs when you are not even looking. So relax. Rushing the process can lead to feelings of disappointment or failure when a hoped-for relationship doesn't work out.

## Preparation

The first step in dating is *preparation*. What does preparation in this context mean? It means you must know what you are looking for. What is the purpose of your search? Are you looking for a serious relationship, marriage and children? Or are you looking for a sexual partner? Companionship? A way to alleviate boredom? The purpose of the relationship will influence what kind of person you will seek and/or attract. For example, if you are looking for excitement, someone who is aloof, mysterious, and gorgeous may be exactly what you are looking for. On the other hand, if you are looking for a more serious relationship, you should choose to emphasize qualities that will continue to be important to you after the thrill of a new relationship wears off, like a sense of humor, shared values, kindness, honesty, stability, responsibility, and respect.

Despite the saying "opposites attract," the cliché "birds of a feather flock together" is probably closer to the truth. Generally, research in social psychology has found that people are most attracted to others who are similar to them with respect to values, appearance, interests, and other attributes. Being aware of your own interests and attributes will help you to know what you are looking for in another person. In addition, being the type of person whom you would like to meet will help you to attract that person. To meet the right person, you need to make a point of being in places where that person is likely to be. For example, if you are interested in meeting someone who loves reading, then make a point of spending time in the library, visiting bookstores, or attending book signings.

## Networking

One very helpful activity for meeting new people is called networking. That is defined as the exchange of information or services among individuals or groups. As shown in the tables above, most people are introduced to their spouses by a third person. Therefore, let your friends and family know that you are interested in meeting someone. If nothing romantic develops, you may add to your circle of friends. By adding new friends (without actually giving up on old friendships), you will increase your chances of finding a partner.

## Personal Ads

Some people have had great success with personal ads, including those in newspapers, telephone personal ad services, and on the Internet. Dating services may also provide you with opportunities to meet new people. If you choose to meet people through these routes, be sure to be cautious before meeting the individual. Initially, get to know the person over the phone. Be sure to get together in a public place the first time you meet. Arrange a short first meeting (e.g., for coffee or tea) so you can leave early if it doesn't work out. Although meetings through personal ads, dating services, and blind dates often do not work out, some great relationships have started this way. Also, using these services may provide you with opportunities to work on your basic communication and dating skills, confront anxiety-provoking social situations, and learn more about the qualities that are important to you regarding a potential partner. The book *25 Words or Less: How to Write Like a Pro to Find That Special Someone Through Personal Ads* (Calvo and Minsky 1998) provides excellent ideas for developing your own personal ad.

### First Dates

When you do meet someone who interests you, the initial "date" can be quite informal. For example, you might go for a walk during a break at work, run an errand together between classes, or offer the individual a ride home. After you have had more contact with that person, you could suggest a more formal outing, like going out for lunch or dinner, seeing a concert or movie, or visiting a gallery or museum. If you are a student, you might suggest taking a class with the other person, to increase your chances of having repeated contact.

On your date, pay attention to small details, especially your physical appearance and hygiene. Dress appropriately for the situation. Wear clothes you like, but err on the side of conservative or classic fashions if you are unsure about the other person's taste. In other words, don't wear your most outrageous outfit on a first date.

### Rejection

Be prepared for rejection. Much more often than not, a particular dating situation does not lead to a long-term relationship. It is normal for one individual to be more interested in pursuing a relationship than the other person is. If the other individual ends up not wanting to continue the relationship, make sure that you keep the rejection in perspective (see chapter 6 for suggestions). A rejection does not mean that there is something wrong with you or that going out on dates will never lead to a long-term relationship. Rather, rejection speaks more to the fit between you and the specific person with whom things didn't work out. Experiencing some form of rejection is a necessary part of dating. The more dating experiences that you seek out, the more rejection you will experience. Nevertheless, increasing the frequency of your dates will also provide opportunities to improve your dating skills and increase the likelihood of developing a positive relationship in the future.

# Presentations and Public Speaking Skills

This section provides a basic primer on public speaking and giving presentations. In particular, it includes suggestions for preparing for presentations or talks and describes ways to improve the quality of your presentations.

For a more detailed treatment of this topic, we suggest that you look through the recommended readings on public speaking at the end of this book and read one or more of them. Although the emphasis in most of these books is on business presentations, many of the skills suggested apply to other types of presentations as well, such as giving a speech at a wedding or party. In addition to providing suggestions for how to organize and deliver presentations, most of these recommended books also provide ideas for managing anxiety during presentations.

## Preparing for Presentations

Preparing for presentations involves seven important steps: (1) identifying the purpose of the presentation, (2) determining the nature of the audience, (3) deciding the subject matter, (4) organizing the presentation, (5) making your talk interesting, (6) compiling supporting materials, (7) rehearsing the presentation, and (8) managing your anxiety.

1. **Determining the purpose of the presentation.** Before preparing a lecture or speech, you must first be clear about the purpose of the presentation. Essentially, presentations can have one or more of the following functions:

   - **To persuade:** For example, a presentation may be designed to sell a particular product or to convince a group of coworkers to change a procedure in the workplace.

   - **To explain:** Examples include a half-day orientation meeting to explain company procedures to new employees, a lecture designed to teach a complex topic to a class of college students, or a seminar to provide in-depth information to colleagues about a particular subject.

   - **To instruct:** These may include presentations regarding how to perform a task (e.g., how to use a new computer program) or how to develop a new skill (e.g., learning to dance).

   - **To brief:** Some presentations are designed to brief an audience regarding some matter. For example, this may include a three- or four-minute presentation to update management about the status of union negotiations, or to brief your customers about changes in the price of a product.

   - **To entertain:** Examples of presentations designed to entertain include theatrical presentations (e.g., stand-up comedy) and sometimes speeches at weddings, anniversaries, or parties.

2. **Determining the nature of the audience.** Before planning a presentation in detail, it is helpful to know something about the nature of your audience. In some cases, you may even need to ask the audience questions about their background at the start of the presentation and adapt your style or content to meet their needs. Some questions that are helpful to answer include the following:

   - How big is the audience?

- What is the likely composition of the audience (e.g., age, gender, professional background)?

- What is the audience expecting?

- How much does the audience already know? What do they still need to learn?

- Why is the audience attending the presentation (e.g., because they have to versus because they want to)?

3. **Deciding the subject matter.** Before giving your presentation, you should have an idea of the main message that you want to convey. In most cases, the main point of the presentation should be simple and clear. The audience should be aware of the key points that you wish to make, so that the content of the presentation can be understood in the proper context. In most cases, it is helpful to pique the group's interest (perhaps with a joke, anecdote, or illustration) early in the talk. If the purpose of your presentation is to persuade the audience regarding some matter, you should ensure that you have gained their confidence (e.g., by making the members of the audience aware of your expertise and credentials). A persuasive presentation should also include specific instructions on how to implement the suggestions you provide (e.g., where to obtain the product you are selling).

4. **Organizing the presentation.** One of the most common suggestions made to people who prepare presentations is to pay close attention to the three phases of the talk: the introduction, the main body of the talk, and the conclusion. The *introduction* should include an overview of the presentation so that audience members know what to expect. The *main body* of the presentation is where you discuss the main content of the talk with all of the important details. At the *conclusion*, you should provide a brief summary, as well as some interpretations and inferences regarding the content (e.g., why the presentation was important).

    If possible, your presentation should be organized so that it tells a story, i.e., think of it as a narrative. For example, before describing a new method of performing some task, you might provide the audience with a history of how that particular task has been performed in the past, so they have a context in which to understand the new information. Or, the presentation can be laid out so that a series of problems are described, each followed by one or more solutions.

5. **Making the presentation interesting.** In addition to making sure your main points are conveyed to the audience, it is important that they are conveyed in a way that is interesting. Strategies that should be considered include these: humor, analogies, personal stories, examples, illustrations, and relevant statistics. Be careful not to use humor that could offend any audience members. You never know who is in your audience

and whether their backgrounds, beliefs, or experiences might cause them to take a joke the wrong way. Another strategy is to involve the audience members in some way. For example, you might ask them questions, or encourage them to ask you questions during your presentation. Or you could have them do something (e.g., demonstrate the skill you are trying to teach, complete a survey or take a test etc.). Supporting materials (discussed below) can be another useful way to bring your presentation to life.

6. **Supporting materials**. Supporting materials often take the form of visuals (e.g., videotapes, blackboards, white boards, flip charts, slides, CD ROMs, computer-generated presentations, overheads). These visuals can include text, photos, illustrations, cartoons, graphics, and maps. Here are a few suggestions to keep in mind regarding supporting materials:

   - If you are going to use cartoons, make sure they are funny. Ask some friends, family members, or coworkers for their opinions about the cartoons you intend to use.

   - In some cases, it may be helpful to have props. For example, if you mention particular books in your presentation, have copies with you for audience members to look at. If you are describing a product, bring it with you and display it during the presentation.

     If possible, provide handouts containing copies of your slides and overheads so that audience members can listen to you instead of having to take notes. Audience members appreciate getting handouts.

   - Make sure that your slides and overheads are attractive and that the type is large enough to be seen from the back of the room.

   - Avoid the temptation to have too much information on your slides and overheads.

7. **Rehearsing the presentation.** If at all possible, rehearse your presentation beforehand. There are several ways of rehearsing. Ideally, you can rehearse in front of an audience of friends, family, or coworkers, preferably in a location similar to where the actual talk will be held. Ask your rehearsal audience for feedback and make changes to the presentation accordingly. If you cannot rehearse in front of a live audience, try rehearsing in front of a video camera or camcorder and watch the tape afterward. If that is not possible, practice out loud in front of a mirror. As you become more experienced in giving presentations, practicing beforehand will become less important.

8. **Managing your anxiety.** Preparing for a presentation should also include strategies for managing your anxiety. Before the presentation, make sure that you have used the cognitive strategies (chapter 6) to challenge your anxious thoughts. In addition, make use of the exposure-based strategies

(chapters 7 through 9) to confront your fears whenever possible. When you are actually in the situation, make sure that your breathing is slow and regular. Overbreathing or holding your breath will increase your anxiety symptoms. Do not fight your fear. Just let the symptoms happen. Fighting your fear is likely to cause anxiety symptoms to intensify. It is okay to be nervous during a presentation. In fact, audience members often expect it. In fact, sometimes, it is helpful to tell the audience you are feeling nervous. Saying so may help you to calm down and it very likely will help to win the audience over to your side.

## Delivering the Presentation

Here are a list of suggestions to keep in mind when you are giving a presentation.

- Pay attention to the way you deliver your speech. Before the talk, check any pronunciations you are not sure about. Make sure that your voice does not drop off at the end of your sentences. To be sure you are projecting at a reasonable volume, imagine you are delivering your speech to the back wall of the room. Speak crisply and pronounce your words clearly. Avoid saying "uh" and "um." Finally, avoid speaking too quickly. Going too fast is one of the most common mistakes people make during presentations, particularly when they are feeling anxious.

- Make eye contact with the audience members during the talk.

- Try to move around when you are speaking. Walk around the front of the room rather than staying planted at a podium. Don't put your hands in your pockets. Instead, gesture with your hands to emphasize key points. However, keep your hands away from your face.

- Presentations are often less interesting when they are read verbatim. If you read a presentation word for word, you also run the risk of panicking if you lose your place. Instead, we recommend speaking from a detailed outline with lots of headings, bullets, etc. An outline will make sure that all the information you need is available and easy to access, even if you lose your place. It will also force you to be somewhat spontaneous during the presentation. If the thought of not reading your speech is too scary, another option is to bring both an outline version and a fully written version. If necessary, you can switch to reading your presentation if using the outline alone doesn't work.

- Don't talk down to your audience. They probably know more than you think they do. Even if the material is new to them, they will not appreciate being talked to like children (unless, of course, they are children!). Make sure your tone of voice and the things you say are not condescending.

- Repeat the main points of the presentation frequently. Audience members will not hear everything you say, and if they miss an important point you may lose them for the rest of the presentation, unless the important points are repeated.

- Keep it simple. Don't try to discuss more than your time allows.

- Make sure you are prepared to handle questions. Consider bringing additional information (e.g., a reference book, notes, etc.) that may be needed to answer certain types of questions. No matter how silly a question is, try to answer it tactfully and show respect for the person who asked the question (e.g., "that's an interesting question . . ."). Finally, repeat all audience questions before you answer them. Chances are good that people in the back of the room will not be able to hear some of the questions the first time they are asked.

- Be yourself during the talk. Audiences prefer a speaker who is down to earth and genuine rather than someone who looks as if he or she is trying too hard to be entertaining or to impress the audience.

## After the Presentation

Following your presentation, it is helpful to evaluate the quality of your performance, basing your evaluation on whether you followed the suggestions provided in this chapter. Don't base your self-evaluation on whether you were anxious during the presentation or whether your anxiety symptoms showed. The presenter's anxiety or lack thereof is only one small aspect of what makes an effective presentation.

Social anxiety is associated with the tendency to be an overly harsh critic of one's own performance. Therefore, we suggest that you obtain objective feedback from your audience members as well. This can be done informally by asking people what they thought of the talk. Or, if appropriate, it can be done more formally by handing out an anonymous evaluation form that requires audience members to rate their impressions of certain aspects of the presentation. In addition, make sure to include space on the form for audience members to write their impressions (strengths of the presentation, areas for improvement) in their own words. Here is an example of a form that can be used to evaluate presentations that you give:

# Presentation Evaluation Form

Speaker: _____    Date: _____

Topic: _____

Please circle the number that best describes your opinion about the presentation. On this scale from 1 to 5, circle (1) for a "poor" evaluation, (5) for an "excellent" evaluation, and (3) for a "neutral" response.

|  | Poor | Neutral | | | Excellent |
|---|---|---|---|---|---|
| (a) Format of presentation was conducive to learning | 1 | 2 | 3 | 4 | 5 |
| (b) Content seemed relevant | 1 | 2 | 3 | 4 | 5 |
| (c) Content was interesting | 1 | 2 | 3 | 4 | 5 |
| (d) Content was at an appropriate level of difficulty | 1 | 2 | 3 | 4 | 5 |
| (e) Content extended my knowledge about the topic | 1 | 2 | 3 | 4 | 5 |
| (f) Presentation skills of presenter | 1 | 2 | 3 | 4 | 5 |
| (g) Lecturer seemed knowledgeable | 1 | 2 | 3 | 4 | 5 |
| (h) Concepts were clearly explained | 1 | 2 | 3 | 4 | 5 |
| (i) Comfortable location (e.g., lighting, temperature) | 1 | 2 | 3 | 4 | 5 |
| (j) Use of audiovisual resources | 1 | 2 | 3 | 4 | 5 |
| (k) Quality of handouts | 1 | 2 | 3 | 4 | 5 |
| (l) Overall rating of presentation | 1 | 2 | 3 | 4 | 5 |

**Comments and Suggestions for Improvement**

_____

_____

_____

_____

_____

_____

# Chapter 11

# Maintaining Your Improvements and Planning for the Future

The purpose of this final chapter is to discuss strategies for ensuring that the gains you have made so far are maintained over the coming months and years. Perhaps the most important suggestion we can offer is that you should continue to use the strategies described in the first ten chapters. Continuing to use approaches that were helpful in getting you to where you are now will ensure that you maintain your gains and that your anxiety continues to decrease over time.

## Why Does Fear Return and What You Can Do About It

Most people who receive treatment for social anxiety experience long-lasting improvements in their anxiety, particularly following cognitive and behavioral treatment. Nevertheless, there are a number of different reasons why fear may return for some individuals. If your fear returns, the best thing to do is to resume using the strategies that were most helpful to you the first time you overcame your fear. Social anxiety that comes back some time after improving is often easier to overcome the second time around.

## Discontinuing the Treatment Strategies Too Early or Too Quickly

Discontinuing your cognitive therapy and exposure practices may increase the likelihood of experiencing a return of fear, particularly if you stop using these techniques before you have completely overcome your fear. We recommend that you continue to challenge your anxious thoughts from time to time for as long as you continue to feel anxious. When your fear has decreased significantly, you can stop using the cognitive diaries. However, you should continue to use the cognitive techniques informally, by silently asking yourself appropriate questions (e.g., is there some other, nonanxious way of interpreting this situation?).

In addition, you should take advantage of opportunities to expose yourself to previously feared situations even after your fear has been reduced. Sometimes, life circumstances (e.g., being busy at work or school, recovering from the flu) make it hard to practice exposure on a regular basis. Whenever possible, from time to time try to confront your feared situations.. Occasional exposures will help to prevent your fear from returning.

Stopping medication too early may also increase the risk of your anxiety returning. As discussed in chapter 5, relapse following discontinuation from treatment with antidepressants is believed to be less likely when treatment has continued for six months to a year, or longer. So, it is best not to stop medication treatment the moment you start to feel better.

Coming off medication suddenly may also increase the risk of your fear returning. Discontinuation from some antidepressants, and from almost all antianxiety medications, is associated with symptoms of withdrawal, which often mimic the symptoms of anxiety. These withdrawal symptoms may prompt some people to resume their old habits of avoidance and fearful thinking. The best way of preventing withdrawal symptoms following discontinuation from medication is to reduce the dosage very slowly over time. We strongly recommend that you not reduce or stop your medication without first consulting with your doctor.

## Life Stresses

Sometimes, an increase in the stress in your life can lead to a return of anxiety and fear. For example, if you experience a stressful life event (e.g., increased hours at work, relationship problems, financial difficulties, health problems, family tensions, death of a close friend), you may find that your anxiety in social situations gets worse. Sometimes, this worsening of anxiety occurs while the stress is ongoing; other times it may occur shortly after the stress has subsided.

The relationship between stress and increased social anxiety is not surprising. Most people respond to stress in characteristic ways. Some tend to respond physically by experiencing more colds, headaches, increased blood pressure, and other physical ailments. Others may fall into bad habits, such as smoking more, increasing alcohol or caffeine consumption, eating unhealthy foods, or exercising less. Still others may respond emotionally, by becoming more anxious, depressed, or irritable. If your natural pattern has been to experience anxiety in social situations, stress may cause some of your old responses to resurface.

Stress tends to increase a person's arousal level, so breathing becomes heavier, heart rate increases, and other symptoms of arousal become more pronounced. When you are under stress, it doesn't take much change in your anxiety level for the feeling to become more noticeable than usual. Situations that are normally okay may seem overwhelming when you are experiencing other stresses in your life.

Most of the time, the increase in social anxiety following stress is temporary; when the stress improves, the anxiety decreases again. However, if you respond to your increased anxiety by falling back into your old habits of anxious thinking and avoidance behaviors, you may find that the increased social anxiety continues, even after the stress has passed. If your anxiety returns following a stressful life event, the best thing to do is to reread the relevant sections of this book and resume using some of the strategies that you found helpful the first time around.

## Encountering a New and Unexpectedly Difficult Situation

Although you may think you have overcome a particular fear, it is possible that some fear remains, but that you just haven't had a chance to encounter a sufficiently challenging situation until now. One of our clients was recently surprised to experience intense fear while unexpectedly having to give a toast at his father's birthday party. He had worked very hard to overcome his fear of public speaking at work. After a few months of practice, he found he could speak comfortably in meetings and he even gave long presentations to groups of 200 or more with almost no fear.

One day, he was asked on the spur of the moment to make a toast at his father's birthday party to about thirty friends and relatives whom he had known for his whole life. This made him very nervous. Although he had successfully overcome his fear of speaking in formal work situations, he had never had the opportunity to speak in front of an informal and personal situation like a family party. For him, giving a toast in front of friends and relatives was actually a new situation, which he hadn't had the chance to practice previously.

## Experiencing a Trauma in the Feared Situation

Sometimes, experiencing a "trauma" in a social situation may lead to a return of fear. For example, if your audience during a presentation is particularly cold and unfriendly, if you are rejected by someone whom you care about, or if your boss is extremely critical of your performance in a meeting, you may find that the next time you return to the situation that you are more anxious. The fact that you had a particular fear in the past, makes it more likely that your fear will return if you experience a negative event in the situation that was previously feared.

If you experience a negative event in a situation that you previously feared, the best thing to do is to return to the situation as soon as possible. If you begin to avoid the situation, your fear will be more likely to return. In addition to exposure, try challenging your anxious beliefs by considering alternative, nonanxious interpretations of the negative event you experienced.

# Preventing Your Fear from Returning

Although your fear is unlikely to return after you have learned to be more comfortable in social and performance situations, there are no guarantees. Nevertheless, there are a number of things that you can do to improve your chances of maintaining your gains.

## Continue to Use the Cognitive Therapy and Exposure Strategies

As discussed throughout this chapter, continuing to challenge your anxious thoughts informally and to practice exposure from time to time will help you to maintain the improvements that you have made so far. We also recommend that you reread relevant sections from this book occasionally to reinforce what you have learned and to make sure that you have not forgotten any important principles.

## Practice Exposure in a Range of Situations and Contexts

Your gains are likely to last longer if you practice exposure in a wide variety of situations and contexts. For example, if you are fearful of starting conversations, rather than practicing making conversation only at work, we recommend that you practice making conversation in other situations as well (e.g., at home, at parties, at the bus stop, in the elevator, etc.).

## Take Advantage of Opportunities to "Overlearn"

*Overlearning* involves (1) practicing exposure so many times that it becomes boring and second nature, and (2) practicing exposure in situations more difficult than those you encounter in your everyday life. For example, if a person with a spider phobia is fearful of seeing a spider on her wall, treatment should continue until she is comfortable having a spider crawling up her arm. If someone with a phobia of heights is fearful of eating dinner on his third floor balcony, exposure practices should continue until the individual can comfortably stand in much higher places (e.g., a twentieth-floor balcony).

Overlearning is thought to offer protection from experiencing a return of fear. There are several advantages of practicing exposure to more difficult situations than those you normally encounter. First, practicing in more challenging situations will automatically make the less challenging situations seem easier. Second, practices in difficult situations will further challenge your anxious beliefs. For example, if you learn that nothing bad happens even if you purposely make a big mistake during a presentation, you may become less fearful of accidentally making a small mistake when speaking in public. Finally, overlearning provides room for some of your fear to return, without causing significant impairment in your life.

## *Spread Out Your Exposure Practices Toward the End of Your Treatment*

Chapter 7 discusses the importance of making sure that your exposure practices are spaced close together to get the maximum benefit. After your fear has decreased, however, we recommend that you continue to practice exposure, but that you spread out your practices somewhat. There is some evidence (although more research is needed regarding this issue), that increasing the time between practices during the later phases of treatment decreases the likelihood of one's fear returning. So, if you have been practicing exposure to a particular situation several times a week, try spreading out the practices to once a week after your fear has improved. After several weeks of once-a-week practices, try spreading out the practices to once every few weeks.

Of course, this strategy will work only for situations that you don't encounter frequently in your daily life. If you have to attend meetings every day, we are not suggesting that you start to skip meetings just so you can spread out your practices.

# Where to Go for More Information

For those who want additional information on social anxiety and related topics, we have included more useful information at the back of the book. A list of recommended readings includes references for books, chapters, and articles on social anxiety, cognitive behavior therapy, and associated subjects. Readings are included both for lay people and professionals. We have also included a section filled with web sites and Internet addresses that have information on social anxiety and effective treatments. Finally, we have included a resource list of national organizations that provide information (including referrals to experienced therapists) to people who suffer from social anxiety and for professionals who have an interest in this topic.

We hope that you have found the strategies described in this book helpful. Chances are that you will need to continue to use the tools you have learned about for some time before experiencing a reduction in social anxiety that has a noticeable impact on your day-to-day life. We recommend that you reread the sections that were particularly useful or inspiring to you. Most of all, we wish you good luck as you learn to deal with stressful social situations with a new confidence that you have earned by your hard work.

# References

The American Psychiatric Association. *Diagnostic and Statistical Manual of Mental Disorders,* Fourth Edition (DSM-IV). 1994. Washington, DC.

Antony, M. M., and D. H. Barlow. 1996. Emotion theory as a framework for explaining panic attacks and panic disorder. In *Current Controversies in the Anxiety Disorders.* Edited by R. M. Rapee. New York: Guilford Publications.

———1997. In *Psychiatry.* Social and specific phobias. Edited by A. Tasman, gentlemen. Kay, and gentlemen. A. Lieberman. Philadelphia: W. B. Saunders company 1037–1059.

Antony, M. M., and R. P. Swinson. 1998. *When Perfect Isn't Good Enough: Strategies for Coping with Perfectionism.* Oakland, CA: New Harbinger Publications.

———. 2000. *Phobic Disorders and Panic in Adults: A Guide to Assessment and Treatment.* Washington, DC: American Psychological Association.

Antony, M. M., C. L. Purdon, V. Huta, and R. P. Swinson. 1998. Dimensions of perfectionism across the anxiety disorders. *Behaviour Research and Therapy* 36: 1143-1154.

Beck, A. T. 1963. Thinking and depression: 1. Idiosyncratic content and cognitive distortions. *Archives of General Psychiatry* 9:324-333.

———. 1964. Thinking and depression: 2. Theory and therapy. *Archives of General Psychiatry* 10:561-571.

———. 1967. *Depression: Causes and Treatment.* Philadelphia: University of Pennsylvania Press.

————. 1976. *Cognitive Therapy of the Emotional Disorders.* New York: New American Library.

Beck, A. T., Emery, G., and R. L. Greenberg. 1985. *Anxiety Disorders and Phobias: A Cognitive Perspective.* New York: Basic Books

Beidel, D. C., and S. M. Turner. 1998. *Shy Children, Phobic Adults: Nature and Treatment of Social Phobia.* Washington, D C: American Psychological Association.

Bolton, R. 1979. *People Skills.* New York: Simon & Schuster.

Briggs, S. R. 1988. Shyness: Introversion or neuroticism? *Journal of Research in Personality* 22:290-307.

Burns, D. D. 1999. *The Feeling Good Handbook, Revised Edition.* New York: Plume.

Calvo, E. T., and L. Minsky. 1998. *25 Words or Less: How to Write Like a Pro to Find That Special Someone Through Personal Ads.* Lincolnwood (Chicago), IL: Contemporary Books.

Carducci, B. J., and P. G. Zimbardo. 1995. Are you shy? *Psychology Today,* November/December, 34–82.

Chambless, D. L., and E. J. Gracely. 1989. Fear of fear and the anxiety disorders. *Cognitive Therapy and Research* 13:9–20.

Cheek, J. M., and A. K. Watson. 1989. The definition of shyness: Psychological imperialism or construct validity? *Journal of Social Behavior and Personality* 4: 85-95.

Davidson, J. R. T., and K. M. Connor. 2000. *Herbs for the Mind: What Science Tells Us About Nature's Remedies for Depression, Stress, Memory Loss and Insomnia.* New York: Guilford Publications.

Davidson, J. R. T., N. Potts, E. Richichi, R. Krishnan, S. M. Ford, R. Smith, et al. 1993. Treatment of social phobia with clonazepam and placebo. *Journal of Clinical Psychopharmacology* 13:423–428.

Ellis, A. 1962. *Reason and Emotion in Psychotherapy.* Secaucus, NJ: Lyle Stuart.

————. 1989. The history of cognition in psychotherapy. In *Comprehensive Handbook of Cognitive Therapy,* edited by A. Freeman, K. M. Simon, L. E. Beutler, and H. Arkowitz. New York: Plenum Press.

————. 1993. Changing the name of rational emotive therapy (RET) to rational emotive behavior therapy (REBT). *The Behavior Therapist* 16:257-258.

Emmelkamp, P. M. G., and H. Wessels. 1975. Flooding in imagination vs. flooding in vivo: A comparison with agoraphobics. *Behaviour Research and Therapy* 13:7-15.

Garner, A. 1997. *Conversationally Speaking: Testing New Ways to Increase Your Personal and Social Effectiveness,* Third Edition. Los Angeles, CA: Lowell House.

Gelernter, C. S., T. W. Uhde, P. Cimbolic, D. B. Arnkoff, B. J. Vittone, and M. E. Tancer. 1991. Cognitive-behavioral and pharmacological treatments of social phobia: A controlled study. *Archives of General Psychiatry* 48:938-945.

Gould, R. A., S. Buckminster, M. H. Pollack, M. W. Otto, and L. Yap. 1997. Cognitive-behavioral and pharmacological treatment for social phobia: A meta-analysis. *Clinical Psychology: Science and Practice* 4:291-306.

Greenberger, D., and C. A. Padesky. 1995. *Mind Over Mood: A Cognitive Therapy Treatment Manual for Clients*. New York: Guilford Press.

Hartley, L. R., S. Ungapen, I. Dovie, and D. J. Spencer. 1983. The effect of beta-adrenergic blocking drugs on speakers' performance and memory. *British Journal of Psychiatry* 142:512-517.

Heimberg, R. G., M. R. Liebowitz, D. A. Hope, F. R. Schneier, C. S. Holt, L. A. Welkowitz, et al. 1998. Cognitive-behavioural group treatment versus phenelzine in social phobia: 12 week outcome. *Archives of General Psychiatry* 55:1133-1141.

Henderson, L., and P. Zimbardo. 1999. Shyness. In *Encyclopedia of Mental Health*. Edited by H. S. Friedman. San Diego, CA: Academic Press.

Hope, D. A., R. G. Heimberg, H. R. Juster, and C. L. Turk. 2000. *Managing Social Anxiety*. San Antonio, TX: The Psychological Corporation.

James, I. M., W. Burgoyne, and I. T. Savage. 1983. Effect of pindolol on stress-related disturbances of musical performance: preliminary communication. *Journal of the Royal Society of Medicine* 76:194-196.

Kessler R. C., K. A. McGonagle, S. Zhao, C. B. Nelson, M. Hughes, S. Eshleman, H. U. Wittchen, and K. Kendler. 1994. Lifetime and 12-month prevalence of DSM-III-R psychiatric disorders in the United States: Results from the National Comorbidity Survey. *Archives of General Psychiatry* 51:8-19.

King, R. J., I. N. Mefford, and C. Wang. 1986. CSF dopamine levels correlate with extraversion in depressed patients. *Psychiatric Research* 19:305-310.

Laumann, E.O., J. H. Gagnon, R. T. Michael, and S. Michaels. 1994. *The Social Organization of Sexuality: Sexual Practices in the United States*. Chicago, IL: University of Chicago Press.

Lazarus, P. J. 1982. Incidence of shyness in elementary-school age children. *Psychological Reports* 51:904-906.

Lewis, M. H., J. Gariepy, and L. L. Devaud. 1989. Dopamine and social behavior: A mouse model of "timidity." Paper presented at the meeting of the American College of Neuropsychopharmacology, Maui, Hawaii. December.

McKay, M., M. Davis, and P. Fanning. 1995. *Messages: The Communication Skills Book*, Second Edition. Oakland, CA: New Harbinger Publications.

Meichenbaum, D. H. 1977. *Cognitive Behavior Modification: An Integrative Approach*. New York: Plenum Press.

Mulkens, S., P. J. de Jong, A. Dobbelaar, and S. M. Bögels. 1999. Fear of blushing: Fearful preoccupation irrespective of facial coloration. *Behaviour Research and Therapy*, 37:1119-1128.

Nesse, R. M., and G. C. Williams. 1994. *Why We Get Sick: The New Science of Darwinian Medicine*. New York: Vintage Books.

Plomin, R. 1989. Environment and genes: Determinants of behavior. *American Psychologist* 44:105-111.

Safren, S. A., R. G. Heimberg, and H. R. Juster. 1997. Clients' expectancies and their relationship to pretreatment symptomatology and outcome of cognative-behavioral group treatment for social phobia. *Journal of Consulting and Clinical Psychology* 65:694-698.

Schmidt, L. A. 1999. Frontal brain electrical activity in shyness and sociability. *Psychological Science* 10:316-320.

Schmidt, L. A., and J. Schulkin, eds. 1999. *Extreme Fear, Shyness, and Social Phobia: Origins, Biological Mechanisms, and Clinical Outcomes*. New York: Oxford University Press.

Stein, M. B., J. R. Walker, and D. R. Forde. 1994. Setting diagnostic thresholds for social phobia: Considerations from a community survey of social anxiety. *American Journal of Psychiatry* 151:408-412.

Stein, M. B., M. J. Chartier, A. L. Hazen, M. V Kozak, M. E. Tancer, S. Lander, P. Furer, D. Chubaty, and J. R. Walker. 1998. A direct-interview family study of generalized social phobia. *American Journal of Psychiatry* 155:90-97.

Suls, J., and T. A. Wills. 1991. *Social Comparison: Contemporary Theory and Research*. Hillsdale, New Jersey: Erlbaum.

Tancer, M. E. 1993. Neurobiology of social phobia. *Journal of Clinical Psychiatry* 54 (Suppl 12):26-30.

Tancer, M. E., R. B. Mailman, M. B. Stein, G. A. Mason, S. W. Carson, and R. N. Golden. 1994/1995. Neuroendocrine responsivity to monoaminergic system probes in generalized social phobia. *Anxiety* 1:216-213.

Taylor, S., W. J. Koch, and R. J. McNally. 1992. How does anxiety sensitivity vary across the anxiety disorders? *Journal of Anxiety Disorders* 6:249-259.

Tessina, T. 1998. *The Unofficial Guide to Dating Again*. New York: Macmillan.

*Toronto Star*. October 10, 1998. "Born to Be Bashful." L1, L2.

Toropov, B. 1997. *The Complete Idiot's Guide to Getting Along with Difficult People*. New York: Alpha Books.

Widiger, T. A. 1992. Generalized social phobia versus avoidant personality disorder: A commentary on three studies. *Journal of Abnormal Psychology* 101: 340-343.

Wong, A. H. C., M. Smith, and H. S. Boon. 1998. Herbal remedies in psychiatric practice. *Archives of General Psychiatry* 55:1033-1044.

Zimbardo, P. G., P. A. Pilkonis, and R. M. Norwood. 1975. The social disease of shyness. *Psychology Today* 8:68-72.

# Additional Recommended Readings

## Social Anxiety: Self-Help Books

Carducci, B. J. 2000. *Shyness: A Bold New Approach*. New York: HarperCollins.

Desberg, P. 1996. *No More Butterflies: Overcoming Shyness, Stage Fright, Interview Anxiety, and Fear of Public Speaking*. Oakland, CA: New Harbinger Publications.

Markway, B. G., C. N. Carmin, C. A. Pollard, and T. Flynn. 1992. *Dying of Embarrassment: Help for Social Anxiety and Phobia*. Oakland, CA: New Harbinger Publications.

Rapee, R. M. 1998. *Overcoming Shyness and Social Phobia: A Step-by-Step Guide*. Northvale, NJ: Jason Aronson.

Schneier, F., and L. Welkowitz. 1996. *The Hidden Face of Shyness: Understanding and Overcoming Social Anxiety*. New York: Avon Books.

## Social and Communication Skills: Self-Help Books

### Dating and Meeting New People

Browne, J. 1997. *Dating for Dummies*. Foster City, CA: IDG Books Worldwide.

Burns, D. D. 1985. *Intimate Connections*. New York: Signet (Penguin Books).

Kuriansky, J. 1999. *The Complete Idiot's Guide to Dating*, Second Edition. New York: Alpha Books.

### Public Speaking and Presentations

Bowman, D. P. 1998. *Presentations: Proven Techniques for Creating Presentations That Get Results*. Holbrook, MA: Adams Media Corporation

Buchan, V. 1997. *Make Presentations with Confidence*, Second Edition. Hauppauge, NY: Barron's Educational Series.

Dickinson, S. 1998. *Effective Presentations*. London: Orion Business Books.

Kushner, M. 1996. *Successful Presentations for Dummies*. Foster City, CA: IDG Books Worldwide.

Morrisey, G. L., T. L. Sechrest, and W. B. Warman. 1997. *Loud and Clear: How to Prepare and Deliver Effective Business and Technical Presentations,* Fourth Edition. Reading, MA: Addison-Wesley.

### Other Communication Skills

Fleming, J. 1997. *Become Assertive!* Kent, United Kingdom: David Grant Publishing.

## Cognitive Behavioral Therapy and Related Topics: Self-Help Books

Bourne, E. J. 1995. *The Anxiety and Phobia Workbook*, Second Edition. Oakland, CA: New Harbinger Publications.

Butler, G., and T. Hope. 1995. *Managing Your Mind: The Mental Fitness Guide*. New York: Oxford University Press.

Copeland, M. E. 1992. *The Depression Workbook: A Guide for Living with Depression and Manic Depression*. Oakland, CA: New Harbinger Publications.

Davis, M., E. R. Eshelman, and M. McKay. 1995. *The Relaxation and Stress Reduction Workbook*, Fourth Edition. Oakland, CA: New Harbinger Publications.

Johnson, S. 1997. *Taking the Anxiety Out of Tests: A Step-By-Step Guide*. Oakland, CA: New Harbinger Publications.

McKay, M., M. Davis, and P. Fanning. 1997. *Thoughts and Feelings: Taking Control of Your Moods and Your Life,* Second Edition. Oakland, CA: New Harbinger Publications.

## Social Anxiety: Professional Readings

### Chapters and Review Papers

Antony, M. M. 1997. Assessment and Treatment of Social Phobia. *Canadian Journal of Psychiatry* 42:826-834.

Antony, M. M., and D. H. Barlow. 1997. Social and specific phobias. In *Psychiatry*. Edited by A. Tasman, J. Kay, and J. A. Lieberman. Philadelphia: W. B. Saunders Company.

Chambless, D. L., and D. A. Hope. 1996. Cognitive approaches to the psychopathology and treatment of social phobia. In *Frontiers of Cognitive Therapy*. Edited by P. M. Salkovskis. New York: Guilford Press.

Clark, D. M. 1997. Panic disorder and social phobia. In *Science and Practice of Cognitive Behaviour Therapy*. Edited by D. M. Clark and C. G. Fairburn. New York: Oxford University Press.

Hope, D. A., and R. G. Heimberg. 1993. Social phobia and social anxiety. In. *Clinical Handbook of Psychological Disorders*, Second Edition. Edited by D. H. Barlow. New York: Guilford Press.

Scholing, A., P. M. G. Emmelkamp, and P. Van Oppen. 1996. Cognitive-behavioral treatment of social phobia. In *Sourcebook of Psychological Treatment Manuals for Adult Disorders*. Edited by V. B. Van Hasselt and M. Hersen. New York: Plenum Press.

Turner, S.M., M. R. Cooley-Quille, and D. C. Beidel. 1996. Behavioral and pharmacological treatment for social phobia. In *Long-term Treatments of Anxiety Disorders*. Edited by M. R. Mavissakalian and R. F. Prien. Washington, DC: American Psychiatric Press.

### Books

Heimberg, R. G., M. R. Liebowitz, D. A. Hope, and F. R. Schneier, eds. 1995. *Social Phobia: Diagnosis, Assessment, and Treatment*. New York: Guilford Press.

Rapee, R. M., and W. C. Sanderson. 1998. *Social Phobia: Clinical Application of Evidence-based Psychotherapy*. Northvale, NJ: Jason Aronson.

Stein, M. B., ed. 1995. *Social Phobia: Clinical and Research Perspectives*. Washington, DC: American Psychiatric Press.

## *Anxiety Disorders and Cognitive Behavior Therapy: Professional Readings*

Andrews, G., R. Crino, C. Hunt, L. Lampe, and A. Page. 1994. *The Treatment of Anxiety Disorders: Clinician's Guide and Patient Manuals*. New York: Cambridge University Press.

Antony, M. M., S. M. Orsillo, and L. Roemer, eds. In press. *Practitioner's Guide to Empirically-based Measures of Anxiety*. New York: Kluwer Academic/ Plenum.

Barlow, D. H. 1988. *Anxiety and Its Disorders: The Nature and Treatment of Anxiety and Panic*. New York: Guilford Press.

Barlow, D. H., J. L. Esler, and A. E. Vitali. 1998. Psychosocial treatments for panic disorders, phobias, and generalized anxiety disorder. In *A Guide to Treatments*

*That Work*. Edited by P. E. Nathan and J. M. Gorman. New York: Oxford University Press.

Beck, J. S. 1995. *Cognitive Therapy: Basics and Beyond*. New York: Guilford Press.

Craske, M. G. 1999. *Anxiety Disorders: Psychological Approaches to Theory and Treatment*. Boulder, CO: Westview Press.

Persons, J. B. 1990. *Cognitive Therapy in Practice: A Case Formulation Approach*. New York: Norton.

Rapee, R. M., ed. 1996. *Current Controversies in the Anxiety Disorders*. New York: Guilford Press.

Roy-Byrne, P. P., and D. S. Cowley. 1998. Pharmacological treatment of panic, generalized anxiety, and phobic disorders. In *A Guide to Treatments That Work*. Edited by P. E. Nathan and J. M. Gorman. New York: Oxford University Press.

Salkovskis, P. M., ed. 1996. *Frontiers of Cognitive Therapy*. New York: Guilford Press.

Wells, A. 1997. *Cognitive Therapy of Anxiety Disorders: A Practice Manual and Conceptual Guide*. New York: John Wiley and Sons.

## Video Resources

Padesky, C. *Guided Discovery Using Socratic Dialogue* (videotape). Oakland, CA: New Harbinger Publications.

———. *Testing Automatic Thoughts with Thought Records* (videotape). Oakland, CA: New Harbinger Publications.

Rapee, R. M. *I Think They Think . . . Overcoming Social Phobia* (videotape). New York: Guilford Publications.

# Resources: National Organizations

**Anxiety Disorders Association of America**

11900 Parklawn Drive, Suite 100
Rockville, MD 20852
Tel: (301) 231-9350
Fax: (301) 231-7392
Email: anxdis@aol.com
Web Page: www.adaa.org

- Newsletter
- Information on support groups in the United States, Canada, South Africa, and Australia
- Names of professionals who treat anxiety disorders in the United States, Canada, and elsewhere
- Book catalog

**American Psychological Association**

Office of Public Affairs
750 First Street, N.E.
Washington, DC 20002-4242
Tel: (202) 336-5700
Referral Line: 1-800-964-2000

Email: public.affairs@apa.org
Web Page: www.apa.org

- Listings of state or provincial psychological associations that can provide psychologist referrals

## American Psychiatric Association

Division of Public Affairs, Attention Marcia Bennett
Dept. NASD, 1400 K Street, N.W.
Washington, DC 20005
Tel: (202) 682-6000
Email: mbennett@psych.org

- Referrals for psychiatrists

## Freedom From Fear

308 Seaview Avenue
Staten Island, New York 10305
Tel: (718) 351-1717
Fax: (718) 667-8893
Email: fffnadsd@aol.com

- Information

- Newsletter

- Information on support groups

## National Anxiety Foundation

3135 Custer Drive
Lexington, KY 40517-4001
Tel: (606) 272-7166
Web Page: www.lexington-on-line.com

- Information packages

- Names of professionals who treat anxiety disorders in the United States, Africa, China, and France

## Association for the Advancement of Behavior Therapy (AABT)

305 Seventh Avenue – 16th Floor
New York, NY 10001-6008
Tel: (212) 647-1890 or 1-800-685-AABT
Fax: (212) 647-1865
Email: mailback@aabt.org (under subject header insert "menu")
Web Page: www.aabt.org/aabt

- Names of professionals who treat anxiety disorders

- Information and brochures on specific phobias and social phobia

# Internet Resources

Although the information in this section was up to date when this book went to press, note that web pages come and go and addresses for Internet resources change frequently. For additional information on Internet resources, we suggest doing a search using key words like social phobia, social anxiety, and shyness.

### Web Pages on Social Anxiety and Related Topics
### Anxieties.com

www.anxieties.com/home.htm

Anxiety and Panic Book Store
www.wellnessbooks.com/anxiety

Anxiety-Panic.com (Internet links)
anxiety-panic.com/default.cfm

### Anxiety and Panic Internet Resource: Social Phobia Page

www6.pair.com/algy/anxiety/social.html

### Anxiety Disorders Association of America

www.adaa.org

*Anxiety Disorders and their Treatment: A Critical Review of the Evidence-based Literature*, by M. M. Antony and R. P. Swinson (Health Canada, 1996)
www.hc-sc.gc.ca/hppb/mentalhealth/pdfs/anxiety_review.pdf

**Anxiety Disorders Cyberpsych Penpals**

www.cyberpsych.org/cgi-bin/penpals.pl

**Anxiety Network International**

www.anxietynetwork.com

**CBT Website**

www.cognitivetherapy.com

**DIRECT – Anxiety Information Centre**

www.fhs.mcmaster.ca/direct/anxiety/anxiety.html

**Doctors Guide to Anxiety Disorders Information and Resources**

www.pslgroup.com/anxiety.htm

**Internet Mental Health**

www.mentalhealth.com

National Anxiety Foundation
www.lexington-on-line.com/naf.html

**NIMH Anxiety Disorders Education Program**

www.nimh.nih.gov/anxiety

**Paxil Anxiety Disorders Page**

www.panicattack.com

**Shyness Home Page**

www.shyness.com

**Social Phobia/Social Anxiety Association**

www.socialphobia.org

**Social Anxiety Network**

www.social-anxiety-network.com

**Internet Newsgroups**

Alt.support.anxiety-panic

Alt.support.shyness

alt.support.social-phobia

## Martin M. Antony, Ph.D.

Dr. Antony is Associate Professor in the Department of Psychiatry and Behavioural Neurosciences at McMaster University. He is also Chief Psychologist and Director of the Anxiety Treatment and Research Centre at St. Joseph's Hospital in Hamilton, Ontario. He received his Ph.D. in clinical psychology from the University at Albany, State University of New York and completed his pre-doctoral internship training at the University of Mississippi Medical Center in Jackson, MS. Dr. Antony has published several books, including *When Perfect Isn't Good Enough* and *Phobic Disorders and Panic in Adults: A Guide to Assessment and Treatment*, with Dr. Richard Swinson, *Obsessive-Compulsive Disorder: Theory, Research and Treatment*, with Drs. R. Swinson, S. Rachman, and M. Richter, and *Mastery of Your Specific Phobia* (patient and therapist manuals) with Drs. Michelle G. Craske and David H. Barlow. He has also published numerous research papers and book chapters in the areas of cognitive behavior therapy, panic disorder, social phobia, specific phobia, and obsessive compulsive disorder. Dr. Antony has received new researcher and young investigator awards from the Canadian Psychological Association (in 1999) and the Anxiety Disorders Association of America (in 2000). He is currently President of the Anxiety Disorders Special Interest Group of the Association for Advancement of Behavior Therapy (AABT) and will be Program Chair for the 2001 AABT meeting. Dr. Antony is actively involved in clinical research in the area of anxiety disorders, teaching and education, and maintains a clinical practice.

## Richard P. Swinson, MD

Richard P. Swinson is Professor and Morgan Firestone Chair of the Department of Psychiatry and Behavioural Neurosciences, Faculty of Health Sciences, McMaster University. He is also Professor in the Department of Psychiatry at the University of Toronto, and Psychiatrist-in-Chief at St. Joseph's Hospital in Hamilton, Ontario. Previously, he held several appointments at the Clarke Institute of Psychiatry, including Vice President Medical Affairs, Chief of Medical Staff, and Head of the Anxiety Disorders Clinic. Dr. Swinson was recently chair of the Examination Board in Psychiatry for the Royal College of Physicians and Surgeons of Canada. He has published approximately 200 scientific papers, book chapters, and reports, mostly on behavior therapy, anxiety disorders, and related topics. He has also published several books, including *When Perfect Isn't Good Enough* and *Phobic Disorders and Panic in Adults: A Guide to Assessment and Treatment, with Dr. M. Antony, and Obsessive-Compulsive Disorder: Theory, Research and Treatment*, with Drs. M. Antony, S. Rachman, and M. Richter. In addition, Dr. Swinson was a member of the DSM-IV subcommittees for obsessive compulsive disorder and for panic disorder and agoraphobia.

# More New Harbinger Titles

## WHEN PERFECT ISN'T GOOD ENOUGH

**Strategies for Coping with Perfectionism**
Psychologists Martin M. Antony and Richard P. Swinson help you challenge unrealistic expectations and work on the situations in your life where perfectionism is a problem.   *Item PERF $14.95*

## THE SELF-ESTEEM COMPANION

Over 60 simple exercises to help you unmask a punishing inner critic and begin to celebrate your personal strengths.   *Item SECO $10.95*

## THE SECRET MESSAGE OF SHAME

Explores what feelings of shame really tell us about our hidden yearnings and concept of ourselves.   *Item SHME Paperback, $13.95*

## BETTER BOUNDARIES

**Owning and Treasuring Your Life**
If you feel like you have trouble saying no to others, this book can help you establish more effective boundaries.   *Item BB Paperback, $15.95*

## DON'T TAKE IT PERSONALLY

**The Art of Dealing with Rejection**
Reveals the power of negative childhood messages and shows how to depersonalize responses and develop a new sense of self-acceptance and self-confidence.   *Item DOTA Paperback, $15.95*

Call **toll-free 1-800-748-6273** to order. Have your Visa or Mastercard number ready. Or send a check for the titles you want to New Harbinger Publications, 5674 Shattuck Avenue, Oakland, CA 94609. Include $4.50 for the first book and 75¢ for each additional book to cover shipping and handling. (California residents please include appropriate sales tax.) Allow four to six weeks for delivery.

*Prices subject to change without notice.*

# Some Other
# New Harbinger Titles

*Freeing the Angry Mind,* Item 4380 $14.95

*Living Beyond Your Pain,* Item 4097 $19.95

*Transforming Anxiety,* Item 4445 $12.95

*Integrative Treatment for Borderline Personality Disorder,* Item 4461 $24.95

*Depressed and Anxious,* Item 3635 $19.95

*Is He Depressed or What?,* Item 4240 $15.95

*Cognitive Therapy for Obsessive-Compulsive Disorder,* Item 4291 $39.95

*Child and Adolescent Psychopharmacology Made Simple,* Item 4356 $14.95

*ACT\* on Life Not on Anger,* Item 4402 $14.95

*Overcoming Medical Phobias,* Item 3872 $14.95

*Acceptance & Commitment Therapy for Anxiety Disorders,* Item 4275 $58.95

*The OCD Workbook,* Item 4224 $19.95

*Neural Path Therapy,* Item 4267 $14.95

*Overcoming Obsessive Thoughts,* Item 3813 $14.95

*The Interpersonal Solution to Depression,* Item 4186 $19.95

*Get Out of Your Mind & Into Your Life,* Item 4259 $19.95

*Dialectical Behavior Therapy in Private Practice,* Item 4208 $54.95

*The Anxiety & Phobia Workbook, 4th edition,* Item 4135 $19.95

*Loving Someone with OCD,* Item 3295 $15.95

*Overcoming Animal & Insect Phobias,* Item 3880 $12.95

*Overcoming Compulsive Washing,* Item 4054 $14.95

*Angry All the Time,* Item 3929 $13.95

*Handbook of Clinical Psychopharmacology for Therapists, 4th edition,* Item 3996 $55.95

*Writing For Emotional Balance,* Item 3821 $14.95

*Surviving Your Borderline Parent,* Item 3287 $14.95

*When Anger Hurts, 2nd edition,* Item 3449 $16.95

*Calming Your Anxious Mind,* Item 3384 $12.95

*Ending the Depression Cycle,* Item 3333 $17.95

*Your Surviving Spirit,* Item 3570 $18.95

*Coping with Anxiety,* Item 3201 $10.95

*The Agoraphobia Workbook,* Item 3236 $19.95

Call **toll free, 1-800-748-6273,** or log on to our online bookstore at **www.newharbinger.com** to order. Have your Visa or Mastercard number ready. Or send a check for the titles you want to New Harbinger Publications, Inc., 5674 Shattuck Ave., Oakland, CA 94609. Include $4.50 for the first book and 75¢ for each additional book, to cover shipping and handling. (California residents please include appropriate sales tax.) Allow two to five weeks for delivery.

*Prices subject to change without notice.*